Siddhas of Ga

Siddhas of Ga

Remembered
by Khenpo Karthar Rinpoche

Written by Lama Karma Drodhul
Translated by Lama Yeshe Gyamtso

KTD Publications
Woodstock New York USA

Published by KTD Publications
335 Meads Mountain Road
Woodstock, NY 12498, USA
www.KTDPublications.org
Distributed by: www.NamseBangdzo.com

Photo on back cover by Jangchub Gurung

ISBN 978-1-934608-37-1
LCCN: 2013932048
Printed in the USA on 30% PCR, acid-free paper

Contents

Foreword
by Khenpo Karthar Rinpoche

Our teacher, the kind Buddha, taught the holy dharma out of compassion. Although a great deal of time has passed since then, people with great renunciation, compassion, purity of outlook, and diligence have continued to unfailingly give rise to authentic experience and realization ever since. The stories in this book are evidence of this, especially since most of the holy beings whose lives are recounted here began as ordinary people like us, and were not recognized emanations of buddhas or bodhisattvas.

This book clearly demonstrates that we can, through diligence, achieve the same result. In particular, most of the events recounted here occurred during my lifetime, and were either witnessed by me or told to me at the time; these accounts are therefore trustworthy. My nephew, Lama Karma Drodhul, wrote these stories down with the best intentions and composed the book's introductory homage and concluding dedication. Lama Yeshe tirelessly translated this book into English. My students — Maureen McNicholas, Peter van Deurzen, and others — published it. I want to thank all of them from my heart.

Through the virtue of this, may the Gyalwang Karmapa Ogyen Trinley Dorje and all holders of the teachings live long; may their activity flourish. May all the sickness, famine, violence, and strife in this world be pacified. May everyone in the world be happy and live in joy. May all who pass from this life, including my sisters Pema Lhakhyi and Tashi Wangmo, be born in Sukhavati.

I thank you who read this, and pray that you give rise to the same experience, realization, and virtues as the holy beings whose lives are described in this book.

Khenpo Karthar Rinpoche

May the stainless rays of virtue's light dispel the darkness of bad karma in these decadent days.

May those who impartially and unwaveringly uphold the life-tree of the teachings live long.

May all beings with whom I have good or bad connections live in glorious joy.

May we all give meaning to our lives through the bodhichitta so pleasing to the victors.

A Bouquet of Utpalas

Brief accounts of the lives of siddhas of Ga whom my guru actually met or whose stories he heard from trustworthy sources, set forth here as medicine to restore faith.

Namo Guru!

You utterly renounced all the stains of the two veils,
The darkness that ruins the world.
You fully realized the greatest wisdom,
The knowledge of what there is and how things are.
Buddha, you perfectly crossed the turbulent river
Of the three levels of existence.
I bow at your feet, our teacher, for you show all beings,
Humans and devas, the path to freedom.

With powerful wisdom you saw your own face,
self-awareness.
With loving compassion you brought holy dharma to Tibet.
With might you tamed vicious, aggressive devas and
rakshasas.
I bow to you, Lake-Born Vajra, the single protector of
all Tibetans.

Your teaching of all sutras and tantras was unhindered.
Your debating overcame all opposition.
Your compositions are superior to all other explanations of the victor's intentions.
I bow to Sakya Pandita, Mañjushri in person.

The fame of your scholarship filled all of Tibet.
Your nobility opened a hundred doors to the vinaya.
Your benevolent deeds led us to call you a second victor.
I bow to the buddha called Lobzang Drakpa.

You upheld the lineage of the victor's words.
You fostered the lotus garden of disciples
With the instructions of the Kadampas and Mahamudra.
You brought the Samadhirajasutra to Tibet.
I bow to Gampopa, Chandraprabhakumara.

By properly practicing with unflagging diligence
The dharma of tradition and realization taught by our peerless teacher,
The blessings of your unbroken lineages have entered your hearts.
Who could fail to respect you, impartial great beings?

In hidden valleys and isolated, pleasant retreats
You cultivated the hidden meaning of dharmata.
Hidden yogis, I prostrate at your toes
With unhidden faith and devotion from my heart.

The best path for the achievement of unity in one life
Is reliance on the blessing of realized gurus.
As that requires diligent study of their lives,
I will write briefly here of their lives for the good of myself and others.

In that way I have cast flowers of words in veneration of holy beings and as a promise.

Our teacher, the peerless Siddhartha, generated bodhichitta in the presence of the peerless Mahashakyamuni. Starting then, he undertook countless greater and lesser austerities. Finally, he eradicated the stains that are the two obscurations and achieved manifest awakening at Vajrasana in India. In accordance with the faculties of different disciples he gradually turned the three dharmachakras, enabling innumerable devas, humans, and others to achieve the perfect renunciation and realization of the three vehicles. Eventually, through the kindness of the abbot Shantarakshita, the master Padmasambhava, the dharma king Trisong Detsen, and others, the dharma of peace spread north from Vajrasana in India to Tibet. This opening of the gate of dharma led to the appearance of the Eight Great Chariots of the Accomplishment Lineage and others. The well-known four great traditions, the Sakya, Geluk, Kagyu, and Nyingma, became widespread. The holders of their teachings became ubiquitous.

However, due to various adverse circumstances the lives of those holy beings, and especially the lives of hidden yogis and yoginis, are not that well-known. Therefore, I will now set forth with benevolence and devotion a few stories about holy beings of various traditions that I have heard from my kind guru Khenpo Karthar Rinpoche.

1 The First Karma Sabchu

The First Karma Sabchu was a monk of Thrangu, a Kagyu monastery, who achieved siddhi because of water.

Your renunciation of existence is the ground of freedom.
Through your guru's instructions, the life-tree of freedom,
You came to live in holy solitude, the immediate cause of freedom.
I bow from my heart to you who became drunk with the joy of freedom.

This holy being was born in Dzakok, which is near Doti Gankar in Gyam, a sacred place in Paltang in Kham. At an early age he exhibited a diligence in worldly endeavors throughout day and night far greater than that of others. He also appeared to be extremely aggressive. One day, while he was driving twenty burdens of goods to be sold, he came to the Pal River. It was in full spate, and its current was very fast. Without thinking, he rashly tried to cross the raging river along with his beasts of burden, but was carried off to a great distance by the current. Terrified, he thought, "Up to now I have only thought of worldly endeavors; I have never thought of dharma. If I survive this, I will devote myself exclusively to holy dharma!" With that vow in mind, he managed to grab onto a large rock just when he was about to drown.

As soon as he had freed himself from the river he abandoned all his previous worldly endeavors, such as his burdens of goods, as completely as one would abandon one's spittle in the dust. At Thrangu Monastery he received instruction from the Lord Refuge Thrangu Kunkhyap

Nyima. Afterward he practiced diligently, without distinction between day and night, at isolated hermitages such as the Vairochana of Bi and Lepje Karyak. For the rest of his life he principally practiced the Six Dharmas of Naropa and nyungnes. Through those practices he gained siddhi.

At that time Doshul Khandro, a woman who repeatedly returned from the dead, was alive. After Karma Sabchu passed away she visited hell, and discovered that Karma Sabchu had gone there as well. She overheard him say the following to Yama Dharmaraja:

I am a bedraggled old monk from Thrangu.
I come from Doti Gangkar.
I have gathered the accumulations with my body by doing a thousand nyungnes.
With my speech I have recited more than three hundred million MANIs.
My mind never strays from dharmata.
I will absolutely not let anyone connected to me be born in a lower realm.

After saying that, Karma Sabchu promised to remain there until everyone connected to him had died. This story was told by Doshul Khandro herself.

Renunciation is the ground of freedom.
The accumulations are the immediate cause of freedom.
Practice pleases the guru.
I dedicate the virtue of those three things.

2 The Second Karma Sabchu

The second Karma Sabchu was a monk of Thrangu, a Kagyu monastery, who achieved siddhi because of imprisonment. Author's note: The second Karma Sabchu was my kind guru's uncle.

You were as tough as Lord Marpa the Translator.
Your commitment rivaled Jetsun Milarepa's.
The depth of your bodhichitta equaled Chenrezik's.
I bow to you, holy being drunk on realization.

The second Karma Sabchu was extremely aggressive in his youth, always fighting and invariably victorious. Because he was well-known for this, he was also arrogant. One day he got into a fight with a Chinese man. Although Karma Sabchu won the fight, the other man charged him with assault. As a result Karma Sabchu was imprisoned and beaten with a bamboo flail that is called "bedzi" in Chinese. This flail causes the victim's skin to split open; Karma Sabchu was subjected to five hundred blows with it. This caused him to think, "Up to now my every deed has been worldly; there isn't even a trace of virtue in me. Even worse, I'm putting my own life at risk! I will definitely devote however much life remains to me exclusively to holy dharma!"

With that stable vow, he practiced for the duration of his life in the Red Retreat on the north side of Thrangu Monastery. When he passed away, although he had been a tall man, his body shrank to the length of one cubit. This amazed and inspired everyone.

This holy dharma is profound.
Through pure, holy samaya
You, holy being, were victorious.
I dedicate this in threefold holiness.

3 Namkha Drakpa

Namkha Drakpa was a monk of Kyergu, a Sakya monastery. He was a hidden actionless yogin with a tranquil demeanor.

You renounced all the spoils of existence.
Your mind is moist with love and compassion.
Holy one, you love beings as your own children.
Please dwell smiling in our hearts of faith.

Namkha Drakpa undertook both renunciation and completion. After doing so, he renounced even the use of a hearth fire or dwelling. As he had only one set of robes, they soon became ragged; he replaced them with a calfskin that covered his front and back. He had no shoes. In the summer he would journey to various isolated hermitages and allow insects to feed on his body. When he returned to the villages in the winter it was observed by everyone that his entire body was covered by insect bites. He would say, "This past summer my whole body was bitten by insects!"

When he begged in the villages he would only eat once a day. No one knew where he slept at night, except that he never slept in any villager's home. He was always gentle, and inspired everyone who met him. People often said, "He is not ordinary." Author's note: My aunt Pema Lhakyi met

Namkha Drakpa in her youth. Because he slept at the side of the road, she and other children used to throw stones at him. Speaking kindly and without the slightest trace of anger, he would say, "Children, don't mistreat me." When she later heard more about him, my aunt regretted and confessed this. She told me this story herself.

Regardless of the social standing of whomever he met, Namkha Drakpa always spoke kindly to them. When he was around sixty, he announced, "I have now completed the deeds of a renunciate. It is time for me to begin the life of a householder!" When he went begging thereafter, unlike before he asked for tea and scarves, and carried a clay pot. In a field he set up three rocks as a hearth and lit a fire. He placed the clay pot on top of this and boiled some tea. Once the tea was ready he drank a bit of it and poured the rest around the hearth. He then divided the tea leaves into three equal portions, placed them on the three hearth stones, and covered each of them with a scarf. He then announced, "I have made a home!" He did these things one hundred and eight times. Author's note: According to my guru, this was definitely skillful tantric behavior.

Finally he asked the custodian, "Everything I needed to do in this life is now done, so tonight please allow me to sleep in the Kyergu prayer-wheel temple."

The custodian answered, "That wouldn't be right; you have a lot of lice."

Namkha Drakpa replied, "You would have been correct in the past, but now I have not even a single louse." In the end he was allowed to sleep in the temple. On the next morning, when the custodian next saw him, Namkha Drakpa had passed away, and was seated in the vajra posture with his hands in equipoise. His body was floating an inch above his mat, which everyone there saw.

When his remains were cremated, his heart, tongue, and eyes emerged unburnt from the fire. A statue of him was placed in the prayer-wheel temple, and his heart, tongue, and eyes were placed in the statue. By that time everyone realized that he had been a holy being. They regretfully confessed their previous treatment of him. His statue became their focus for the accumulation of merit.

Although you perfected the actions of the six paramitas,
Your actions for beings' benefit were unpredictable.
Some, judging you by your actions, called you good or bad,
But you proved to be beyond the actions of our
  judging minds.

4 The Mad Siddha of Talung

The mad siddha of Talung, a Sakya monastery, exhibited the discipline of wrathful freedom from action.

Although your heart was moist with the water of
  compassion,
Your external discipline was that of wrathful behavior.
The magic dance of such lord siddhas, such great beings,
Is beyond the reach of thought.

After undertaking renunciation, the mad siddha wandered from place to place. He was a large man and always appeared, judging by his facial expression, to be angry. He spoke aggressively to everyone he met, regardless of their social status; everyone feared him. However, his heart was actually moistened by the water of compassion. He would carry the corpses of the poor and of people who had died of contagious diseases such as leprosy to the charnel grounds. Whenever the corpse he was carrying was particularly heavy he would fiercely scold the corpse, saying "Why are you so heavy?" and "What did you eat?" He would also strike the corpse. After doing so, he would announce "You're lighter now!," easily sling the body over his shoulder, and bring it to the vultures.

He would collect the clothing from the corpse, regardless of its condition or quality, give the better clothing to the poor, and himself wear the oldest of the clothes.

When he was about to pass away, he demanded to be allowed to sleep in the temple of Talung, his monastery. He was refused, and so said to the temple custodian, "If you don't let me sleep here I will have to vomit in the temple or cast other filth into it!" This made the custodian even angrier than before, and he expelled the mad siddha from the temple.

The mad siddha went to the nearby home of a wealthy family and told them, "They won't let me sleep at Talung Monastery. I will sleep in your shrine room tonight." He slept there that night. On the next morning he was discovered to be seated with his legs crossed in vajra posture, his hands in equipoise, and his eyes gazing into space; he had passed away in that posture. When his monastery was informed of this, they understood for the first time that he was a yogin who had attained siddhi. Regretting and confessing their previous treatment of him, they brought his remains back to the monastery with an elaborate procession. His remains became a basis for disciples' accumulation of merit.

Nowadays monasteries expect
Siddhas to be monastic lamas
Who are impressive upon first sight.
May these biographies eradicate doubt!

5 Jamyang Gyaltsen

Jamyang Gyaltsen was also a monk from Talung, a Sakya monastery.

Realized one, you accomplished a celestial rainbow body.
You realized that all things are like rainbows.
You were received by rainbow-bodied dakinis
In an expanse of rainbow light and rays. I bow to you.

Jamyang Gyaltsen lived in a retreat adjacent to Talung Monastery. He was attended by a nun; as a result people had little faith in him. One year he became ill and remained so for a long time. One day during his illness he asked that the officials of the monastery come to see him, which they did. They found him sitting in his retreat with a cup filled with his own blood set before him. He told them, "The chieftain of the Drau clan was very nice to me; please give him this blood. Please give everything else I have to this nun, for she has been the kindest to me. Without leaving a single drop of water or morsel of food, please lock and seal my door and hold onto the key. After seven days, as soon as the sun shines into my room, please open the door."

Some of the monks said that it would be better if they left

him a little food and drink, but the other monks insisted that they follow his final requests. They agreed to give the key to the nun, who could enter the retreat if the need arose. They instructed her accordingly.

At sunrise on the seventh day his door was opened. On his bed were his hair, nails, and clothing; his body had transformed into a rainbow body, leaving nothing behind. Seeing this, everyone understood that he had been a siddha; his clothing and nails were kept as supports for faith.

Although the foul breath of evil times pollutes our
world these days,
The power of the tantric teachings blazes like fire.
Therefore abandon wrong views of actionless hermits,
No matter what company they keep!

6 Karma Gyalwang

Karma Gyalwang was a realized monk of Benchen, a Kagyu monastery, who achieved siddhi because of a knife.

You accomplished the destined deity of Tibet,
The great treasure of compassion.
Realized Karma Gyalwang,
You are worthy of veneration by all!

As a young monk, Karma Gyalwang was a herdsman for the family of the chieftain of the Rada clan. He always kept an extremely sharp knife under his pillow, although he never used it. One fall, while many of the chieftain's yaks and sheep were being slaughtered for consumption during the following winter and spring, one of several people who knew about Karma Gyalwang's knife took it from under his pillow and used it in the slaughtering. That evening Karma Gyalwang discovered that his knife was missing and began to search for it. One of the butchers said to him "Here's your knife!" and returned it to him, covered in blood.

Karma Gyalwang immediately began to weep, saying, "I have done terrible wrong!" He quickly journeyed to Benchen Monastery, where he entered the presence of the Lord Refuge Nyenpa Rinpoche and received instruction from him. In retreat there he mainly practiced the meditation and recitation of Mahakarunika, through which he eventually achieved siddhi. Every year, accompanied by more than a thousand disciples, he would carve the MANI mantra on mountains and in stone all over the place. In winter he would write the MANIs with sand on the ice. He also convened accomplishment assemblies for the recitation of one hundred million MANIs in many places. He left his footprints in stone on every mountain and rock he visited, and displayed precognition of future events. He became widely famous for these and other miracles; the evidence of his siddhi was visible.

One karmically destined being
Can bring an entire land to dharma.
One karmically doomed wrongdoer
Can darken an entire land.
Unlimited interdependence
And relativity are undeniable.

7 The Retreat Master Karma Tsultrim

Karma Tsultrim, or Yönpel, was a lifelong retreatant. He was a retreat master at Thrangu, a Kagyu monastery, who achieved siddhi through having his feet chained for thirteen years.

A devoted and diligent disciple,
You were accepted by your kind lord guru.
Your mind mixed inseparably with your father guru's.
I bow to you, a second Lord Tilopa.

The guru of this lifelong retreatant was Dru Jamyang Drakpa, a direct disciple of Jamgön Kongtrül Yönten Gyamtso. Jamyang Drakpa prophesied to Karma Tsultrim, "Practice for thirteen years with your feet in chains. Your wisdom will equal Tilopa's!"

Accordingly, in the Colorful Cave of Tselung, a hermitage near Thrangu Monastery, Karma Tsultrim practiced one-pointedly. When the prophesied thirteen years were almost over, the region entered into a great conflict with armed forces from Lhasa. As the local forces suffered a devastating defeat, everyone in the area began to flee in any direction they could. Because of his guru's command, Karma Tsultrim alone remained where he was. He was discovered and beaten by the invading soldiers, some of whom said, "This man seems to have been imprisoned here!" and started to remove his chains. Karma Tsultrim insistently explained to them that he was practicing in obedience to his guru's command, and barely managed to escape the forced removal of his fetters.

Realizing that there was no hope of his being able to

remain in the area, he went to the peak of Dzam Kyangpo, an isolated, snow-covered mountain. On his journey there he had to cross the Palchu River, which was in full spate and appeared impossible to cross. However, because Karma Tsultrim had withdrawn his prana into his avadhuti and did not need to breathe, he amazingly crawled across the river bottom, grabbing onto rocks as he went, and reached the other side. He regularly walked from Thrangu Monastery to its Vairochana Retreat while holding a single vase breath. When he went to other places he would walk in a straight line, without avoiding any of the mountains or rivers in his way. He displayed the siddhi of quickly reaching any destination, no matter how distant. When people were watching, however, he always seemed to walk slowly; he kept his abilities hidden.

The remote mountain to which he went, Dzam Kyangpo, was so high that no one had ever climbed its peak. Karma Tsultrim easily climbed the mountain's face. When he was later asked how he did this, he said, "I would grip the snow with my fingers and flip my lower body upward; then I would grip the snow with my feet and throw my upper body forward."

He also said, "I've heard it said that the entire peak of Dzam Kyangpo is formed of crystal. It isn't crystal; it's snow."

He fulfilled his vow to practice there for one month, relying only upon samadhi for food and chandali for clothing. After that, his chains fell off spontaneously without having to be struck off.

He would often say, "No matter what I do, whether walking, sitting, standing, or lying down, I never stray from luminosity. This is very convenient, since I have no need for any additional, effortful practice."

I venerate you who with stable diligence
Raised the precious command of your father guru
To the peak of the victory banner of unchanging devotion,
Raining down the unfailing fruition of all that is wanted
or needed.

8 Trimey Özer

Trimey Özer was a yogin of the great perfection.

The fasting practice of the thousand-handed and -eyed
protector of beings
Is a virtuous endeavor that certainly closes the doors to birth
as the six types of beings.
You regard beings with love beyond focus.
Actionless refuge of beings, I bow to you.

The yogin Trimey Özer was originally from Serta in Golok. He undertook renunciation in his youth and traveled through various places as an actionless mendicant. He eventually reached the area of my kind guru's birth, where he practiced in a small cave at the peak of the mountain Anye Dorje Nyengyal. This cave had been an accomplishment site of Geri Chögyal Dorje, and this mountain is identified with the local deity whose name it bears. Author's note: Geri Chögyal Dorje was a tertön associated with the Fourteenth Gyalwang Karmapa Tekchok Dorje. The Fourteenth Karmapa and the tertön opened the way to both the mountain and lake at Anye Dorje Nyengyal and performed a ganachakra in this cave. While they were doing so the rock melted, taking the form of the eight auspicious signs and the seven articles of royalty. A rain of crystal fell. It was from that cave that the tertön retrieved both *White Jambhala Prosperity Protection* and the *Sadhana of the Blue Wrathful Guru* as terma; they are both still in circulation. There are also many of the tertön's footprints and body imprints in the cave. However, the people of the area misunderstood Chögyal Dorje. They accused him of removing the source of the area's prosperity and chased him out of the region. As a result he was unable to fill the aperture left in the cave by his removal of terma, as is customarily done. It is said that the large aperture that therefore remains in the cave accounts for the poverty of the villagers of Nyengyal.

When Trimey Özer first settled there, no one knew about it. Then one day an older man named Kori Karma Namgyal, while herding sheep on the mountainside, saw a peaceful and gentle young monk meditating there. Karma Namgyal thought, "I wonder if he is a local deity of this mountain." He looked carefully at the monk and saw that his eyes were closed. Walking around outside the place where the monk was sitting, he noticed that there were no human footprints in the ground. This made him certain that the monk was a deity. He went back to look at him again, and saw that he was still meditating as before. He asked the monk, "Who are you?"

The monk replied, "I am a monk from Golok. Because of my aspirations, I must remain here. Please don't tell anyone I'm here!"

The old man searched the hollow in the rocks where the monk was living and found only one cup of tsampa in a sack and no other provisions, so he offered the monk some yoghurt. Trimey Özer made an offering of it with his hand and put one drop of it on his tongue, and then returned the rest. Karma Namgyal was delighted and, without telling anyone of the monk's presence there, returned to see him after a month. He found Trimey Özer seated in meditation as before, and with only the tsampa as a provision. He again offered him some yoghurt. This time the monk, after making an offering with it, accepted a spoonful of it. He again asked Karma Namgyal to tell no one of his presence there. One month later it was autumn, with winter not far away, so Karma Namgyal went again to see Trimey Özer. The monk was seated as before, with his bag of tsampa hanging on a wooden peg that he had driven onto the rock. This time Trimey Özer told the old man, "You no longer need to keep my presence here secret; you can tell others."

Delighted, Karma Namgyal said to the monk, "Not far from here is the old Nyengyal Cave where the great tertön Geri Chögyal Dorje gained accomplishment. Will you live there and be the lama of this area?"

Trimey Özer agreed to do so, so the old man told the people of the area. With joy and devotion they repaired the cave, which had become dilapidated, and made it habitable. Thirteen mounted men rode up the mountain to escort Trimey Özer there. They met with him, received his blessing, and asked him to ride with them to the cave on horseback. He laughed, suddenly got up, broke off the peg stuck into the rock, and began to walk, carrying his tsampa bag under his shawl and refusing to ride a horse.

The others kept the stub of the peg he had broken off as a support for their faith. When they pulled it out they noticed that the hole left in the rock by the wooden peg disappeared, leaving only a faint impression, like that of a peg removed from butter. Seeing this increased their faith, and they knew from then on that he was an actual siddha.

From that year onward Trimey Özer led one hundred nyungnes and one week of ejection practice for the elderly every year. Everyone who attended these achieved the signs. He never wasted whatever was offered to him, using it to sponsor the engraving of MANI stones, the presentation of lamp offerings, and the raising of prayer flags. For the rest of his life he remained immersed in deeds of offering and generosity, and always lived as an actionless renunciate.

From upper Beru he extracted engraving stone as treasure. He used this for the engraving in stone of the entire Kangyur. In general engraving stone was extremely rare in that area, so when Trimey Özer began to speak of his intention to engrave the Kangyur, people of the region said things like, "How could one ever find enough of the stone to do this?"

Trimey Özer told them, "Dig right here and you will find engraving stone." They found the stone, as flat and smooth as paper in a book. The engravers stayed where the stone was found and engraved the Kangyur into it, day after day. At night they slept in the excavation pit, covering it with a felt curtain. It took about a hundred engravers two years to complete the Kangyur.

This holy being was gentle and noble in his behavior; he demonstrated all the attributes of the holy. He usually remained in dark retreat in his cave. When he was around seventy he was invited to a place called Namshipu by various patrons among his disciples, some of them farmers and some of them nomads. He led eight nyungnes there, which were attended by a great many people. When he bestowed the nyungne vows the walls of his tent were lifted up so that everyone could see him. At the end of the eight nyungnes, when he bestowed the vow of silence, he supported his head with his hand and transmitted the vow in a loud voice. Afterward, he straightened his posture and prepared to pass into parinirvana. Others lowered the walls of his tent, so onlookers were unable to see him clearly. My guru told me that he heard this story from his father, whose root guru was Trimey Özer.

The benefits of nyungnes are immeasurable.
Beings, don't fear nyungnes!
Sufferings a thousand times worse than a nyungne
Are said to be purified by a single nyungne.
Through the virtue of writing this,
May this be correctly understood.
May this practice be the best refuge
In this and future lives.

9 Lama Tapkay

Lama Tapkay was a monk from Ayang, a monastery of the Drikung Kagyu.

In solitude, so extolled by the victor,
You practiced with a carefree mind at ease.
You gained confidence beyond hope and fear.
Yogi, you are worth of homage.

There are prophetic indications that Lama Tapkay was an emanation of the great tertön Chögyal Dorje. When he undertook renunciation, Lama Tapkay saw indications in both waking and hypnogogic experience that if he were to practice in isolation at Kyogyal Ngangma, the dwelling of the local deity of his birthplace, he would achieve siddhi. Accordingly he journeyed there in secret, and practiced there for twelve years, emphasizing the six dharmas of Naropa. He didn't achieve much during that time, but began thereafter to frequently hear the sound of a pleasant female voice saying to him, "Have fortitude!"

He increased his efforts, but still continued to hear the voice, so one day he performed yogic exercises on bare rock without any mat or cushion. His body became covered in blood, and he felt great pain, so he meditated on the illusory body. He became free of all pain, and his mind gave birth to extraordinary realization; he achieved siddhi.

Later, out of necessity, he married; his wife's name was Drölma. One day, while she was milking dris, a ferocious hailstorm occurred. She was wearing a cotton hat, which was struck by lightning, producing a flow of molten metal over her hat that did her no harm. This incident led to her nickname Lightning-Proof Drölma.

For yogis who bring adversity to the path
Sickness, demons, and obstructors are just mental drama.
Although they seem real to ordinary people,
They reveal the very meaning of relativity.

10 Koru Topchu

Koru Topchu was a lama of the Drukpa Kagyu.

Although you achieved awakening many kalpas ago,
In order to free many beings from samsara
You perfected austere practice over many years.
With many bodies, lord, I bow at your feet.

Koru Topchu was a monk in a Drukpa Kagyu monastery. He gave rise to weariness toward samsara and relied upon Dzigar Dorje Drakpo, a siddha of the Drukpa Kagyu who was an emanation of Guru Padmasambhava. Koru Topchu received all of Dorje Drakpo's instructions and guidance, and then went to Dzikung, an extremely isolated, high mountain. On its upper slopes he lived on a single sheep's liver for three years, engaged in rasayana. At the end of that period he achieved siddhi.

The Fifteenth Gyalwang Karmapa Khakyap Dorje prophesied that Koru Topchu was an emanation of the peerless Gampopa. This prophesy was bestowed upon a man named Yushu Tritok Pema Dorje, who was from Yushu and had killed seven people. Pema Dorje went on pilgrimage to Lhasa in order to purify his obscurations, and met Gyalwang Khakyap Dorje there. When he told the Karmapa of his terrible sins and asked him for a way to purify them, Khakyap Dorje told him, "As you and I share no karmic connection I am unable to lead you to freedom. Return to Kham and purify your obscurations relying upon Drukpa Topchu, an emanation of the peerless Gampopa; and Yönten Chöpel, a monk from Rapshul Lungshö Monastery who is an emanation of the victor Maitreya."

After Koru Topchu left his retreat he became very famous and received the patronage of many donors. In particular, he founded a new abbey for women that housed more than three hundred nuns. When he was on the point of passing away he said to his future mother, "I will soon visit your home; I will need you to provide me with lodging."

A year after his passing he was reborn as her son, as he had predicted. He was given the name Karma Damchö and became a monk of Thrangu Monastery. Author's note: He was known as Bentra Karma Damchö. Bentra is the name of a place, but was also used as the name of his family, which was called the Bentra family. There were two branches of the Bentra family, the greater and lesser; Karma Damchö was born to the greater Bentra family. The Seventh Traleg Kyabgön Rinpoche, Karma Rangjung Kunkhyap Nyima, was also born to the greater Bentra family.

From an early age Karma Damchö was gentle. Because of his immeasurable compassion, everyone believed that he was the rebirth of Koru Topchu. He became known as a bodhisattva.

Along with the Lord Refuge Thrangu Rinpoche and my kind guru, Karma Damchö studied for five years in the college at Thrangu. During this time he also exhibited the wisdom of meditation; he immediately recognized the nature of his mind simply through receiving instruction on mahamudra and other guidance on the mind. He eventually became a khenpo of Thrangu Monastery. While he was presiding in that capacity over a summer retreat the monastery was invaded by the Communists, and he was arrested. Along with many other khenpos and tulkus he was sent to Siling. He jumped out of the vehicle in which he was being transported and was shot twice by the soldiers, killing him.

Victorious through genuine love and compassion for all
And the pure three trainings that pleased your guru,
You quickly gathered the two accumulations
And saw naked, primordial, self-arisen wisdom.

11 Yönten Chöpel

Yönten Chöpel was a monk of Lungshö, a Gelukpa monastery.

Through the heart-jewel of the Kadampas,
Mind training, the good path to awakening,
You gave rise to unmistaken realization
Of emptiness and compassion. I bow to you!

Yönten Chöpel undertook renunciation in his youth. Extremely disciplined, he entered the Denmakang College at Drepung Monastery near Lhasa. He eventually became the Master of Discipline for great assemblies at Drepung. After completing his term of duty he returned to his birthplace. In an isolated hermitage he principally meditated on the gradual path of awakening and on mind training. His compassion was unlimited. He would often say, "Since all beings have sugatagarbha, they are all buddhas."

Whenever he saw another person, no matter who it was, he would immediately rise and join his palms in respect. He even did this toward birds and other animals. Most of the offerings he received from donors were in the form of treacle, butter, and a type of ornamental bracelet, called "ngoney," worn by nomad women in Eastern Tibet. Yönten Chöpel would smear butter on the rocks and decorate it with the bracelets. He would roll the treacle into balls and scatter them. Rodents would eat the butter and treacle and carry off the bracelets. Delighted, he would say, "I have presented offerings to the rodents!" and then bow with respect.

When donors came to see him, he would always correctly answer whatever question they intended to ask before they asked it; his wisdom was unlimited. When he passed away his heart and tongue survived the cremation fire, and many shariram emerged from his remains. As stated above in the biography of Drukpa Topchu, the Fifteenth Gyalwang Karmapa Kakhyap Dorje prophesied to Tritok Pema Dorje that Yönten Chöpel was an emanation of the victor Maitreya.

Although you had completed the guiding of others
with your actual body,
You still planted the seed of liberation
In all who formed a connection with you
By means of your heart, tongue, and shariram.

12 Katak Ogyen Chöpel

Katak Ogyen Chöpel was a retreat master at Thrangu Monastery.

Although you were wealthy in samsara you were unattached
to it.
In the presence of your kind guru, peerless in samsara,

You gained the confidence to shatter the wheel of samsara.
I will bow to you with devotion until samsara is empty.

Ogyen Chöpel was born in Rapshul Borok; his father was the leader of that community. In his twenty-second year he and his brother took a wife. In his family it was common for disaster to strike when they reached their twenty-fifth year, so when he got close to that age he went with a servant to see the Drukpa Kagyu Lama Koru Topchu in order to request a divination. The lama told him, "Unless you undertake renunciation, you will certainly die and go to hell. If you undertake renunciation, you will live."

Ogyen Chöpel asked, "May I go home and discuss this with my parents and family?"

The lama replied, "No. You must change your clothes and undertake renunciation right now."

Drukpa Topchu gave Ogyen Chöpel a felt robe to wear. Accepting it, he changed into it on the spot and gave his fine clothing, knife, bow and arrows, and horse to his servant to return to his family. Terrified and saddened, the servant pleaded with Ogyen Chöpel to change his mind, but he refused.

His lama then said to him, "Throughout beginningless time your mind has been polluted by distraction and entertainment. You must first meditate on tranquility." He taught him tranquility meditation, and Ogyen Chöpel practiced it for a month. Afterward, he requested permission to visit his home just once, but his lama refused. He then meditated on tranquility for four more months, becoming extremely stable. In order to test him, his lama stuck him with a needle; he didn't feel it. His lama told him that his tranquility was now sufficiently stable. He instructed him to meditate in the accomplishment cave in Kardong Riwoche, the mountain behind that area.

Accordingly, he meditated there one-pointedly for three years. One day he saw a raven fighting with a hawk; in the end the raven killed the hawk. Other than that he saw no special signs. When he told his lama about this, Drukpa Topchu said, "The raven represents the dharmapalas; the hawk represents the spirit that was going to take your life. You are now victorious over the obstacles of Mara!"

After his lama passed away, he relied upon Palden Khyentse Özer, the Second Jamgön Rinpoche, for three years at the hermitage at Palpung Monastery. Once he experienced that, while everything seems real to us in our delusion, there exists not so much as an atom of anything. When he touched the wall of his cave, the clear imprint of his hand appeared. Elated, he told Jamgön Rinpoche of this. Rinpoche told him, "Check and see if your handprint is really there."

When he looked, he saw that there was no imprint of his hand there. Rinpoche told him, "Don't mistake transitory experience for realization. Meditate with fortitude!"

Accordingly, from then on he cast clinging to any experience behind him. Finally, Rinpoche praised him and assured him that he had achieved the realization of Beyond Embellishment.

Ogyen Chöpel later spent a few years in the Vairochana Retreat at Thrangu Monastery, and in particular was the retreat master of the Six Dharmas of Naropa Retreat for twelve years. Then, because of the changing times, he had to flee to India along with the Lord Refuge Thrangu

Rinpoche, my kind guru, and others. He became gravely ill upon reaching India; his entire lower body swelled, and the pain was unbearable. Four monks, my kind guru among them, carried him to a hospital on a blanket. As soon as they hoisted him up, he sat up on the blanket and began to cheerfully and loudly sing the vajra doha of Marpa the Translator in which the latter described how in a dream he was carried on a palanquin by four dakinis to Mount Shriparvata in southern India, where he met the mahasiddha Saraha.

After Ogyen Chöpel had been in the hospital for two days, my kind guru went to see him. He said to my guru, "Last night I dreamed that a white snake bit my big toe and sucked out all my sickness. After doing so the snake told me, 'You will have a slight scar on your toe, but other than that you're cured.' Have a look." When my guru looked, there was a slight wound on his toe, but he was otherwise recovered. Ogyen Chöpel did not have to stay in the hospital after that.

At the time they were living in a refugee camp along with many other monastics, including monks from the great monastic seats. Ogyen Chöpel said, "Were I to meditate during the day others would see; it would be nothing more than hypocrisy." During the day he would sneak into other monks' rooms and carry off their most prized possessions. He would keep them for a few days and then return them to their owners. This is said to have been his skillful way of destroying the basis for their self-fixation, and helped them a great deal.

At night, he would sit up at midnight and briefly chant Calling the Guru From Afar in a haunting melody. He would then rest evenly in samadhi. In the morning, at seven, he would arise from meditation and delightedly perform the dance of dharma. He would also spontaneously sing many previously unheard songs based on his experience.

Finally, in the year 1969, his seventy-eighth year, he passed away. For three days afterward he remained in meditation. By that time all of the monks from the great seats had tremendous faith in him; after his passing they assiduously collected his hair and clothing, and treasured them greatly. It had become obvious that he was a holy being.

Through the virtue of eulogizing your utter liberation
On utterly white paper
With utterly few words,
May the teachings of our utterly perfect guide spread.

13 Droril the Yogini

Droril was a yogini from Rima.

Through the unchanging faith and devotion in your heart
For the supreme deity, the great treasure of nobility of heart,
And your repetition of his six-syllable heart-essence,
You revealed the heart of everything. Yogini, I bow to you!

This yogini was from Rimar in Kham. She was called Droril because her hair was whiter than a conch, and she usually bundled herself in an outer garment of white felt. Droril means "wheat-colored and round." As she worked constantly as a shepherd, she never learned to read. However, she continuously recited the MANI with stable faith and trust, and eventually recited more than three hundred million. Her brother recited one hundred million and had a good practice.

When Droril herded her sheep in cold weather she would recite MANIs on the mountain slopes and then, imagining a fence surrounding her flock, would blow air in their direction. She would say, "Through the compassion of Arya Avalokita, they'll be fine." Then she would sleep through the day, without checking on the sheep even once. The sheep would never stray from the area she had blessed for them as pasture. In the evening she would imagine summoning them to her, and they would follow her home.

When the weather was fine she would circumambulate the mountain's peak while reciting MANIs.

At that time my kind guru was about ten years old, and loved to accompany her when she tended her flocks. He told me that there were several reasons for this. As she was a bodhisattva who had perfected love and compassion she was loving to all beings, including him. In addition, because she blessed her sheep they were protected from all harm, including the predation of wolves. They therefore did not require much actual shepherding, so accompanying her was free of stress. Also, although he had barely enough clothing to survive the weather, she would let him lie down to sleep inside her outer garment.

Because she used her mala so much, its cord was always breaking. He often helped her restring it with yarn.

She cured the blindness of both humans and animals simply by blowing on them; her benefit of others was not inconsiderable. It is said in authoritative sources that those who complete one hundred million MANIs will grow a new tooth even if they are advanced in age; accordingly, she grew three. They were as bright and white as a conch; everyone who saw them was amazed and inspired. I have heard from others that she passed away while sitting up with her palms joined in prayer.

It is said that in these times of decadence and short lives it is better to accumulate a spark of merit than a mountain of learning. I have never heard of a source of merit greater than meditating on the single deity Avalokita and reciting the single mantra of six syllables. Unfortunately, most people are like me; they neglect the accumulation of merit in favor of elevated, empty words about the view, meditation, and conduct while abandoning their bodies, speech, and minds to mediocrity. This is our worst problem, both for this life and for the future. I have not seen this do anyone any real good, only bring about their ruin and that of others.

Through the virtue of writing this may beings in the
six states
Rely upon the six syllables, the king of mantras;
Purify the six kleshas that cause rebirth;
And reach the state of Vajradhara, the sixth buddha.

14 Karma Tendzin

Karma Tendzin was a lama and lifelong retreatant from Thrangu Monastery.

Threefold guru drunk on the taste of the nature of being,
You bring unprotected, tormented beings
To bliss beyond being through nonreferential compassion
Beyond coming, going, or being. Realized one, I bow to you.

Karma Tendzin was from Bi in the vicinity of Thrangu Monastery. After doing a three-year retreat in the Six Dharmas of Naropa Retreat he went on to do continuous solitary retreat in isolated places such as the site of the great image of Vairochana in Bi.

When the livestock of the chieftain of Rongpo were struck by rinderpest, many of them dying, he was invited and went there along with another monk as his attendant. The chieftain separated the animals that had contracted the illness from those that had not and Karma Tendzin inspected them, repeatedly saying, "Poor things, poor things."

He promised to perform severance that evening. When he began, although two lamps had been lit, he pretended from time to time to be unable to see his text. At other moments he pretended to be somewhat illiterate. Then, he suddenly demanded that his attendant bring him a urination pot. Extremely embarrassed but unable to refuse, the attendant brought one and Karma Tendzin promptly urinated into it. The chieftain and his entourage were present for all this; they too became embarrassed and were struggling not to laugh.

In reality, Karma Tendzin was engaged in the essence of severance, which is the eradication of self-fixation, and purification with amrita; he later admitted this.

When he retired for the night he stripped off all of his clothing, including his skirt, and saying "Ow, ow!" he began to scratch his body as though he were covered with lice. Ashamed, his attendant immediately covered him with a blanket.

On the day afterward Karma Tendzin announced that he would make singed offerings and gathered the requisite materials. He formed a lot of representations of horses, people, goats, and livestock. While doing this he described the value of each of the animals and the reputation of each of the people depicted. Then, all of a sudden, he told them to let all of the animals go. Everyone was shocked, but they didn't dare disobey him.

In the middle of the night he appeared to become very ill with diarrhea. When he was repeatedly asked what was going on, he told them that he was practicing taking and sending. Although rinderpest never spreads from animals to humans, he was able to take the animals' illness into himself.

On the next day he returned to Thrangu Monastery. Afterward, it was discovered that all of the livestock were completely cured of their illness. The chieftain and all his subjects became Karma Tendzin's devoted disciples. He passed away amidst wondrous signs when my kind guru was around thirty.

With the stream of your compassion free from samsaric reference points,
You cooled unprotected beings tormented by samsaric heat,
Knowing them to have been your parents, kind beyond samsaric repayment.
I pray to emulate your deeds and bring samsaric beings to bliss.

15 Arkham Serbal and his Wife

Arkham Serbal and his wife were hidden siddhas.

Although you reached the hidden meaning, dharmata's exhaustion,
In the unhidden perception of beings
You displayed the deeds of hidden siddhas.
May you be victorious, hidden yogin and yogini!

Arkham Serbal was a water carrier at Dzodzi, a Kagyu monastery. His wife herded dzos for the monastery. One day a monk of that monastery saw them sitting and talking where they usually drew water. In front of them was a bloody human skull filled with brains, which they were eating with their hands. Shocked, the monk told the monastery about this, and they, along with their son, daughter, goats, and dogs were evicted from the monastery. They were brought to a narrow valley surrounded by high mountains and rocks on all sides. It seemed impossible for them to escape from the valley, but they were also forbidden to leave it. Guards were posted on watch at all times.

Whenever the curious secretly spied on them they always appeared relaxed and at ease, but as soon as they detected that they were being observed they would start to quarrel furiously with one another.

After several days they began to quarrel so loudly that the sound of their shouting filled the entire valley. People gathered to watch, and saw that this time they were fighting with more than words; they had actually come to blows. The father of the family was seen seizing his daughter and striking his wife with her. The girl then dissolved into her mother, who shouted, "You've killed my daughter!"

Wailing loudly, she grabbed their son and struck her husband with him. The boy dissolved into his father, who exclaimed, "You've killed my son!" Weeping, the father seized his wife as though to wrestle with her. She seized her husband at the same time. The moment they did so, they dissolved into one another, seemed to ascend the rocks behind them, and disappeared. Their goats and dogs, bleating and barking, also seemed to ascend the rocks and then disappeared. Afterward, people could see clear human footprints and goat hoof-prints on the rock wall. Recognizing that they had failed to appreciate the family's holiness and had treated them poorly, the entire monastery felt great regret and faith.

Although to our dim vision without clarity
You seemed impure, without virtue,
You had realized the nature without artifice
And passed into rainbow bodies without exception.
This revealed the state without knowledge
Of beings' ignorance, which is without awareness.
Let us never again point our finger without hesitation
In rash judgment without careful examination.
I dedicate whatever virtue is here, without reservation,
To the happiness of all my mothers, without exception.

16 Khenpo Gangshar

Khenpo Gangshar was from Shechen, a Nyingma monastery.

The clean face of wisdom present from the beginning
Was concealed by dirt and unseen by anyone.
You washed it on the spot with the water of mahamudra
and dzokchen
And bejeweled it with the trikaya. I bow to you.

Khenpo Gangshar was born at Shechen in Kham. He was descended from Adro Dra Rapjampa, who was a disciple of the Eighth Tai Situpa Chökyi Jungney. When the Gelukpa monastery Labrang Tashi Khyil asked the Tai Situpa to send his disciple Belo Tsewang Kunkhyap there, he sent Adro instead. This led to a lineage of instruction based on the Tai Situpa's *Great Exegesis of Grammar* at Labrang Tashi Khyil that still exists today. Adro was a tantrika, not a monastic, and therefore had descendants. Among them was Khenpo Lodrö Rapsal of Shechen, who was a nephew of Shechen Gyaltsap Rinpoche. Khenpo Gangshar was Khenpo Lodrö Rapsal's nephew.

Khenpo Gangshar's parents had many sons and daughters, but they all died. For that reason, on the day after his birth his father gave him to a relative. When he later learned to speak he clearly described his father bringing him to the relative, including the mountains they passed on their journey and what he was wearing at the time. There were other extraordinary signs as well. One day there was a great snowfall, and many birds gathered, picking at seeds. Khenpo Gangshar threw a large flat rock from the roof of his home, crushing many birds underneath. When his mother scolded him, he immediately went outside and lifted up the stone. All the birds flew off unharmed. From an early age he did wondrous things.

He soon went to Shechen Monastery, where he studied reading, writing, and other subjects with his uncle, Khenpo Lodrö Rapsal. From there he went to the college at Katok Monastery, where he completed his studies under the guidance of Khenpo Nüden.

Khenpo Gangshar was an extremely gentle person, and in particular upheld the vinaya in an exemplary manner; he had all the qualities of the holy.

The Eleventh Trungpa Rinpoche went to Shechen Monastery in order to study. Afterward, he spoke to Khenpo Lodrö Rapsal of the lack of a khenpo for the college at Surmang Dutsi Til Monastery. He insistently asked that Khenpo Gangshar be sent there. Khenpo Lodrö Rapsal acceded to his request and wept with wonder, saying, "It is amazing that you are already taking on such great responsibility for the teachings!" Trungpa Rinpoche was only fourteen at the time.

So Khenpo Gangshar went to Surmang Dutsi Til. After he had been there for about two years he became extremely ill and passed away. While Khenpo Gangshar was in samadhi, Trungpa Rinpoche kept a vigil in the room. Khenpo Gangshar's remains were behind a curtain, which Trungpa Rinpoche eventually lifted in order to view his teacher's body. Khenpo Gangshar was seated upright in meditation, but when the curtain was lifted a breeze struck his face; he blinked and arose from samadhi.

He said, "Although my karmic lifespan is completed, I

encountered Jamgön Kongtrul Yönten Gyamtso and Jamyang Khyentse Wangpo after my death; they have sent me back to complete the liberation of their remaining disciples.

"In addition, I am the final emanation among the hundred and eight tertöns prophesied by Guru Rinpoche. Most tertöns reveal statues, books, and scepters from mountains and rocks. I am unlike them; I must reveal the treasure of the trikaya by directly pointing out through instruction the treasure-like sugatagarbha that lies hidden in everyone's mind.

"Very soon the times will change; there will be no leisure for the practice of preliminaries." Having said that, Khenpo Gangshar directly pointed out the nature to whomever he met by means of mahamudra and dzokchen. Of necessity he accepted a consort.

Once he convened a great ganachakra, saying, "We will need the feast substances described in the tantras." The corpse of a small child was brought from a distance of three days' journey, and excrement and so forth were gathered.

Khenpo Gangshar announced, "Whoever tastes these feast substances will achieve the state of Vajradhara in this life!" Everyone believed what he said and enjoyed the feast with devotion. Not only did they not perceive the feast as disgusting; they found it to have an amazingly fine taste and fragrance. All of the monastics and laity who partook of that feast had from then on little craving for the world; they delighted only in the practice of meditation. In addition, that area became free from illnesses of both humans and livestock, and became more prosperous. There were amazing signs.

Wherever he went, Khenpo Gangshar bestowed guidance on the mind. He visited Thrangu Monastery for two days and gave instruction on the mind to about five hundred monks. My kind guru was there then, and has told me, "As soon as I saw him I was overwhelmed by feelings of devotion as intense as if meeting a mahasiddha such as Tilopa or Naropa."

Khenpo Gangshar taught that, since sugatagarbha is present within everyone's mind, we need to look directly at the nature of our minds using mahamudra and dzokchen. He taught that looking at one's mind is extremely convenient; even when undergoing the hardships brought by the changing times that were soon to come, looking at one's mind would be easier than any other form of practice. He also strongly advised those he taught to abstain from any violent resistance against the Communist occupation.

He gave instruction on the mind to everyone he met. He would begin by directly describing each person's individual faults; his knowledge of their faults caused everyone to feel unfabricated devotion. Then he would point out the nature of their mind. His compassion and blessing were so great that most of those who met him were liberated on the spot.

The instruction on the mind that he gave to a retreat master of Thrangu Monastery was to say to him, "First turn your back to this column. Now turn to face it. Now turn your back to it again."

The retreat master did this. Khenpo Gangshar then asked him, "Do you understand?"

The retreat master answered, "I do."

Years later my kind guru asked the retreat master, "What did he mean?"

The retreat master told him, "What he meant is very easy to understand. The meaning of turning my back to the column was that through not realizing the unity of things and their nature we turn our backs on it. My then facing the column was a symbol of the unity of things and their nature. My once again turning my back to the column was a symbol that through correctly realizing that unity one turns one's back on samsara."

Khenpo Gangshar gave many such skillful pointing-out instructions.

He continued to act in this way for more than a year. Then he sent his consort back to her family and returned to Shechen Monastery, where he resumed his former modest demeanor and observance of the vinaya.

Then the changing times of which he had spoken occurred. He, Khenpo Lodrö Rapsal, Shechen Kongtrul Rinpoche, and others were imprisoned in Dartsedo. It appears that he passed away there.

Yogis who realize that all that appears or exists is mind
Freely perform the illusory dance of birth and death.
This ability is born from the blessings of a realized guru
In the lake of their own unfabricated devotion.

17 Karma Dargye

Karma Dargye of Kori was a retreat master at Thrangu, a Kagyu monastery.

Everything that appears or exists is illusory drama.
Realizing this, you holy beings can transform it at will.

Help us, so bound by our belief in its reality,
To achieve freedom from fixation in this life.

Karma Dargye of Kori was born in upper Rongpo. He undertook renunciation at Thrangu Monastery at a young age. When he was in the retreat there his room was adjacent to that of the presiding retreat master. He practiced with diligence and recited mantras loudly and distinctly. From time to time, while reciting mantras, he would circumambulate the retreat. The retreat master heard him and wondered how he had got out, as the gate to the retreat was locked. The retreat master went out to look and found that Karma Dargye was seated in his room reciting mantras as before. The retreat master heard him do this many times, and concluded that Karma Dargye had stabilized the practice of the illusory body. Later, after the retreat was concluded, many people witnessed Karma Dargye sometimes leaving his room through the walls, unobstructed by them.

When Lama Ganga was young Karma Dargye was his tutor. From time to time Karma Dargye would get up late at night after going to sleep and announce that it was time for his supper; on such days he ate supper twice.

Karma Dargye was the retreat master who trained Ogyen, who was later Lama Ganga's retreat master. One day Ogyen got hold of some clay in the retreat and made a statue of Jetsun Milarepa. He placed it on his table and was looking at it during a meditation session when his retreat master Karma Dargye suddenly opened his door, rushed into his room, and threw the statue to the ground. Karma Dargye then realized that it was an image of Milarepa, so he quickly placed it on his head and then threw it outside.

During the next day's assembly the retreat master Karma Dargye scolded Ogyen, saying, "Yesterday Ogyen not only wasted a meditation session; he also made me kill Milarepa!"

While Karma Dargye was the retreat master the discipline in the retreat was somewhat unsteady. One day he needed to go out, and did so. While the retreatants were assembled, performing Renewal and Purification of the Three Vows, the retreat attendant was seen pulling on the end of a rope. Then Karma Dargye returned, leading a dri. He said, "I have saved this dri from slaughter; do you all rejoice?"

Everyone replied, "We rejoice!"

Karma Dargye asked them, "Do you really rejoice?"

Everyone replied, "We really rejoice!"

Karma Dargye said, "In that case you must all contribute grain to pay for the dri."

One monk was saving grain to pay for the woodblock printing of Traleg Rinpoche's biography, so he said, "I don't have enough grain to be able to contribute to this."

Karma Dargye said, "In that case touch heads with me." They did, and then Karma Dargye said, "By touching heads with me you said goodbye, so I'm going." He started to prepare to leave, so everyone asked him to remain. In particular the monk who had objected to paying for the dri now promised to contribute.

There was an old monk named Nyenpa Rapgye. Although he was lame, he had been the best at the physical exercises among all the retreatants in the Six Dharmas of Naropa Retreat. One day he said to his attendant Karma Sönam, "I am definitely going to die tomorrow. Please invite Kori Karma Dargye here." Karma Dargye was brought there and spent quite some time conversing with Nyenpa Rapgye; then he left. Nyenpa Rapgye said, "They say Kori Karma Dargye is realized. He seems to be; he has helped me. Karma Sönam, please make my supper tonight. You won't have to make my breakfast tomorrow; I'll be dead by then." His attendant agreed to this, but didn't really believe what Nyenpa Rapgye said. The next morning when the cock crowed Karma Sönam heard Nyenpa Rapgye coughing and thought, "He said he was going to pass away, but he's still alive."

As soon as he thought that, Nyenpa Rapgye asked him, "Karma Sönam, has the cock crowed?"

Karma Sönam replied, "He has crowed."

Nyenpa Rapgye said, "Oh, good!" Then he was quiet.

Karma Sönam thought "What's happening?" and went to look. He found that Nyenpa Rapgye had put on his meditation hat and his formal robe, and was seated upright in posthumous samadhi.

In the shining mirror of mind-itself
Appear the reflections of outer and inner objects.
Ordinary beings are trapped in the net of delusion.
The noble ones realize them to be unreal illusions.
May this net of grasping, fixation, and delusion
Be cut by the razor of realization.

18 Shagö the Severance Master

Shagö was a monk of Thrangu Monastery.

You severed the bonds of grasping at objects.
You severed fixation, internal kleshas.

You gained confidence in realization beyond dirty
and clean.
Yogi, to you I prostrate!

When Shagö was around twenty his uncle told him to slaughter a pack animal. The beast took a long time to die, and lay there with tears streaming from its eyes. Seeing this caused Shagö to relinquish all worldly activity from then on. He undertook renunciation and spent one year in the Vairochana Retreat and three years in the Six Dharmas of Naropa Retreat. Whenever he practiced severance he would cry.

In order to practice the all-victorious conduct he took to wearing just a loin cloth and let his hair grow long and unbound. Practically naked, he began to wander around the area of Thrangu Monastery, blowing a thighbone trumpet. At the time my kind guru was around eleven years of age, and encountered Shagö while fetching water. Frightened, my guru hid behind a boulder. A woman with the marks of a dakini was relieving herself there; as soon as she saw Shagö she ran away in fear, yelling. Without hesitation Shagö ate her steaming excrement; by doing so he properly established the interdependence of all-victorious conduct.

Your habit of renunciation, accumulated over many kalpas,
Was awakened in an instant by the slightest thing.
You entered the supreme path beyond hope and fear,
And reached the state of peace. I rejoice!

19 Ju Mipham Jamyang Namgyal Gyamtso

Adorned by the fine jewelry of relinquishment and realization,
You are world-famous for your learning, nobility, and goodness.
You are the supreme crown-jewel of all the scholars and siddhas of Tibet.
I bow to the great Mipham, Mañjushri in person.

Ju Mipham Namgyal Gyamtso was a direct disciple of both Jamyang Khyentse Wangpo and Jamgön Kongtrul. His full biography can be found elsewhere; here I wish to tell briefly of the five years he spent living at the Palace of Supreme Bliss in Ga. This was on the site of the present location of the Vairochana Retreat at Thrangu Tashi Chöling Monastery.

As soon as he moved there, Mipham painted a sword, representing Mañjushri, and a two-headed bird, representing the great translators, on the wall of his residence; these are also insignia of the Nyingma tradition. He later said that the isolated location of his residence was geomantically excellent, and that his experience and realization had flourished there. He named it Solitary Palace of Supreme Bliss.

While Mipham was living there several monks of Thrangu Monastery, including the lifelong retreatant Karma Tashi, met him. They said Mipham was tall and handsome, with reddish brown skin. It was while he was living there that he wrote the *Gateway to Knowledge* and his *Great Explanation of the Kalachakra*. He also wrote his

Response to Criticism and his *Final Response* there. One day a man with the appearance of being from Amdo brought him several books and said, "I will need your response to these within a month from now." Mipham Rinpoche placed the books on his head and then set them aside. About a month later the man returned and asked Mipham to return the books. They were exactly where Mipham had put them a month before; he had not touched them since, and they were a little dusty.

Mipham said, "Please wait here today." Then he opened the books for the first time and, laughing a bit, added a few notes to them here and there and returned them.

His guest thought, "These books were written in committee by many great scholars such as Palri Lobzang Rapsal over many months. How could Mipham respond to them by adding a few notes one day?"

He returned to Labrang Tashi Khyil Monastery and offered the books to Palri Lobzang Rapsal, who immediately placed them on his head and then blessed all of his disciples with them, saying, "We must pray to become disciples of Mipham Rinpoche, the dharma king of the three realms, in our next lives!"

While telling me this story my kind guru shed tears.

Jamgön Mipham Rinpoche and his attendant Ösal kept a few dzos. They were tended by a monk of Thrangu Monastery called Bengap Dara.

Mipham Rinpoche would often tell Bengap Dara, "Eat whatever food you have; don't hoard it!" Hearing this, Bengap Dara would think, "I eat as well as I can, and never hoard food. What does he mean?" He told this to many other monks.

Years later, when Bengap Dara was old, he began to hoard the butter and other foodstuffs he received in the assemblies at Thrangu Monastery. Not daring to consume them, he became pallid and wore shoddy clothing. When he died and it was discovered that all the butter he had saved had become rotten and turned blue, the truth of Mipham's prophecy became evident.

One day the previous Lord Refuge Thrangu Rinpoche, attended by the lifelong retreatant Karma Tashi, rode to Mipham Rinpoche's residence, the Palace of Great Bliss, in order to meet with him before he left the Thrangu area. He brought many offerings, a pot of ink, a pen, and several sheets of blank paper, and told Mipham, "Although, greatest of scholars and siddhas, you have been living here for several years, because of my advanced age, chronic ailments, and ceremonial duties in local communities I have been unable to study under your guidance. I regret this deeply. I am also unsatisfied by my service to the teachings. Please hold me in your compassion so that in my next life I serve the teachings and purely uphold your dharma lineage." Saying that, he held onto Mipham's clothing and wept.

Jamgön Mipham Rinpoche, extremely pleased, replied, "Certainly! Your offering of pen, ink, and paper is extremely auspicious. The sun is about to set, but I will help you pull it back up into the very center of the sky!" At the time, the meaning of what Mipham said then was unknown. However, if we now consider that at this time when the Kagyu teachings have been seriously threatened the present Thrangu Rinpoche's activity in upholding, sustaining, and spreading the Buddhadharma and especially the Kagyu teachings through instruction, practice, and work has been peerless, the meaning of Jamgön Mipham's prophecy is extremely clear.

When the lord of scholars Mipham was about to pass away, he instructed his attendant Ösal to offer a fragment of his bones to Thrangu Rinpoche. When Thrangu Rinpoche received it, he enshrined part of it in a stupa that he kept in his room; part of it is in the locket that the present Thrangu Rinpoche wears at his throat to this day.

In the Palace of Great Bliss, a hermitage in Ga,
Mañjushri in person, Mipham Rinpoche,
Jampal Gyepay Dorje, bestowed the blessing
Of his luminous three secrets.

20 Khenpo Lodrö Rapsal

Lodrö Rapsal was a khenpo from Shechen, a Nyingma monastery.

From the peak of the mountain of learning, discipline, and goodness
You sent forth the roar of tradition, reasoning, and practical instruction,
Causing the foxes of dispute to flee to the darkness.
I bow to you who spread the impartial teachings of the victors.

Shechen Khenpo Lodrö Rapsal was born at Shechen to the family of Adro Dra Rapjampa. His sister was a nun; she was the steward of both Shechen Gyaltsap and Shechen Rapjam. Shechen Gyaltsap Gyurmey Pema Namgyal, who was a disciple of both Jamgön Kongtrul Lodrö Thaye and Mipham Jamyang Namgyal Gyamtso, was both Lodrö Rapsal's uncle and his guru.

Once Lodrö Rapsal, his sister the nun, and more than thirty pilgrims went on pilgrimage to Lhasa and Samye. Lodrö Rapsal told his companions that it would be unfitting for him not to visit Daklha Gampo, Gampopa's seat. As all the pilgrims were Nyingmapas and might say they didn't want to make the journey (in which case he would have been unable to go), he and his sister went there alone. They visited every part of it. According to Lodrö Rapsal's sister, while they were viewing an image of Gampopa, the eyes of the statue gazed intently at her brother. Later, Khenpo Lodrö Rapsal said that he had had three visions of Gampopa while he was at Thrangu Monastery.

Once, while Khenpo Lodrö Rapsal was singing the *Ocean of Songs* with his students, he suddenly began to gaze into space and dropped his text to the ground. He stayed in meditation for a little while, and then appeared surprised, saying, "I'm like a crazy person! What did I just do?" It seems that this was one of his visions of Gampopa.

Once, while the shrine custodian was walking to the college, he saw Khenpo Lodrö Rapsal gazing into the sky while dancing. Unable to avoid him, the custodian was observed by Khenpo, who immediately came over to him, touched heads with him, and walked away. According to my guru, this seems to have been another occasion when Khenpo had a vision of Gampopa.

As other philosophical schools had a strong dislike for the dharma lineage of Mipham, when the Thrangu college was studying Mipham's writings under the guidance of Khenpo

Lodrö Rapsal he said that there was a strong malignant magical influence present. They therefore invited the Drikung tertön Ösal Dorje, who showed up wearing a mirror over his heart. When he was asked to perform a protection blessing the tertön pulled a text out of his robe and began to chant a blessing. However, he appeared unable to read his text properly, and his voice became hoarse; he seemed unable to perform the ceremony. Khenpo Lodrö Rapsal had the thought, "This tertön is either a charlatan or a sophist!"

As soon as Khenpo had that thought, the tertön replaced his text in his robe and, while rubbing his mirror up and down, began to spontaneously tell many wondrous accounts of how he and Khenpo had been guru and disciple throughout many lives. As there were neither recording devices nor writing materials present, these were not recorded or written down. However my kind guru, who was there, has said that he clearly remembers the tertön saying that Khenpo Lodrö Rapsal was a rebirth of Dakpo Tashi Namgyal. Khenpo Lodrö Rapsal often remarked that he was certain that he was the rebirth of a Kagyu lama.

The Drikung tertön Ösal Dorje was closely connected to Thrangu Monastery; in particular, his mind and that of Traleg Rinpoche were mixed as one. Ösal Dorje once predicted, "In the future Thrangu Monastery will expand greatly; I have seen the golden spire of its temple from the source of the Dragyal River." Later, when my kind guru went to the source of the Dragyal River and looked, he said he was able to see the temple's spire.

When Traleg Rinpoche passed away the Second Jamgön Rinpoche, Palden Khyentse Özer, was invited to the monastery and performed his funeral observances for a month. During that time Jamgön Rinpoche remarked, "Traleg Rinpoche is now hale and hearty, happily living at the Glorious Copper-Colored Mountain in the company of Guru Rinpoche. Meanwhile I am left here, pallid and weak! I don't want to live here anymore! I'm going there!" Immediately after completing the month-long funeral, Palden Khyentse Özer passed away in the hermitage Palace of Great Bliss. When he was cremated, the smoke from the fire rose into the blue sky and gradually formed a tent of rainbow light; this was seen by my kind guru and all of the monastics and laypeople present. Many relics appeared around the place where the cremation was performed. A stupa was built to enshrine Jamgön Rinpoche's remains.

Once, after Jamgön Rinpoche's passing, while Khenpo Lodrö Rapsal and his students were singing the *Ocean of Songs* at the college, he suddenly joined his palms at his heart and exclaimed, "Children! The perfect Buddha has actually come here! It is certain that whatever aspirations you make will be accomplished, so make them!" When they subsequently asked him about this, he told them that Jamgön Palden Khyentse Özer had actually come there.

Later, after the invasion, Shechen Kongtrul Rinpoche, Khenpo Gangshar, and Shechen Khenpo Lodrö Rapsal were captured by the soldiers. They were later seen in the prison at Dartsedo by a monk who was also being held there. When Khenpo Lodrö Rapsal was dying he asked to be brought to Thrangu Monastery, but no one was able to do this. According to my kind guru, it is likely that he died in the prison at Dartsedo.

Shechen Kongtrul Rinpoche once said, "Although

Khenpo Lodrö Rapsal was always extremely intelligent and learned in philosophy and logic, he had no realization. When he returned from Thrangu Tashi Chöling Monastery in upper Ga, however, he was no longer merely learned; he had become a great lord of realization. Thrangu Tashi Chöling in upper Ga is a place with blessing unlike that of anywhere else!"

The renowned Karmapa, the Buddhas' activity,
Has blessed with his three secrets the best place in Ga.
It is Thrangu Tashi Chöling Monastery in upper Ga.
Simply seeing it brings one to the path to freedom.

21 Gongpen the Protector Lama

Gongpen the protector lama was a monk of Thrangu Monastery.

Dharmapala Bernakchen, you are the play of the victors' activity.
If accomplished through offering, praise, and faith you bestow siddhi.
Although in your outer rupakaya you performed the dance of a poor monk,
You were inwardly and really the wisdom dharmapala. I bow to you!

Gongpen was an impoverished monk without wealth or possessions who continuously lived in the protector temple. Whenever there were thunder, lightning, and hail he would call out to the local deity Rakma Bukur, "Rakma Bukur, settle down! You are under my control!" As long as he lived, no one there was harmed by hail.

When he went to the bathroom at night he would make loud cracks with a sling. He said that he was shooting stones into the cauldrons of hell. People didn't believe him, and joked that his excrement roared and cracked.

When he was about to pass away he said, "On the fifteenth day of this month I will die. Thrangu Monastery has been very kind to me, so although I have nothing else to offer, I will leave you my skull. You will need to cremate my body, but if you can place my skull in the Yak Stupa there will be the greatest benefit. I cannot supply or pay for the wood and so on for my cremation; you will need the assistance of the local families and communities." He then passed away.

His skull survived his cremation unburnt, so it was placed in the Yak Stupa as he had directed.

For the sake of beings, our mothers,
You accomplished the Mother and Lord, the dharmapalas,
And led all our mothers out of hell
And to the path to freedom, like a mother.

22 Sherap Gyaltsen

Sherap Gyaltsen was a monk of Langchen, a Sakya monastery.

You realized the natural state, ultimate wisdom.
With great wisdom you traversed the stages and paths in one life.
You raised the victory banner of freedom over this whole earth.

The victory banner of your fame has reached the peak of existence; I bow to you.

Sherap Gyaltsen was originally a monk of Kyergu, a Sakya monastery. His incompetence while serving as the monastery's steward caused him to be expelled from Kyergu, so he went to Darjay, also a Sakya monastery, where he also served as the steward. He again proved incompetent, and was expelled from that monastery as well. He then went to Langchen, another Sakya monastery, where he took up residence. An elderly woman there with influence in the government protected him from punishment after the invasion. When he was dying he told her, "Langchen Monastery has been very kind to me. Burn my body, but preserve my skull as a support for the monastery."

He died wearing his dharma robe. The elderly woman gathered wood and cremated his remains as he had requested, but his robe wouldn't burn, so she removed it and laid it aside on a rock. After his cremation, his skull remained unburnt, his robe disappeared, and countless shariram arose. She gave these to all the faithful who wanted them. It is said that once it was decided that she had given too many away and should charge a bit of money for them, they stopped multiplying, and in some cases disappeared from within the paper in which they'd been wrapped.

You secretly traversed the pure stages and paths,
Revealing the pure, primordial nature.
Your pure remains gave birth to shariram.
I dedicate your pure and holy virtue!

23 The Blacksmith's Wife An Emanation of Vajravarahi

Supremely changeless great bliss
Appears as all types of rupakayas for the good of beings.
These guide pure and impure beings.
I devotedly bow to the mother of the victors.

In the region of Sakya, in Tsang, there lived a blacksmith and his wife. In those days to be a blacksmith was considered the lowest of occupations, and blacksmiths were little esteemed. In particular, no one liked the wife of a blacksmith. In the uplands nearby there lived in retreat a yogin and his disciple. Whenever the yogin performed a ganachakra, the disciple heard the sound of a beautiful female voice speaking, but never saw the speaker. When he told his guru that he wanted to see her, the yogin said, "She is a dakini; seeing her requires a little realization."

The disciple insisted that he wanted to meet her, so the guru told him, "Go into the village today. Prostrate yourself without hesitation to whomever you meet; you will receive a bit of siddhi."

The disciple walked to the village. On his way he encountered the blacksmith's wife, who was walking toward him. She had removed her upper garments, exposing her breasts, and was carrying a few radishes. He immediately prostrated himself to her. She appeared displeased and loudly exclaimed, "You dull monk! What are you doing, prostrating to me?" She then rubbed a piece of turnip against her nipples and saying, "Here! Take this!," threw it at him.

The disciple returned to his guru and told him what had

happened. The yogin said, "As siddhi you received that piece of radish." The disciple again insisted that he wanted to meet the dakini, so the guru told him, "Tonight go to the blacksmith's home and sleep among the pigs in the pigsty there. No matter who shows up there, don't think too much. Have faith!"

The disciple lay down to sleep that night in the blacksmith's pigsty. Around midnight the pigs began to squeal and grunt loudly and run around. When the disciple got up and looked he saw that the pigs' heads were blazing with fire. All of a sudden, amongst them was a naked woman with upswept hair; Vajravarahi was really there! Terrified, he covered his eyes with his hands. When he looked again after a moment, he saw none of this.

When he related this story to his guru, the yogin appeared displeased and said, "Too bad! This is not good! Vajravarahi actually came to you, and you not only failed to have faith, you were afraid! You have impaired your samaya! This is inauspicious; Vajravarahi is now going to depart for other realms. Tomorrow go to the charnel ground and meet her there!"

The next day, when the disciple went to the charnel ground as the yogin had instructed him, he discovered that the blacksmith's wife had died, and her corpse had been brought to the charnel ground. It was being consumed by vultures. The disciple saw that the vultures were really viras and virinis. They threw him a piece of one of the woman's ribs and told him, "Samaya-breaker, this is all you get!"

Yogins and yoginis who've completed the stages and paths
Place disciples on the path to freedom in appropriate ways

Through skillful magical displays, pure and impure.
I rejoice in this with unchangeable great faith and devotion.

24 Dorje Gyaltsen

The Upasaka Dorje Gyaltsen is a protector of Thrangu Monastery.

Guru Padmasambhava, the Second Buddha;
Nyima Gyurmey, Saltong Shogom's emanation;
And all the wise and accomplished have appointed you
To protect the victor's teachings. I bow at your feet, great Upasaka!

The Upasaka of Thrangu Monastery is one of the twenty-one upasakas commanded by Guru Rinpoche to protect the teachings. When Nyima Gyurmey, the Second Traleg Kyabgön, attempted to cross the iron suspension bridge at Sok, the Upasaka didn't allow it, and caused an earthquake, a hailstorm, and thunder and lightning in protest. While Traleg Rinpoche's party camped there for one day, he bound the upasaka to samaya and led him, like an owner leading a dog, back to Thrangu Monastery, appointing him as its protector.

There is a story that when the siddha Tangtong Gyalpo began to build that bridge the resident gods, out of jealousy, tried to prevent him. The siddha then composed and performed the Lhamo Dance, which delighted the gods. While they were thus distracted, the siddha completed the construction of the bridge. It is near Sandalwood

Monastery, a large Gelukpa monastery.

When Jamgön Mipham first came to Thrangu he observed the monastery supplicating the Upasaka of Thrangu. He thought, "Even this monastery propitiates an aggressive spirit!" One day, when a number of young monks were gathering juniper, he saw the Upasaka holding each of the monks with his hand, preventing them from falling over a precipice. He asked Bengap Dara, "What is the name of your local deity?"

The monk answered, "He is called Dorje Gyaltsen." Mipham then wrote this activity entrustment:

HRIH Powerful, mighty lord of this place,
Known as Upasaka Dorje Gyaltsen,
Appearing as a wealth-lord along with your beloved consort, the nagini:
Come here! I offer you purely-prepared torma, select beverages,
Gifts, dress, and clouds and oceans of all you desire.
May your heart be filled with pleasure!
Always protect and assist us as you would your own children.
Guard us against all enemies and harm.
Though your mastery of magical transformation—
Into a divine white yak, a terrifying great serpent,
And a ferocious nagamara riding a crocodile—
Protect us and utterly defeat our enemies.
If I venerate and praise you, mighty one,
Cause the teachings of all the accomplishment lineage and this monastery,
The sangha, grain, livestock, and prosperity to increase.
Accomplish everything that is truly good!

After the invasion of Tibet and before the lamas and monks began to flee, several lamas of Thrangu Monastery and several religious villagers dreamed of the Upasaka, who told them, "Flee, taking the lamas with you. I have to remain in China for the time being." Then he cleansed them with water from a vase and blessed them. As a result of their dreams, many lamas and monks of Thrangu Monastery safely reached India.

Years later, when the Lord Refuge Thrangu Rinpoche was building a college at Namo Buddha in Nepal, the work became subject to many difficulties. There was a lama there called Lama Kundrak, who regularly saw spirits and had visions. Once, in a dream or vision, he saw the traditional protectors of Thrangu Monastery. They appeared angry, and said, "Since Thrangu Rinpoche fled to India he has not only neglected our supplication; he doesn't even remember us!"

Lama Kundrak informed Thrangu Rinpoche of his vision. Up to then Thrangu Rinpoche had been privately supplicating the Upasaka and the Five Bodies of the King, longtime protectors of Thrangu; from then on he made sure that all the lamas and monks recited their daily supplications without fail. The construction work was soon completed without obstacle.

The reconstruction of the temple at Thrangu Monastery destroyed during the cultural revolution was undertaken with great exertion by the monks who remained there, including Dara Karma Rinchen, Bentra Tutop, Bentra Karma Chöpel, Gyara Düdül, and Rinchen Norbu. During the reconstruction Dara Karma Rinchen and other young monks went to Surmang to cut wood for the temple. While there, they stayed in a tent. People of Surmang told them, "Every night a light brown yak with a white blaze sleeps beside your tent. It also circles the tent, snorting."

One day the local people told them, "Be careful today! That yak is snorting and striking the ground with his horns; he seems agitated!" This was at the time when they were bringing the cut wood to Thrangu Monastery. That day one of the loads of wood became unbalanced and started to lean to the right. However, other than leaning it didn't fall over, so neither the driver nor any of the monks were injured. The local people saw the load start to lean, and said they saw the same light brown yak with a white blaze they'd seen before support the load, preventing it from falling over, and protecting those transporting it. However, while the local people saw it, none of our monks did.

Thrangu Tashi Chöling in upper Ga
Is the source of millions of scholars and siddhas.
Its guardian, the great Upasaka,
Is the foremost protector of the teachings of
accomplishment.

25 Lama Tsoknyi and the Hermit of Miyul

Lama Tsoknyi and the hermit of Miyul were lifelong retreatants associated with Thrangu Monastery.

Grounded in great renunciation for samsara,
With great courage you gathered the two accumulations
on the path.

You gained great fame for achieving the result, the two bodies.
Realized yogins, I prostrate to you!

Lama Tsoknyi was from Kutse in Derge; he was born to a poor family. He eventually became a mule driver for a merchant from Derge called Karma Zöpa. Traveling with the merchant Tsoknyi passed through Kyergu and reached Thrangu Monastery, where he undertook renunciation. As he never stopped talking he was given the derogatory nickname Parakha, which means the cup in which dice are shaken with a clattering sound.

When Lama Tsoknyi was accepted into the Six Dharmas Retreat, Karma Zöpa came and offered him a pack load of food for the winter that he had purchased. On the next morning, while beating the gong signaling the beginning of a meditation session and singing the call to meditation, Lama Tsoknyi gave rise to true renunciation. He returned the pack load of provisions to the merchant so that they could be used to sponsor life-release, and gave up eating meat. After the completion of the retreat Lama Tsoknyi entered a lifelong retreat, during which he performed a thousand nyungnes. His merit brought many offerings to him; he used them to sponsor the painting of eighty thangkas for the new temple at Thrangu Monastery. He hired an artist from the lowlands, and the paintings were completed within three years. He paid the artist three measures of gold for each painting. Since the thangkas were sized to fit the pillars of the new temple, he intended each of the pillars to have a painting hung on it. However, because of the invasion the paintings were never installed, and Lama Tsoknyi died in prison.

His rebirth was born in Nupri in Nepal and was recognized by the Lord Refuge Thrangu Rinpoche. From the time when he could first speak he repeatedly declared, "I will go to Thrangu Monastery!" This caused his mother to bring him to Thrangu Rinpoche. She asked Rinpoche to allow her son to undertake renunciation and to take care of him. This was just after Rinpoche first arrived in Nepal, and he lacked any facilities, so he told her that it would be very difficult to assemble the resources needed for her son's care and upbringing.

After a few days she came to see Rinpoche again with her son. This time she was insistent in her request. Nevertheless he did not rush anything, but repeated what he had said during the previous audience about his lack of resources.

Although at the time the tulku was very young, his behavior was unlike that of other small children. In response to Thrangu Rinpoche's reply to his mother's request, he touched his head to Rinpoche's feet, weeping and asking to undertake renunciation. Rinpoche finally agreed, and gave him the name Karma Damchö.

Tulku Damchö studied and served Thrangu Rinpoche for many years with great diligence. In 1998 he was enthroned at Thrangu Tashi Chöling Monastery in Nepal along with the Lord Refuge Lodrö Nyima Rinpoche. He has now completed his studies at Varanasi University and a three-year retreat in the Six Dharmas of Naropa Retreat. You may learn more about him from those who know him well.

Even when your rupakaya was young
Your wisdom was unobscured.
Even though you passed into the dharmadhatu,
Your compassionate activity is unending.

As for the hermit from Miyul:

He gained accomplishment in the Palace of Great Bliss.
He was inseparable from the viras and dakinis.
He appeared and gave prophecy
To countless realized men and women.

Although the hermit from Miyul was quite famous, I don't know much about his life, but here is what my kind guru heard from Sönam Yönpel, the custodian of the Vairochana of Bi:

Sönam Yönpel and the hermit from Miyul were in retreat at the same time in separate cabins at the hermitage called Palace of Great Bliss. One day, as it was a sacred occasion, they were supposed to perform a ganachakra. Sönam Yönpel went to bring a load of feast offering materials to the hermit. As he approached the hermit's door he heard beautiful singing from inside. As the voice he heard was that of a woman, he thought, "He's got a woman in there with him!" Distraught, Sönam Yönpel threw open the door.

He saw the hermit sitting there with several sheets of paper in front of him, in the process of writing something down. Gazing into space, the hermit said to him, "Oh, my friend, it is unfortunate that you have come here right now!" He then burned all that he had just written in his fire.

Sönam Yönpel told me, "The hermit was undoubtedly receiving prophecy from the dakinis. My disapproval ruined the interdependence, which I regret very much."

Because you saw your own unaltered face
The mothers and dakinis offered you unmistaken prophecy,
But the uncontrolled impure thoughts of another
Ruined and undid the interdependence.

26 Gogyu Aku Rinpoche

Gogyu Aku Rinpoche was from Bumgang, a Gelukpa monastery.

The moment the moon of your countenance was revealed,
Self-arisen interdependence was also revealed.
Your fame, revealed, fills the domains of gods and men.
I bow to you who revealed how stainless you were.

My kind guru remembers hearing one day in his seventeenth year that his niece Gyamtso Wangmo was due to give birth in a month. The place where she gave birth a month later was known as Pelungnang. Her labor began while she was milking sheep, so she rushed home, carrying a small bowl of milk, which she placed on the side of the stove. She then gave birth to a son without injury. Later it was discovered that the milk in the bowl had turned into yogurt. Herders and other people saw a tent of rainbows over the tent in which the birth occurred, but no member of the family saw them.

An elder monk from Bumgang Monastery realized that the young boy was extraordinary and attentively undertook his education. One day, while the family was moving its tent to a different pasture, the young incarnation looked back at the site they had vacated and began to rub his hands together. His tutor thought, "He seems to be killing insects, but unless I'm gentle with him he'll be frightened." He went over to the boy and unobtrusively looked at his hands. The incarnation was kneading a rock between his palms, rolling it into a ball and then flattening it out without any difficulty.

The tutor said to the boy, "Please roll that rock into a ball and give it to me." The incarnation did so. Then, seeing a flat rock, the tutor picked it up, removed his boots, and placed his bare feet on the rock. He then told the boy to do the same thing. Laughing, the incarnation took off his boots and placed his bare feet on the rock, leaving clear impressions in it of both his feet.

By his eighteenth year the times had changed, and the communist government issued an order requiring everyone to kill marmots. The incarnation didn't kill any. When he was told that if he didn't kill any marmots he would be punished, he said, "Okay; tomorrow I'll kill the biggest marmot." That night he stabbed the local communist leader with a knife and fled. He was captured and killed by the soldiers, who left his remains where he died.

When his mother heard of this she went looking for his body, grieving terribly. She found that he had carefully folded his clothing and placed it on a rock, and that he had been killed while seated upright in vajra posture, his hands in equipoise; he had remained in that position after death. She later told my kind guru that as soon as she saw her son's remains, all her grief disappeared and she became filled with faith, wonder, and joy.

In the appearances of delusion
You violently liberated the violent.
Yet, because you transcended killing and passing away,
You became an expanse of light, the luminous dharmakaya.

27 Rigyar Sergyi Dorje

Rigyar Sergyi Dorje, the Siddha of Kojo, was from Ranyak, a Gelukpa monastery in Ga.

I bow to Sergyi Dorje,
The siddha of glorious Ranyak Monastery
Where flourished the study and practice
Of the teachings of Tsongkhapa, the second victor.

I have not seen an extensive biography of Kojo Tulku Sergyi Dorje, the siddha of the glorious Ranyak Monastery, but I am certain of the following:

He is known to have been an emanation of Lhalung Palgyi Dorje. The reason for his being known by the name Rigyar is said to be this: Although his birthplace is unknown, when he was around five his mother died and his father remarried. His stepmother constantly beat him. For some time this did not affect his ability, present from an early age, to remember events from his past lives. One day, however, she took her boot in her left hand and struck him nine times on the head; this obscured him so much that he could no longer remember past events as clearly as before. Thinking "Remaining here is pointless!", he fled his home in order to meditate in the mountains. That night he first covered his back with two willow leaves when he went to sleep. Later, two ravens appeared and covered him with their wings while he slept. Starting the next day, while he continued to meditate, he followed the ravens further into the mountains. It is said that because he lived in the mountains and came from a place called Gyar, he came to be called Mountain Gyar, or Rigyar.

He eventually reached Gegye Yushu, where he was adopted by an old woman. Each day he herded sheep, meditating while he did so. One day the old woman died, and a lama with a lot of monks was invited to her home to pray for her. The siddha thought "I wonder how much good these monks are capable of doing her consciousness?" and watched them. The lama and monks sang well and were skilled musicians; they performed their ritual with great pomp. In fact, because of their fine voices and liturgical expertise they recited the ceremony in a state of pride. There was, however, one monk at the end of the row who served as the groom for the rest. While the others were chanting he was thinking, "They are performing an elaborate ritual. I don't know how to do any of it, so I will recite as many MANIs as I can for the good of the deceased." Thinking that, he sat there doing so. Although the consciousness of the deceased woman was flying around among the monks in the form of a flying insect, none of them other than the groom even noticed it. The groom thought, "This insect might be the consciousness of the deceased!" Praying for her, he blew on the insect, which helped her a great deal.

Observing all this the siddha thought, "I must deflate this lama's pride." When it was time for them to eat, the siddha filled the lama's porcelain bowl with rice and then bent it so its mouth was closed. The lama's pride was dispelled; he signaled to the siddha to reopen the bowl's mouth. He did so, leaving it as it was before he bent it closed. However, the rest of the monks saw none of this.

To tell you a little about this siddha's deep connection to Thrangu Monastery, during the time of the Fifth Traleg

Kyabgön Trinley Nyima, a temple with eighty columns called Victory Over Mara Unaffected by the Four Elements was built at Thrangu. The siddha of Kojo promised to provide all of the vermillion needed for the temple, so after the construction was completed the monastery's custodian came to him and asked for the pigment. The siddha gave him just one kidskin bag of vermillion, so the custodian said, "If you had told us that this is all the pigment you have, we could have made arrangements to find more elsewhere. How will this be enough for such a large temple?"

The siddha replied, "Not only will this suffice for the painting of the entire temple; you will have enough left over to fill any cracks in the columns."

As he said, the pigment was enough for the whole temple. Because in those days they lacked modern tools, the columns had many cracks and uneven surfaces. The pigment was also used to fill these, making the columns smooth. Later, when that temple was destroyed, people dug the pigment out from the cracks in the columns and used it to write with.

At one time all attempts to build a bridge across the Jachu River were unsuccessful; every time a bridge was attempted it was carried off by the current. They invited the siddha of Kojo, and together with Traleg Trinley Nyima he visited the Margo Ngakhang Shrine. While circumambulating the shrine the siddha smoked tobacco. He walked to the east of the temple and asked about the names of the mountain and other features to the east. Traleg Rinpoche told him their names, and the siddha dropped his tobacco ash in a pile to the east. He then walked to the south, west, and north of the temple in turn, asking the same questions and leaving some ash in each direction. Then he left.

Traleg Rinpoche's manager asked Rinpoche, "We prepared all the materials for a fire offering, but the siddha didn't recite even one word of liturgy. What should we do now?"

Rinpoche replied, "The siddha performed fire offerings of pacification, enrichment, attraction, and force to the east, south, west, and north. What better fire offering than that could we need?"

That night there was a fierce hailstorm accompanied by thunder and several lightning strikes. The rock on either side of the Jachu River collapsed, leaving self-arisen holes in the rock ideal for the planting of pylons to support the bridge. This time, when the bridge was built, it remained unharmed by the water.

Usually the siddha dressed as a layman. He wore fine clothes and a long sword at his hip. He made his attendant carry a rifle. Whenever he visited nomad communities he would let off a few shots with his rifle at the request of the faithful in order to bless their livestock and sheep. For one year afterward they would never lose any animals to wolves. The faithful would also offer him ammunition; he would present them with a corresponding amount of gunpowder, which they would mix with fumigation substances and use every evening to purify their livestock.

My kind guru told me that when he was a child his father would use this fumigation mixture to purify his livestock, daily circling his corral while burning it. As the gunpowder within the mixture exploded loudly while it was burnt, my kind guru very much enjoyed being given the job of carrying it around.

I have heard that this siddha composed many songs.

When my kind guru was in his fourth and fifth years he often slept in his grandmother's lap. She would always chant "Rigyar Sergyi Dorje Khyenno!" One of his songs begins:

Peerless lord Mila Töpaga,
You are the most splendid of beings.
You are this unprotected beggar's only refuge.
I cry to you from afar; look upon me with compassion!

Disciples who look to me,
Listen with undistracted minds and attentive ears!
Although you've bodies born from past virtue,
You need the complete eight freedoms and ten resources.

After that the song continues, but my kind guru didn't remember the rest, except the conclusion:

I pray that in my next life I return home
To Uddiyana, the dakinis' land.
AH! May this be auspiciously and instantly accomplished
AH AH!

While singing this song to me, my kind guru shed tears.

The chieftain of the Deta clan of Rongpo is said to have been an emanation of Langdarma, the king of Tibet who persecuted Buddhism in the ninth century. As a sign that he was Langdarma's rebirth the chieftain is said to have had little horns growing on his head. Because it was Lhalung Palgyi Dorje who assassinated Langdarma, and because the siddha Rigyar Sergyi Dorje was an emanation of Lhalung, the life-debt incurred by the assassination caused the Deta chieftain to try to kill the siddha. However, no matter what weapons were used he and his men couldn't kill him, so they sewed him into a sack of leather, attached a millstone to his neck, and cast him into the Drichu River. When the leather sack was later recovered, all it contained was a brilliant golden vajra; there were no other remains of the siddha. Everyone agreed that the siddha had turned into a golden vajra. I have already explained the derivation of the name Rigyar; this is the source of the name Sergyi Dorje, Golden Vajra.

One morning not long after the siddha was cast into the Drichu River Traleg Rinpoche's groom noticed that both of Rinpoche's horses were sweating heavily, as though someone had been riding both of them. Afraid that someone was stealing the horses for their own use, the groom slept in the stable that night. Traleg Rinpoche entered the stable and asked the groom what he was doing there; the groom told him what he had seen. Traleg Rinpoche told his groom, "Last night I escorted the siddha of Kojo halfway to Lhasa; that's why both my horses were sweaty!"

There are other accounts of many people seeing the siddha in Lhasa and Tsang after he was cast into the Drichu.

Eventually the Deta chieftain realized what he had done and came to very much regret it. He insistently petitioned both the Ruta Kyabgön, a lama of Ranyak Monastery, and the Traleg Kyabgön to protect him from rebirth in a lower state. They both promised to do so. In order to fulfill their promise they both passed away when the chieftain died. It is also said that because of the connection they formed then the Ruta Kyabgön was sometimes reborn at Thrangu Monastery, and the Traleg Kyabgön at Ranyak Monastery.

You realized the middle way beyond extremes.
In order to guide beings with form and those without
Your display of deeds was like a water-moon.
Siddha, who could fail to respect you?

From a song by Nyima Tashi, the First Traleg Kyabgön:

You men and women of precipitous Kham
Would denigrate even the Buddha if he appeared.
Not knowing how to think, you are sectarian
And partisan about philosophical systems.
How can you refute another's outlook
With mere empty attachment and anger?
You incur a downfall and meander in the dark!

And:

Because you've never developed an impartial, pure outlook,
You've built hell for yourself with your sectarian speech.
For sure, if you don't tame your minds,
Loud talk of dharma is a mass of attachment and hatred.
The service without concealment
Of great centers for the practice of the Buddha's doctrine
And of holy, authentic gurus
Will increase your merit in this and future lives.

And:

From now on, at all times,
Abandon sectarian attachment and hatred
Within the All-Doing's expanse.
Cultivate impartial, pure outlook
Within the All-Doing's expanse.
Virtue and wrongdoing arise from the All-Doing's expanse.

The various philosophical systems that exist nowadays,
Whether they are good or bad,
All come from the All-Doing's expanse.
When virtue arises it is wondrous.
When wrongdoing arises it is depressing.
I have taken many births in Jambudvipa.
I have passed through all four dharma traditions.
I have entered all four of their dharma gates.
I have seen no difference in quality among them,
No reason to say, "This is good and this is bad."
All their dharma leads to buddhahood.
All their dharma comes from the Buddha's mind.
Among all the dharma taught by the Buddha,
He never taught good dharma to one person
And bad dharma to another.
There are no good and bad in the experience of a Buddha.
Good and bad arise in the experience of ignorance.
Through many successive births I have helped beings
Through Mahamudra, the Path and Result, Five-Fold Mahamudra,
The Dictates as Instructions, the Great Perfection,
And each of the dharma traditions and philosophical systems.
I therefore have no sectarianism toward philosophical systems.
I have been liberated through abandoning sectarian attachment and hatred.
Future followers and disciples, abandon sectarianism.
Cultivate impartial, pure outlook.
The sources of refuge are infallible.
Keep this in mind.

As he says here, the magical display of such holy beings' births is inconceivable!

28 Lama Ganga

Lama Ganga was a monk from Thrangu,
a Kagyu monastery.

You anointed the good ground of pure morality
With the amrita of your bodhichitta
And grew the beautiful tree of mantra,
Heavy with the fruit of generation and completion.
I bow a hundred times to you, the threefold vajra holder.

Lama Ganga was born on June 13, 1931. In his thirteenth year he undertook renunciation at Thrangu Monastery in upper Ga. Under the guidance of the retreat master of Kori he began his studies and memorized the liturgies used at Thrangu. In his eighteenth year he received the vows of a bhikshu, the bodhisattva vow, and ripening empowerments of secret mantra from Palden Khyentse Özer, the Second Jamgön Rinpoche. He then entered the Six Dharmas Retreat, which he completed three times under the guidance of the retreat master Katak Ogyen. Because of the changing times, in 1958 he fled to India with other lamas and monks of Thrangu. He lived at Buxa for nine years along with my kind guru. While there he studied the treatises of many Buddhist traditions. He later received the complete empowerments of the *Precious Treasury of Terma* from the Lord Refuge Kalu Rinpoche.

In 1976 he moved to the United States of America, along with my kind guru and others, at the command of the Sixteenth Gyalwang Karmapa. Lama Ganga eventually became the lama of the Karma Teksum Chöling centers in California. Starting in 1980, he served as the retreat master at Kagyu Samye Ling while continuing to oversee the California centers.

When the Sixteenth Gyalwang Karmapa Rigpe Dorje displayed illness while in the United States Lama Ganga served him well, causing the Karmapa to delightedly remark, "Because of our previous karma, this person has helped me a lot!"

In the years 1986 and 1987 Lama Ganga accompanied the Lord Refuge Thrangu Rinpoche when he visited Thrangu Monastery in Tibet. In 1988 Lama Ganga returned to Tibet with my kind guru. Before leaving for Tibet, Lama Ganga told a few of his western disciples, "I will not be coming back from Tibet this time; I'm going to die there."

Also, Yeshe Namdak, an assistant to Tendzinla, the president of Karma Triyana Dharmachakra, told the following story: When he invited Lama Ganga and Khenpo Karthar Rinpoche to his wedding, due to occur after their return from Tibet, Lama Ganga laughed and said, "That would be amazing, because I'll be dead by then!"

A tumor appeared on the back of his neck. He said to my kind guru, "I'm not going to escape this tumor."

My guru jokingly replied, "Why are you whining so much about a tiny growth like that?"

Lama Ganga responded, "This is no ordinary tumor! We'd better hurry up and get to Thrangu Monastery! Once we get there, no matter what happens to me, you won't have any problems." He repeated this often.

After they arrived at Thrangu Monastery, Lama Ganga's tumor began to grow and he became ill, so he was brought to the Kyergu General Hospital. When my kind guru visited him there, Lama Ganga's neck was covered in bandages. Joking a bit even then, and free from any pain, he passed away.

His body was brought to Thrangu Monastery and, dressed in a dharma robe and meditation hat, was placed in a seated position. Although he was seated upright, because by the end of his life he had been unable to raise his head due to the tumor on his neck, his head still fell forward after his passing. A friend of his who had been in the same retreat, Gyara Gegen Karma Düdül, performed the clarification of samadhi. From then on Lama Ganga's head, needing no support, remained upright. He remained in samadhi for five days. His cremation was overseen by his nephew, Gegen Rinchen Norbu, who built a stupa enshrining his uncle's remains.

29 Gyara Gegen Karma Düdül

After completing the Six Dharmas Retreat, Gyara Gegen Karma Düdül had learned all of our ritual traditions, including how to lead our liturgical practices, from his uncle Umdze Gyara Palga. The existence nowadays of an undiminished tradition of proper ritual performance at Thrangu Monastery is primarily due to Karma Düdül's kindness. During his life he served for two terms each as the umdze and master of discipline at Thrangu Monastery.

After the times had changed Dara Karma Rinchen, the retreat master Tsewang Dorje, Bentra Karma Tutop, Karma Chöpel, Mora Gegen Karma Tsultrim, Gegen Kartsa, Denshul Gegen Karma Düdül, and the physician Gegen

Rinchen Norbu gathered at the Vairochana of Bi and through great effort soon rebuilt the Temple at Thrangu.

More recently, for several years Gyara Gegen Karma Düdül was seriously ill. All his attending physicians agreed that he was definitely dying. Karma Düdül, however, repeatedly told them that he was going to wait until he saw Traleg Rinpoche again. In October of 2004, Traleg Rinpoche returned to Thrangu Monastery in order to preside over the opening of the newly completed temple there, called Victory Over Mara Unaffected by the Four Elements. While there, Traleg Rinpoche performed the ejection of consciousness for Karma Düdül's benefit. Afterward, that evening, Karma Düdül said to the retreat master Rinchen Tsering, "Please don't be angry with me for the many harsh words I've spoken to you; I'm short tempered. Go back up to the retreat and sleep well; as I had hoped, I've received the ejection of consciousness from the precious Lord Refuge, so I'm going to sleep well tonight!" After affectionately saying this, Karma Düdül went to sleep. That night he passed away. His remains were dressed in his dharma robe and meditation hat, and he remained in samadhi for several days. Afterward he was cremated at the Hermitage of Great Bliss.

30 Bentra Gegen Karma Chöpel

Bentra Gegen Karma Chöpel also completed a Six Dharmas Retreat. Throughout his life he was harmonious and disciplined, and became like the very life-tree of Thrangu Monastery. Near the end of his life he accompanied Trinley

Palzang, a khenpo of Thrangu Monastery, to Lhasa, Tsurphu, and a long tour of the south. After traveling through much of Nepal and India, Karma Chöpel became ill. At the sacred place of Namo Buddha in Nepal, he geomantically determined the best place for his cremation and, indicating it in his will, passed away. His sister, a nun, also remained in samadhi when she passed away, as did Gegen Kartsa, Denshul Düdül, and Karma Tsultrim, as well as the protector lama of the previous Zuru Rinpoche when he passed away at Namo Buddha in Nepal.

This brief account of the small part of the ocean-like outer, inner, and secret lives of a few siddhas of Kham that has appeared to our common, mundane perception came to be written in the following way: The activity of the learned and accomplished Khenpo Tsultrim Gyamtso, the life-tree of the teachings of our accomplishment lineage, has filled every land, both east and west. While turning the dharmachakra in accordance with disciples' needs, he visited Karma Triyana Dharmachakra Monastery in America, the third seat of the glorious Gyalwang Karmapa, the activity of all victors. While there he discussed with my kind guru, the abbot of the monastery, the lives of siddhas of Ga in Kham. Delighted, my guru described the wondrous deeds of several hidden yogins, in response to which Khenpo Tsultrim Gyamtso enjoined me to write these stories down.

I had already written down some of them in the hope of

collecting them. Further encouraged by Khenpo Tsultrim's instruction, I wrote down all the stories told by my guru and offered them to Khenpo Tsultrim. Not content with that, I have since added the stories told by my guru while teaching in our retreat, and those he told in response to questions posed by retreat lamas while I was in the retreat. I have included all of the stories told by my guru with no exceptions. I have repeatedly questioned him about them, and offered him the manuscript to review after completing it. I have only published it after receiving his assurance of its correctness. I have not trusted my own unsupported recollections, nor have I written down whatever occurred to me in the manner of a mouse gathering grain.

I therefore have no vain sense of personal accomplishment based on having published a few biographies of siddhas, and have written them down honestly. Even the verses of veneration and dedication with which I have preceded and succeeded the accounts are merely expressions of appreciation of these siddhas based on my sense of how rare and precious it is to hear of their deeds.

Many of these accounts concern lamas and retreatants from Thrangu Tashi Chöling Monastery in upper Ga, which is my monastery, but there are also stories here about holy upholders of many other traditions among the Sakya, Geluk, Kagyu, and Nyingma. My great guru said, "Because I am a monk from Thrangu Monastery, I know most about the lives of holy beings from that monastery and have told their stories. I would be delighted if I knew and could tell you of the lives of yogins of all traditions, including the Sakya, Geluk, Kagyu, and Nyingma, so you could write them down, but I only know these stories so there is nothing to be done about it."

The need for this is that if one is able to set down even a few accounts of the lives of holy upholders of the dharma of various traditions, they form a cloud of offerings pleasing to the victors, a repayment of the kindness of one's parents in the six states, amrita for the devoted, a spur for renunciates, a resource for the practice of holy dharma, proof of its greatness, the best way to please the guru, and instruction in the need to have a pure perception of everyone. Especially, such accounts definitely inspire devotion and confidence in holy dharma.

Because I lack extensive learning I am unfamiliar with the norms of elegant composition and poetic imagery, so my writing will undoubtedly embarrass those who are extremely learned. However, I have written this with words easily understood by others like myself. It will be accessible to ordinary, worldly people and will plant the seed of liberation in them by inspiring faith and devotion.

I would also remind learned monastics and laypeople of the future that the worldwide fame of Tibet, our land with such a long history, is primarily due to the holy dharma. That holy dharma was taught by the compassionate Buddha and disseminated by holders of the teachings of many traditions. Therefore, I dare to extol what I have done and assert that to be able to set down even a few honest accounts of the lives of learned and accomplished masters of the Sakya, Geluk, Kagyu, and Nyingma traditions; and especially of hidden yogins and yoginis who are the display of rupakayas in accordance with disciples' needs, is to serve the Buddha's teachings. Why? Because based on these accounts people will develop confidence in and devotion for the holy dharma so well taught by the Buddha, and especially for the quick and profound path of secret mantra.

Anyone who reads these accounts or has them read to them will naturally feel inspiring faith. That is enough to plant the seed of liberation within their being. It is extensively taught in the sutras and tantras that faith is the essence of all the dharma taught by the victor. Especially, it is taught that devotion is the key that opens the door to wisdom and is therefore essential to the realization of natural, connate mahamudra. The authentic term *mahamudra of devotion* is for that reason used by the holy masters of our lineage with great reverence.

Giving birth to it depends upon learning of the lives of these well-known and lesser-known holy beings. If, therefore, Tibetan writers benevolently concerned with the many traditions of the victor's teachings could research and write down, with altruism, devotion, and honesty, the stories of their monasteries, their lamas, and of yogins and yoginis that they hear or learn from others, this would definitely benefit people throughout the world, since Tibet is now so well-known all over the world.

Digressing, I would point out that previously well-known histories of sacred places of accomplishment; of Sakya, Geluk, Kagyu, and Nyingma monasteries; and of their many holy lamas are disappearing or already forgotten. These days it seems that their names and number of incarnations are rarely known, let alone their biographies. It is therefore our responsibility to assiduously research, preserve, and publish accounts of holy beings of the past. I also pray, with a pure motivation and joined palms, that preceded by the relinquishment of antipathy and the contempt born of familiarity, the great deeds and biographies of those khenpos, tulkus, yogins, and yoginis, the marks and signs of whose rupakayas we have the good fortune to still encounter, may be fully written down.

Supreme Buddha Siddhartha, our teacher who accomplished everything,
Saw the dharmakaya's face, accomplishing dual good.
He didn't rest in peace without further accomplishment;
He accomplished the teaching of infinite dharma, vast and profound.

That teacher, whose kindness we could never repay,
Taught his first entourage, the good Group of Five,
And ever since has led beings in appropriate ways
Out of the fearsome dark abyss of samsara.

The three great dharma kings transformed
Tibet, a barbaric land without dharma,
Into a wondrous, holy field of dharma, so that
Tibet is now universally known for its dharma.

Especially, through the kindness of the abbot, master, and king,
The special, superior dharma of secret mantra was taught there.
It filled all Tibet without distinction.
Many special hidden yogins and yoginis have appeared there.

Realized beings who purified thought in dharmakaya

Have displayed all kinds of pure rupakayas.
These wondrous, brief pure biographies
Are worth more than pure gold.

I've no fine or pretty words.
There are no feats of grammatical elegance here,
Nor any long-winded quotations or arguments,
So, scholars of quotes and dispute, read something else.

Those who, with renunciation, seek freedom from the six states of being;
Those who, with love, recognize all beings as their parents;
Those who, with pure perception, recognize all beings as deities:
Please read these biographies of beings' protectors.

Through this virtue, in this life, the future, and in between,
May I and all my parents come to see all the wrong
We have done through self-fixation and confess it from our hearts.
Compassionate deities, please attend my prayer!

May the impartial teachings flourish everywhere and forever.
May impartial great beings live to the end of time.
May all beings, my mothers, without partiality,
Achieve impartial omniscience.

I, the devoted one called Karma Drodhul, possess merely the name of the nephew and disciple of my kind guru, Khenpo Karthar Rinpoche, and am the least of the monks of Thrangu Tashi Chöling Monastery in Ga. After revising the biographies I had written in accordance with my kind guru's wishes, I completed this while engaged in the inner sadhana of Vajravarahi, the mother of all victors, during my second retreat at Karme Yiwong Samten Ling, the glorious Gyalwang Karmapa's retreat in America, on an auspicious day in the ninth month of the Wood Bird year, the Tibetan year 2132, the year 2005 of the Western calendar. Virtue!

༄༅། །ཁམས་སྣ་ཡི་གྲུབ་ཐོབ་དངོས་མཇལ་དང་རྣམ་ཐར་ཁྲུངས་ལྡན་
ཐོས་པ་རྣམས་ཀྱི་རྣམ་ཐར་ཉུང་བསྡུས་དད་པའི་གསོས་སྨན་ཨུཏྤལའི་ཆུན་པོ་
ཞེས་བྱ་བ་བཞུགས།།

༄༅། །ཁམས་སྣ་ཡི་གྲུབ་ཐོབ་དངོས་མཇལ་དང་རྣམ་ཐར་ཁྲུངས་ལྡན་ཐོས་པ་རྣམས་ཀྱི་རྣམ་ཐར་ཉུང་བསྡུས་དད་པའི་གསོས་སྨན་ཨུཏྤལའི་ཆུན་པོ་ཞེས་བྱ་བ་བཞུགས།།

༄༅། །ན་མོ་གུ་རུ། འཇིག་རྟེན་རྒྱུད་པའི་མུན་པ་སྒྲིབ་གཉིས་དྲི་མ༷་མ༷་ལུས་རབ་སྤྱང༷ས་ཤིང་། །ཇི་ལྟ་ཇི་སྙེད་ཚུལ་བཞིན་མཁྱེན་པའི་ཡེ་ཤེས༷་ཤེས༷་རབ་མཐར་རྫོགས་པས། །སྲིད་པ་གསུམ་གྱི་ཆུ་བོའི་རླབས་ལས་ཕ་མཐར༷་མཐར༷་ཕྱིན་སངས་རྒྱས་ཞེས། །ལྷ་མི་འགྲོ་བ་ཡོངས་ཀྱི་ཐར་པའི་ལམ་སྟོན༷་སྟོན༷་པའི་ཞབས་ལ་བཏུད། །མཁྱེན༷་པའི་རྩལ་གྱིས་རང་རིག་རང་ཞལ་མཇལ། །བརྩེ༷་བའི་ཐུགས་རྗེས་བོད་དུ་དམ་ཆོས་སྤེལ། །ནུས༷་པས་ལྷ་སྲིན་དྲེགས་པ་མ་རུངས་འདུལ། །བོད་འབངས་མགོན་གཅིག་མཚོ་སྐྱེས་རྡོ་རྗེར་འདུད། །འཆད༷་པས་མདོ་རྒྱུད་ཀུན་ལ་ཆགས་ཐོགས་བྲལ། །རྩོད༷་པས་ཕས་རྒོལ་ཚོགས་རྣམས་ཟིལ་གྱིས་གནོན། །རྩོམ༷་པས་རྒྱལ་བའི་དགོངས་འགྲེལ་ཀུན་ལས་ལྷག །འཛམ་པའི་དབྱངས་དངོས་ས་སྐྱ་པཎྜིར་འདུད། །མཁས༷་པའི་གྲགས་པ་གངས་ཅན་ཡོངས་ལ་ཁྱབ། །བཙུན༷་པས་འདུལ་བའི་ཆོས་ཀྱི་སྒོ་བརྒྱ་འབྱེད། །བཟང༷་པོའི་མཛད་པ་རྒྱལ་བ་གཉིས་པར་གྲགས། །བློ་བཟང་གྲགས་ཞེས་སངས་རྒྱས་དེ་ལ་འདུད། །རྒྱལ་བའི་བཀའ་བབས་བརྒྱུད་པ་ཡོངས་སུ་འཛིན༷། །བཀའ་ཕྱག་གདམས་པས་གདུལ་བྱའི་བདེ་ཚལ་སྐྱོང༷་། །མདོ་རྒྱལ་ཏིང་འཛིན་གངས་རིའི་ལྗོངས་སུ་སྤེལ༷། །བླ་འོད་གཞོན་ནུ་སྒམ་པོ་པ་ལ་འདུད། །མཉམ་མེད༷་སྟོན་པས་གསུངས་པའི་ལུང་རྟོགས་ཆོས། །ལྷོད་མེད༷་བརྩོན་པས་ཇི་བཞིན་ཉམས་བཞེས་པས། །བར་མེད༷་བརྒྱུད་པའི་བྱིན་རླབས་སྙིང་ལ་འཕོས། །རིས་མེད༷་སྐྱེས་ཆེན་རྣམས་ལ་སུ་མི་གུས། །སྤྲ༷་ཡུལ་དབེན་པའི་རི་ཁྲོད་ཉམས་དགའ་རུ། །སྤྲ༷་དོན་ཆོས་ཉིད་དོན་ལ་རྩལ་སྦྱངས་པའི། །སྤྲ༷་པའི་རྣལ་འབྱོར་རྣམས་ཀྱི་

ཞབས་སེན་དུ། །སྤྲོས་མེད་དད་མོས་སྙིང་ནས་ཕྱག་བགྱིའོ། །ཚེ་གཅིག་ཟུང་འཇུག་བརྙེས་པའི་ལམ་མཆོག་ནི༔ །རྟོགས་ལྡན་བླ་མའི་བྱིན་རླབས་རག་ལས་ཕྱིར། །དེ་ཡང་རྣམ་ཐར་ཐོས་ལ་བརྟེན་དགོས་པས། །རང་གཞན་ཕན་ཕྱིར་རྣམ་ཐར་ཉུང་འགོད་བྱ། །ཅེས་ཡུལ་དམ་པ་ལ་མཆོད་པར་བརྗོད་ཅིང་དམ་བཅའ་བའི་ཚིག་གི་མེ་ཏོག་སྔོན་དུ་འཐོར་ནས། དེ་ཡང་བདག་ཅག་གི་སྟོན་པ་མཉམ་མེད་དོན་ཀུན་གྲུབ་པ་མཆོག །མཉམ་མེད་ཐུབ་ཆེན་གྱི་དྲུང་ནས་བྱང་ཆུབ་ཀྱི་ཐུགས་བསྐྱེད་ནས་བཟུང་སྟེ་དཀའ་བ་ཆེ་ཆུང་རྩིས་ལས་འདས་པ་དང་དུ་བཞེས། མཐར་སྒྲིབ་གཉིས་ཀྱི་དྲི་མ་རྩད་ནས་བྱང་སྟེ་འཕགས་ཡུལ་རྡོ་རྗེའི་གདན་དུ་མངོན་པར་བྱང་ཆུབ་ནས་རིམ་བཞིན་གདུལ་བྱའི་ཁམས་དང་མཐུན་པའི་ཆོས་ཀྱི་འཁོར་ལོ་རིམ་པ་གསུམ་བསྐོར་བས། གང་ལ་གང་འདུལ་གྱི་ལྷ་དང་མི་སོགས་ཐེག་པ་གསུམ་གྱི་སྤྱངས་རྟོགས་མཐར་སོན་པ་གྲངས་ལས་འདས་པ་ཕེབས། དེ་ནས་རིམ་བཞིན་མཁན་སློབ་ཆོས་གསུམ་སོགས་ཀྱི་བཀའ་དྲིན་ལ་བརྟེན་ནས། རྒྱ་གར་རྡོ་རྗེའི་གདན་གྱི་བྱང་གི་ཕྱོགས། བོད་ཀྱི་ཡུལ་ལ་ཡང་ཞི་བའི་ཆོས་ཀྱི་སྒོ་ཕྱེས་ནས་སྒྲུབ་བརྒྱུད་ཤིང་རྟ་ཆེ་བརྒྱད་སོགས་བྱུང་བ་ལས། ཡོངས་སུ་གྲགས་པའི་ས་དགེ་བཀའ་རྙིང་སྟེ་གྲུབ་མཐའ་ཆེན་པོ་བཞི་ཆེས་དར་ནས་བསྟན་འཛིན་གྱི་སྐྱེས་བུ་གང་སར་ཁྱབ་ཀྱང་། མི་མཐུན་གྱི་རྐྱེན་དུ་མ་ལ་བརྟེན་ནས་སྐྱེས་བུ་དམ་པ་དེ་རྣམས་དང་། ཁྱད་པར་དུ་སྦས་པའི་རྣལ་འབྱོར་ཕོ་མོ་རྣམས་ཀྱི་རྣམ་ཐར་ནི་དེ་ཙམ་མ་དར་ལ། ད་ལམ་དྲིན་ཅན་བླ་མ་མཁན་པོ་ཀར་མཐར་རིན་པོ་ཆེ་མཆོག་གི་ཞལ་ནས་གསུངས་པའི་རིས་མེད་ཀྱི་སྐྱེས་བུ་རྣམས་ཀྱི་རྣམ་ཐར་ཁ་ཤས་ཤིག་ལྷག་བསམ་དང་མོས་པའི་བློ་ཡིས་འགོད་པར་བྱའོ།། ༈ ཆུ་ཡི་རྐྱེན་ལ་བརྟེན་ནས་གྲུབ་པ་ཐོབ་པ་བཀའ་བརྒྱུད་ཁྲ་འགུ་དགོན་གྱི་གྲྭ་ཀརྨ་ས་བཅུའི་སྐུ་ཕྲེང་དང་པོ་ནི། ཐར་པའི་གཞི་མ་སྲིད་ལ་ངེས་འབྱུང་ཆེ། །ཐར་པའི་སྲོག་ཤིང་བླ་མའི་གདམ་ངག

མཐུས། །ཐར་པའི་ཉེར་རྒྱུ་དབེན་གནས་དམ་པ་རུ། །ཐར་པའི་བདེ་བས་མྱོས་ལ་སྙིང་ནས་འདུད། དེ་ཡང་དམ་པ་འདི་ཉིད་ནི་ཁམས་དཔལ་ཐང་གནས་ཆེན་རྒྱམ་གྱི་རྡོ་ཧི་གངས་དཀར་གྱི་ཉེ་འགྲམ་ཛ་ཁོག་ཏུ་སྐུ་འཁྲུངས་ཤིང་དགུང་ལོ་ཆུང་ངུའི་དུས་འཇིག་རྟེན་གྱི་ལས་ཁོ་ན་ལ་ཉིན་མཚན་མེད་པར་གཞན་ལས་ཧུར་བརྩོན་ཆེ་ཞིང་ཐུགས་རྒྱུད་ཀྱང་ཤིན་ཏུ་གཏུམ་པོར་སྣང་། ཉིན་ཞིག་ཁོང་གིས་ཁལ་ཉེ་ཤུ་ཙམ་དེད་ནས་ཚོང་ལ་འགྲོ་སྐབས་དཔལ་ཆུ་ཤིན་ཏུ་ཤུགས་ཆེ་ཞིང་རྒྱས་ཀྱང་བརྟགས་དཔྱད་མ་མཛད་པར་ཁལ་དང་མཉམ་དུ་འོལ་ཚོད་ཀྱིས་ཆུ་ལ་བརྒལ་བས་ཆུ་ཡིས་རྒྱུན་རིང་དུ་འཁྱེར་སོང་སྐབས། ཁོང་ཐུགས་སྐྲག་ཆེན་པོའི་ངང་ནས་ཐུགས་བསམ་ལ། རང་གིས་སྔར་འཇིག་རྟེན་གྱི་བྱ་བཞག་ཁོ་ན་ལས་ཆོས་ཕྱོགས་ལ་བསམ་བློ་ཡང་འཁོར་མ་མྱོང་བས་ད་རེས་འཇིགས་པ་འདི་ལས་ཐར་ན་དེས་པར་དུ་དམ་ཆོས་ཁོ་ན་ལ་གཞོལ་སྙམ་པའི་ཐུགས་དམ་བརྟན་པོར་བྱས་པས་མཐར་མ་འདས་ཙམ་དུ་རྡོ་ཆེན་པོ་ཞིག་ལ་འཛུས་ནས་ཐར་ཙམ་བྱུང་། དེ་ནས་ཁལ་སོགས་འཇིག་རྟེན་གྱི་བྱ་བ་ཀུན་སྐད་ཅིག་དེ་ཉིད་ལ་མཆིལ་མའི་ཐལ་བ་བཞིན་དོར་ནས་ཁྲ་དགོན་དུ་སྐྱབས་རྗེ་རིན་པོ་ཆེ་ཁྲ་འགུ་ཀུན་ཁྱབ་ཉི་མ་ལས་གདམ་ངག་ཞུས་རྗེས་དབེན་གནས་འབིས་རྣམ་པར་སྣང་མཛད་དང་། ལེབ་རྗེ་དཀར་ཡག་གི་སྒྲུབ་གནས་སུ་ཉིན་མཚན་མེད་པར་སྒྲུབ་ལ་བརྩོན་ཞིང་སྐུ་ཚེ་གང་པོར་གཙོ་བོ་ནཱ་རོའི་ཆོས་དྲུག་དང་སྨྱུང་གནས་ཉམས་བཞེས་མཛད་བརྟེན་གྲུབ་པ་ཐོབ་ཏེ། དེའི་སྐབས་སུ་འདས་ལོག་རྡོ་ཤུལ་མཁའ་འགྲོ་མ་བཞུགས་ཡོད་པས་ཀརྨ་ས་བཅུ་ཞིང་གཤེགས་པའི་རྗེས་སུ་དམྱལ་བའི་གནས་སུ་ཕེབས། ཀརྨ་ས་བཅུ་ཡང་དམྱལ་གནས་སུ་ཕེབས་ནས་གཤིན་རྗེ་ཆོས་རྒྱལ་ལ་འདི་ལྟར་ཞུས། ང་ནི་ཁྲ་འགུ་བན་རྒན་རྟུལ་པོ་ཡིན། །གནས་ནི་རྒྱམ་གྱི་རྡོ་ཧི་གངས་དཀར་ཡིན། །ལུས་ཀྱིས་ཚོགས་བསགས་སྨྱུང་གནས་སྟོང་ཕྲག་བླངས། །ངག་གིས་མ་ཎི་དུང་ཕྱུར་

གསུམ་ལྷག་འདོན། །སེམས་ནི་ཆོས་ཉིད་དང་ལས་གཡོ་བ་མེད། །འཁྲིལ་ཐོགས་འགྲོ་བ་ངན་འགྲོ་གཏོང་རེ་སྐན། །ཞེས་གསུངས་ནས་ཁོང་ལ་འཁྲིལ་བ་ཐོགས་པའི་འགྲོ་བ་ཐམས་ཅད་འདྲེན་པའི་ཆེད་དུ་དེ་རྣམས་མ་ཤི་བར་དུ་སྐྱུག་པར་ཞལ་གྱིས་བཞེས་སོང་ཞེས་རྗེས་སོར་མོ་རང་གིས་ལོ་རྒྱུས་ཁུངས་ལྡན་གསུངས་སོང་གསུངས། སྨོར་སློས་པ། ངེས་འབྱུང་ནི་ཐར་པའི་གཞི་མ། །ཚོགས་བསགས་ནི་ཐར་པའི་ཉེར་རྒྱུ། །སྒྲུབ་པ་ནི་བླ་མ་མཉེས་རྒྱུ། །དེ་བྱུང་གི་དགེ་བ་བསྔོའོ།།

༼༢༽ ཁྲིམས་ཀྱི་རྐྱེན་ལ་བརྟེན་ནས་གྲུབ་པ་ཐོབ་པ་བཀའ་བརྒྱུད་ཁྲ་འགུ་དགོན་གྱི་གྲྭ་གེ་ཀརྨ་ས་བཅུ་གཉིས་པ་ནི། ༼ཁོང་ནི་དྲིན་ཅན་བླ་མའི་ཨ་ཁུ་ཡིན། མཆན།༽ ཐུགས་རྒྱུད་དཔའ་བ་མངའ་བདག་ལོ་ཙྪ་དང་མཉམ་ཞིང་། །ཐུགས་དམ་བརྟན་པ་རྗེ་བཙུན་རས་པ་ལ་ཟླར་ཞུགས། །ཐུགས་བསྐྱེད་ཟབ་པ་གངས་ཅན་ལྷ་སྐལ་གྱི་ཟླ་བོ། །ཐུགས་རྒྱུད་རྟོགས་པས་སྨྱོས་པའི་དམ་པ་ལ་འདུད་དོ། ཁོང་སྐུ་ཆུང་ངུའི་དུས་ཤིན་ཏུ་གཏུམ་ཞིང་རྟག་ཏུ་འཐབ་འཁྲུགས་ཁོ་ན་མཛད་ཅིང་རྣམ་ཀུན་རྒྱལ་ཞིང་། དེ་ལྟར་སྐན་གྲགས་ཀྱང་ཆེན་པོ་ཡོད་གཤིས་ཁོང་ལ་ཐུགས་རྒྱལ་ཆེན་པོ་མངའ་བས། ཉིན་ཞིག་རྒྱ་མི་ཞིག་དང་འཐབ་འཁྲུགས་མཛད་དེ་ཁོང་རྒྱལ་ཡང་། རྒྱ་མི་དེས་ཁྲིམས་ལ་གཏུགས་རྐྱེན་ཁོང་བཙོན་རར་བཅུག་ཅིང་རྒྱ་སྐད་དུ་བེ་ཇོ་ཞེས་པའི་སྐྱུག་ཁ་གཤགས་པས་བརྡུངས་ནས་མར་འཐེན་སྐབས་ཤ་ཚང་མ་རལ་འགྲོ་བའི་ལག་ཆ་དེས་ཐེངས་ལྔ་བརྒྱ་ཙམ་བྲབས་པས། ད་གཟོད་ཁོང་གིས་སྔར་བྱས་ཀྱི་བྱ་བ་རྣམས་འཇིག་རྟེན་གྱི་བྱ་བ་ལས་དགེ་བའི་ཕྱོགས་དྲི་མ་ཙམ་ཡང་མེད་པའི་ཁར་ཐ་ན་རང་སྲོག་ཀྱང་བོར་ལ་ཐུག་བརྟེན། ད་ནི་ཚེའི་ལྷག་མ་གང་ཡོད་དམ་པའི་ཆོས་ཁོ་ན་མི་སྒྲུབ་རེ་སྐམ་པའི་དམ་བཅའ་བརྟན་པོར་མཛད། དེ་ནས་ཁྲ་དགོན་བྱང་ངོས་མཚམས་ཁང་དམར་པོ་ཞེས་པའི་ནང་དུ་ཚེ་དང་སྒྲུབ་པ་མཉམ་ཞིང་མཐར་འདས་སྐབས་སྤྱིར་ཁོང་གི་སྐུ་གཟུགས་རིང་

པོ་ཡོད་ཀྱང་དེ་དུས་སྐུ་ལུས་ཁྲུ་གང་ཙམ་དུ་གྱུར་པས་ཀུན་ངོ་མཚར་ཞིང་དད་པའི་གནས་སུ་གྱུར་ཏོ། །སླར་སྨྲས་པ། དམ་ཆོས་འདི་ཟབ་ཅིང་། །དམ་ཚིག་ནི་གཙང་བས། །དམ་པ་ཁྲིད་རྒྱལ་དགེས། །དམ་གསུམ་གྱིས་བསྐྱོའོ།། ༼༣༽

བྱ་བྲལ་སྤྲས་པ་ཞི་བའི་བརྟུལ་ཞུགས་ཅན་ས་སྐྱ་སྐྱེ་དགུ་དགོན་གྱི་གྲྭ་ནམ་མཁའ་གྲགས་པ་ནི། སྲིད་པའི་ཕུན་ཚོགས་ཀུན་ལས་ངེས་འབྱུང་ཞིང་། །བྱམས་དང་སྙིང་རྗེའི་ཐུགས་རྒྱུད་རབ་ཏུ་བརླན། །འགྲོ་ལ་བུ་བཞིན་བརྩེ་བའི་དམ་པ་ཉིད། །བདག་ཅག་དད་པའི་སྙིང་དབུས་ཟུམ་ཞིག་གྱི། ཁོང་རབ་ཏུ་བྱུང་སྟེ་བསྙེན་པར་རྫོགས་རྗེས་ཐབ་ལ་མེ་དང་ཁང་ཁྱིམ་སོགས་སྤྱངས་ཏེ་ཐ་ན་ཁོང་གིས་མནབས་པའི་གྲྭ་ཆས་ཐེངས་གཅིག་པོ་དེ་ཡང་རལ་ཞིང་། དེའི་ཚབ་ཏུ་བེའུ་ལྤགས་པ་གཉིས་མདུད་རྒྱབ་ཏུ་བཀབ་ནས་ཞབས་ལྷམ་ཡང་མེད་པ་དང་། དབྱར་ཀའི་དུས་སུ་དཔེན་པའི་རི་ཁྲོད་ངེས་མེད་དུ་གཤེགས་ཤིང་སྐུ་ལུས་འབུ་ལ་སྦྱིན་པས་དགུན་གྱི་དུས་སུ་མར་གྲོང་དུ་ཕེབས་སྐབས་སྐུ་ལུས་ཡོངས་རྫོགས་རྨ་ཡིས་ཁེངས་པ་ཀུན་གྱིས་མངོན་སུམ་དུ་མཇལ་དུ་ཡོད་པ་དང་། ཁོང་གི་ཞལ་ནས་ཀྱང་ད་ལོ་དབྱར་ཁར་གཟུགས་པོ་ཚང་མ་འབུས་སོ་རྒྱབ་སོང་ཞེས་གསུངས་གནང་། གྲོང་དུ་བསོད་སྙོམས་མཛད་དེ་ཞལ་ལག་ཐེངས་གཅིག་ལས་མི་བཞེས་ཤིང་དགོང་མོར་གཟིམས་ཡུལ་ངེས་མེད་ལས་གྲོང་པའི་ཁྱིམ་ཚང་དུ་གཏན་ནས་མི་བཞུགས་ཤིང་། རྣམ་ཀུན་ཁོང་ཉིད་ཐུགས་དུལ་ཞིང་མཇལ་བ་ཙམ་གྱིས་དད་དབང་ངང་གིས་འཕེལ་ནུས་པ་དང་། མི་རྣམས་ཀྱིས་ཀྱང་ཁོང་ཕལ་པ་ཞིག་མིན་པར་ཐག་ཆོད་ཅེས་རྒྱུན་དུ་ལབ་ཅིང་། ༼ཨ་ནེ་པདྨ་ལྷ་སྒྲིད་མོ་རང་ཆུང་དུའི་སྐབས་སུ་མཇལ་མྱོང་ཞིང་། ཁོང་ལམ་སྲང་གང་སར་གཟིམས་མཛད་བརྟེན་མོ་རང་སོགས་ཕྲུག་གུ་རྣམས་ཀྱིས་རྡེའུ་སོགས་ཁོང་གི་སྟེང་དུ་གཏོར་སྐབས༑ ཁོང་ཐུགས་ཁྲོའི་རྣམ་པ་ཙམ་ཡང་མེད་པར་ཞི་བའི་གསུང་གིས། ཕྲུག་གུ་ཚོ། ང་ལ་སྡུག་པོ་མ་གཏོང་སོགས་གསུངས་མྱོང་ཞིང་། དུས་ཕྱིས་ཁོང་གི་རྣམ་ཐར་ཐོས་

སྐབས་མོ་རང་ཡང་འགྲོད་ནས་བཤགས་པ་བྱས་པ་ཡིན་ཞེས་རང་ལ་ལབ་བྱུང་། མཆན།༽ ཁོང་མཆོག་དམན་སུ་དང་འཕྲད་ཀྱང་བྱམས་བརྩེའི་ཚིག་ཁོ་ན་གསུངས་ཤིང་མཐར་དགུང་གྲངས་དྲུག་ཅུའི་སྐོར་སླེབས་སྐབས། ཁོང་གི་ཞལ་ནས་ད་ནི་རབ་བྱུང་གི་བྱ་བ་མཐར་ཕྱིན་ཟིན་པས་ཁྱིམ་གྱི་ལས་ལ་འཇུག་དགོས་ཞེས་གསུངས་ཤིང་བསོད་སྙོམས་སྐབས་སྔར་དང་མི་འདྲ་བར་ཇ་དང་ཁ་བཏགས་སློང་ཞིང་སྣོད་ཀྱང་ཛ་ཕྲུག་ཞིག་བསྣམས་ཏེ། ཐང་དུ་རྡོ་རིལ་གསུམ་བཞག་མཛད་ཅིང་མེ་འབུད་པ་དང་། དེའི་སྟེང་དུ་ཛ་ཕྲུག་བཞག་ཏེ་ཇ་བཀོལ་ཞིང་། ཇ་འཁོལ་རྗེས་ཅུང་ཟད་བཞེས་ཤིང་ལྷག་མ་ཐབ་ཀྱི་མཐའ་སྐོར་དུ་བླུགས་མཛད། དེ་ནས་ཇ་སྙིགས་རྣམས་རྡོ་གསུམ་གྱི་སྟེང་དུ་མཉམ་པར་བསྒོས་རྗེས་ཁ་དར་རེ་བཞག་མཛད་ནས། ད་ནི་ཁྱིམ་གཅིག་གྲུབ་པ་ཡིན་ཞེས་གསུངས་ཤིང་དེ་འདྲ་བ་བརྒྱ་དང་བརྒྱད་གྲུབ་མཚམས། ༼དེ་ནི་གསང་སྔགས་ཀྱི་ཐབས་མཁས་པའི་སྤྱོད་པ་ཞིག་ཡིན་ངེས་གསུངས། མཆན།༽ ཁོང་གིས་ད་ནི་མི་ཚེའི་བྱ་བ་གྲུབ་པ་ཡིན་པས་དོ་ནུབ་སྐྱེ་དགུའི་གྲོང་སྡེའི་འཁོར་ཁང་དུ་གཟིམ་དུ་བཅུག་རོགས་ཞེས་ལྷ་གཉེར་ལ་གསུངས་པས། ལྷ་གཉེར་གྱིས་སྐུ་ཉིད་ལ་སྐྲ་ཤིག་མང་བས་འཐད་ཀྱི་མ་རེད་ཞུས་པས། སྔར་ཡིན་ན་བདེན་ཡང་ད་ནི་ཕྲན་ལ་ཤིག་གཅིག་ཀྱང་མེད་ཅེས་གསུངས་མཐར་ཁོང་འཁོར་ཁང་དུ་གཟིམས་བཅུག །ཕྱི་ཉིན་སྔ་དྲོར་ལྷ་གཉེར་གྱིས་མཇལ་སྐབས་ཁོང་སྐུ་མྱ་ངན་ལས་འདས་ཟིན་ཅིང་ཞབས་རྡོར་དཀྱིལ་དང་ཕྱག་མཉམ་བཞག །སྐུ་ལུས་སོར་གང་ཙམ་གདན་ལ་མ་རེག་པར་བཞུགས་པར་ཀུན་གྱིས་མངོན་སུམ་དུ་མཇལ། དེ་ནས་སྐུ་གདུང་མེ་ལ་བསྲེགས་སྐབས་ཐུགས་ལྗགས་སྤྱན་གསུམ་འཁྲུངས་པས་འཁོར་ཁང་དེར་ཁོང་གི་འདྲ་སྐུ་ཞིག་བཞེངས། དེའི་ནང་རྟེན་དུ་ཐུགས་ལྗགས་སྤྱན་གསུམ་བཞུགས་སུ་བཅུག ད་གཟོད་ཀུན་གྱིས་སྐྱེས་བུ་དམ་པ་ཡིན་པར་ཤེས་རྟོགས་བྱུང་ནས་སྔར་བྱས་འགྲོད་བཤགས་དང་། རྟེན་དེ་ལ་བསོད་ནམས་ཀྱི་

ཚོགས་བསགས་པའི་ཞིང་དུ་གྱུར་པའོ། །སླར་སླུས་པ། སྤྱོད་པ་ཕྱིན་དྲུག་ཕ་མཐར་སོན་ཡང་། །སྤྱོད་ཚུལ་མ་ངེས་འགྲོ་དོན་སྟོན་འདི། །སྤྱོད་ལམ་དཔགས་ནས་བཟང་ངན་སླ་བའི། །སྤྱོད་ཡུལ་མིན་པའི་སློབ་སྟོན་འདུག་གོ། ༼༩༽ བྲ་བྲལ་དྲག་པོའི་བརྟུལ་ཞུགས་ཅན་ས་སྐྱ་ཐག་ལུང་དགོན་གྱི་གྲུབ་སྨོན་ནི། ཐུགས་སྙིང་རྗེ་ཆུ་ཡིས་བརླན་ཀྱང་། །ཕྱི་བརྟུལ་ཞུགས་ཁྲོ་བོའི་སྤྱོད་པ། །རྗེ་གྲུབ་བརྙེས་སྐྱེས་ཆེན་རྣམས་ལ། །སྐུ་སྒྱུ་མའི་རོལ་གར་བསམ་འདས༏ ཁོང་རབ་ཏུ་བྱུང་རྗེས་གནས་ངེས་མེད་དུ་ཕེབས་ཤིང་། སྤྱིར་ཁོང་ཉིད་སྐུ་ལུས་ཆེ་ཞིང་ཞལ་རས་གནག་པ་དང་། མི་མཐོ་དམན་སུ་དང་ཐུག་ན་ཡང་མི་སྙན་པའི་གསུང་ཚིག་དྲག་པོ་ཁོ་ན་འབྱིན་སྐབས་མི་ཀུན་འཇིགས་དགོས་པར་བཞུགས་ཤིང་། ཡིན་ན་ཡང་ཐུགས་རྒྱུད་ལ་སྙིང་རྗེས་ཆུ་ཡིས་བརླན་པའི་མཐུས་རྒྱུན་གྱི་མཛད་སྤྱོད་ནི། མི་དབུལ་པོའི་རོ་དང་མཛེ་སོགས་འགོ་ནད་ཅན་གྱི་རོ་ཁོ་ན་དུར་ཁྲོད་དུ་འཁྱེར་མཛད་པ་དང་། རོ་ལྟོ་བའི་རིགས་རྣམས་ལ་འདི་ལྟ་བུ་ལྟོ་དགོས་པའི་རྒྱུ་མཚན་གང་ཡིན་དང་ག་རེ་ཟེར་བ་ཡིན་སོགས་བཀའ་བསྐྱོན་དྲག་པོ་དང་ཕྱག་འབེབས་ཆེན་པོ་གནང་མཐར། ད་ནི་སྔར་ལས་ཡང་སོང་ཞེས་གསུངས་ཏེ་ལས་སླ་པོའི་ངང་ནས་སྐུ་རྒྱབ་ཏུ་བསྣམས་ཤིང་བྱ་རྒོད་ལ་སྦྱིན་མཛད། གཤིན་པོ་དེ་དག་གི་གོས་བཟང་ངན་གང་ཡོད་བསྡུས་ཏེ་བཟང་བ་རྣམས་དབུལ་པོར་སྦྱིན་ཞིང་རྙིང་པ་རྣམས་ཁོང་གིས་མནབས་མཛད། མཐར་སྐུ་མྱ་ངན་ལས་འདའ་ཁར་རང་དགོན་ཐག་ལུང་དགོན་གྱི་ལྷ་ཁང་དུ་གཟིམས་དགོས་གསུངས་ཀྱང་གཟིམ་དུ་མ་བཅུག་པས། གལ་ཏེ་གཟིམ་མ་བཅུག་ན་ཡང་ལྷ་ཁང་དུ་སྐྱུག་པའམ་མི་གཙང་བ་ཞིག་འདོར་དགོས་ཞེས་གསུངས་སྐབས་ལྷ་གཉེར་སྔར་ལས་ཀྱང་ཁྲོས་ཏེ་ཁོང་ཕྱི་རུ་སྒྲུད་པ་དང་། དེ་ནས་ཡུལ་དེའི་མི་ཚང་འབྱོར་ལྡན་ཞིག་ལ་ང་རང་ཐག་དགོན་གྱིས་ཉར་འདོད་མི་འདུག་པས་ཁྱེད་རང་གི་མཆོད་ཁང་ནང་དུ་དོ་ནུབ་ཉལ་གྱི་ཡིན་ཞེས་གསུངས་པ་བཞིན་གཟིམས་བཅུག

།ཕྱི་ཉིན་ཞོགས་པར་ཁོང་ཞབས་རྗེར་སྐྱེལ་དང་ཕྱག་མཉམ་བཞག །སྤྱན་ནམ་མཁར་ཧྲིག་གེར་གཟིགས་ཏེ་སྐུ་མྱ་ངན་ལས་འདས་འདུག་རྐྱེན་དེ་བཞིན་དགོན་པར་ཞུས་པས། ད་གཟོད་ཁོང་གྲུབ་པ་ཐོབ་པའི་རྣལ་འབྱོར་ཡིན་པར་རྟོགས་ནས་སྔར་བྱས་ལ་འགྱོད་བཤགས་དང་བཅས་དགོན་པའི་སེར་སྦྲེང་གིས་ཁོང་གི་སྐུ་གདུང་དགོན་དུ་སྤྱན་དྲངས་ཏེ་གདུལ་བྱའི་བསོད་ནམས་བསགས་པའི་ཞིང་དུ་གྱུར་པའོ། །སླར་སླས་པ། དེང་སང་དགོན་སྡེ་རྣམས་ཀྱི་ལྷ་ཚུལ་ལ། །གྲུབ་ཐོབ་ཞེས་པ་བླ་གྲྭ་གཟི་བརྗིད་ཅན། །མིག་མཐོང་ཙམ་ལ་རེ་བ་བྱེད་འདུག་པས། །རྣམ་ཐར་འདི་ཚོས་ཐེ་ཚོམ་ཆོད་པར་ཤོག། ༼༥༽ ཡང་ས་སྐྱ་ཐག་དགོན་གྱི་གྲྭ་འཇམ་དབྱངས་རྒྱལ་མཚན་ནི། འཛའ༷་ལུས་མཁའ་སྤྱོད་གྲུབ་པའི་རྟགས་ལྡན། །འཛའ༷་ཚོན་ལྷ་བུར་ཆོས་རྣམས་རྟོགས་པས། །འཛའ༷་འོད་ཟེར་གསུམ་ཐིག་ལེའི་གློང་ནས། །འཛའ༷་ལུས་ཀླ་གིས་བསུ་ལ་འདུད་དོ༔ །ཁོང་དགོན་པའི་ཉེ་འགྲམ་དུ་སྐུ་མཚམས་ལ་བཞུགས་ཤིང་ཞབས་ཞུ་བཙུན་མའམ་ཨ་ནི་གཅིག་ཡོད་ཅིང་། རྒྱུན་དུ་ཁོང་ལ་ཨ་ནི་ཞབས་ཞུ་ཡོད་རྐྱེན་གྱིས་མི་རྣམས་ཀྱིས་དད་པ་དེ་ཙམ་མེད། ལོ་གཅིག་ལ་ཁོང་རྒྱུན་རིང་པོར་སྟོང་ནས་ཉིན་ཞིག་དགོན་གྱི་ལས་བྱེད་པ་རྣམས་ཕེབས་རོགས་ཞེས་གསུངས་ནས་ཕེབས་སྐབས༔ ཁོང་གིས་སྐུ་ཁྲག་ཕོར་པ་གང་བཞག་མཛད་འདུག་ཅིང་ཞལ་ནས། རང་ལ་གྲྭ་ཞུའི་དཔོན་སྐུ་དྲིན་ཤིན་ཏུ་ཆེ་བས་ཁྲག་འདི་ཁོང་ལ་འབུལ་རོགས་ཞུ། གཞན་རྒྱུ་ཟས་གང་ཡོད་བཙུན་མ་འདི་བཀའ་དྲིན་ཆེ་གཤིས་འདི་ལ་གནང་རོགས་གནང་། ཁོང་གི་གཟིམ་ཆུང་དུ་ཆུ་ཐིག་གཅིག་དང་ཟས་ཁམ་གང་ཙམ་ཡང་མ་བཞག་པར་སྒོ་ལ་གཟེར་ལྕགས་རྒྱབ་ཏེ་ལྡེ་མིག་ཀྱང་འཛིན་པར་ཞུ། ཞག་བདུན་མཚམས་སུ་ཁང་པའི་ནང་དུ་ཉེ་མ་ཤར་མ་ཐག་སྒོ་དབྱེ་རོགས་གནང་ཞེས་གསུངས་པས་གྲྭ་ཁ་ཤས་ཀྱིས་བཟའ་བཏུང་ཅུང་ཟད་བཞག་ན་དགའ་ཚུལ་སླས་ཀྱང་གྲྭ་གཞན་རྣམས་ཞལ་འཆམས་ཏེ་ཁོང་གི་གསུངས་བཞིན་

བྲེད་ལ། དགོས་པ་བྱུང་ན་ལྡེ་མིག་བཙུན་མར་སྤྲད་དང་ཞབས་ཞུ་བྲེད་ཀྱི་རེད་ཅེས་ཀུན་དེ་ལྟར་བགྲོས་ཏེ་བཙུན་མར་དེ་བཞིན་སློབ་པོ། །དེ་ནས་ཞག་བདུན་གྱི་སྔ་དྲོར་ཉི་མ་ཤར་བ་དང་དུས་མཉམ་སློ་ཕྱེ་སྐབས། གཟིམ་མལ་དུ་དབུ་སྐྲ་དང་ཕྱག་སེན་ན་བཟའ་ཙམ་ལས་སྐུ་ལུས་ལྷག་མེད་དུ་འཇའ་ལུས་གཤེགས་ཟིན་པས། ད་གཟོད་ཀུན་གྱིས་གྲུབ་པ་ཐོབ་པ་ཡིད་ཆེས་ཤིང་དད་རྟེན་དུ་ན་བཟའ་དང་ཕྱག་སེན་གདན་དྲངས་པའི་སྐལ་པ་བྱུང་བའོ། །སྒྲར་སྒྲས་པ། དེང་སང་དུས་ངན་ཁ་རླངས་བདོ་ན་ཡང་། །གསང་སྔགས་བསྟན་པའི་ནུས་པ་མི་ལྟར་འབར། །དེ་ཕྱིར་བྱ་བྲལ་རི་ སྲུལ་གནས་རྣམས་ལ། །སུ་དང་འགྲོགས་ཀྱང་ལོག་ལྟ་སྤོངས་ཤིག་ཨང་ ||

༼༨༽ གྲི་ཡི་རྐྱེན་ལ་བརྟེན་ནས་གྲུབ་པ་ཐོབ་པ་བཀའ་བརྒྱུད་བན་ཆེན་དགོན་གྱི་གྲྭ་རྟོགས་ལྡན་ཀརྨ་རྒྱལ་དབང་ནི། གངས་ཅན་བོད་ཀྱི་ལྷ་སྐལ། །སྙིང་རྗེ་གཏེར་ཆེན་གྲུབ་པའི། །རྟོགས་ལྡན་ཀརྨ་རྒྱལ་དབང་། །ཀུན་གྱི་མཆོད་གནས་ཁྱེད་རྒྱལ། ཁོང་གྲྭ་ཆུང་གི་སྐབས་རྭ་གདའ་འམ་རྭ་རྫ་དཔོན་ཚང་གི་ཕྱུགས་རྫི་ཡིན་ཞིང་ཁོང་གིས་རྟག་པར་དབུ་སྐྲ་འོག་ཏུ་གྲི་ཤིན་ཏུ་རྣོན་པོ་ཞིག་པེད་སྤྱད་མེད་པར་ཉར་མཛད་ཡོད་པས། སྔོན་གྱི་སྐབས་དཔོན་ཚང་གིས་དགུན་དཔྱིད་ཀྱི་ཆེད་གཡག་ལུག་མང་པོ་བཤས་ནས་མི་ཁ་ཤས་ཀྱིས་རྒྱུས་ཡོད་བྱས་ཏེ་ཁོང་གི་གཟིམས་སྟུས་འོག་གི་གྲི་པེད་སྤྱད་བྱས་པ་དང་། དགོང་མོར་ཁོང་གིས་གྲི་མེད་པ་གཟིགས་ནས་རྩད་གཅོད་མཛད་སྐབས། ཤན་པ་ཞིག་གིས་ཁྱེད་ཀྱི་གྲི་འདིར་ཡོད་ཅེས་ཁྲག་དང་བཅས་ཕུལ་བས། ཁོང་དེ་མ་ཐག་བཤུམས་ཤིང་སྡིག་པའི་ལས་ཚབས་པོ་ཆེ་བསགས་སོང་ཞེས་གསུངས། མྱུར་བར་བན་ཆེན་དགོན་དུ་སྐྱབས་རྗེ་མཉན་པ་རིན་པོ་ཆེའི་དྲུང་དུ་ཕེབས་ཏེ་གདམས་ངག་ཞུས་ཤིང་རི་ཁྲོད་དེར་གཙོ་བོ་ཐུགས་རྗེ་ཆེན་པོའི་བསྒོམ་བཟླས་བྱས་མཐར་གྲུབ་པ་ཐོབ་ཅིང་། ལོ་རྟག་པར་སློབ་མ་སྟོང་ཕྲག་བརྒྱལ་བ་དང་མཉམ་དུ་ཕྱོགས་མེད་ཀྱི་རི་བྲག་ཀུན་ལ་མ་ཆི་བཀོ་བར་མཛད།

དགུན་གྱི་སྐབས་འཁྱགས་རོམ་གྱི་སྟེང་དུ་བྱེ་མས་མ་ཆེ་བྲི་བ་དང་། ས་ཕྱོགས་གང་སར་མ་ཆེ་དུང་སྒྲུབ་བཙུགས་མཛད་ཅིང་རི་བྲག་ཀུན་ལ་ཞབས་རྗེས་དང་། མ་འོང་འབྱུང་འགྱུར་གྱི་མངོན་ཤེས་སོགས་ཐོགས་མེད་ཡོད་པའི་མཚན་སྙན་ཕྱོགས་མེད་དུ་ཁྱབ་ཅིང་གྲུབ་པའི་རྟགས་དངོས་སུ་གསལ་བའོ། །སླར་སྨྲས་པ། ལས་ཅན་སྐྱེས་བུ་རེ་རེས། །ཡུལ་ཁམས་ཆོས་ལ་བསྒྱུར་མཛད། །ལས་ངན་སྡིག་ཅན་རེས་ཀྱང་། །ཡུལ་ཁམས་ནག་པོར་གཏོང་སོང་། །རྟེན་འབྲེལ་ལྟོས་བཞག་ཆོས་ལ། །ཅིར་ཡང་སྣང་ལ་བསྒོན་མེད།། ༼༧༽ མི་ལོ་བཅུ་གསུམ་ཞབས་ལ་ལྕགས་སྒྲོག་གསོལ་ནས་གྲུབ་པ་ཐོབ་པ་བཀའ་བརྒྱུད་ཁྲ་འགུ་དགོན་གྱི་སྒྲུབ་དཔོན་ཀརྨ་ཚུལ་ཁྲིམས་སམ་ཡོན་འཕེལ་ཚེ་མཚམས་ནི། ཐུགས་མོས་བརྩོན་ལྡན་པའི་སློབ་མ། །རྗེ་དྲིན་ལྡན་བླ་མས་རྗེས་འཛིན། །ཕ་བླ་མའི་ཐུགས་དང་དབྱེར་མེད། །མགོན་ཏི་ལོ་གཉིས་པར་འདུད་དོ། ཚེ་མཚམས་ཀྱི་བླ་མ་ནི་གོང་སྤྲུལ་ཡོན་ཏན་རྒྱ་མཚོའི་དངོས་སློབ་འབྲུ་འཛམ་དབྱངས་གྲགས་པ་ཡིན་ཞིང་། བླ་མའི་ཞལ་ནས་ལོ་བཅུ་གསུམ་རིང་ཞབས་ལ་ལྕགས་སྒྲོག་གསོལ་ནས་སྒྲུབ་པ་གྱིས་དང་བུ་ཏི་ལོ་པ་དང་དགོངས་པ་མཉམ་ཞེས་ལུང་བསྟན་གྱི་དབུགས་དབྱུང་བ་བཞིན། ཁྲ་འགུ་དགོན་གྱི་ཉེ་འགྲམ་དབེན་གནས་ཚེ་ལུང་ཕུག་ཁྲའམ་ཕུག་པ་ཁྲ་བོ་རུ་སྒྲུབ་པ་རྩེ་གཅིག་མཛད་ནས་མི་ལོ་བཅུ་གསུམ་ཚང་ལ་ཉེ་བའི་སྐབས་ལྷ་ས་དམག་དང་འཐབ་འཁྲུགས་ཆེན་པོ་ཞིག་བྱུང་སྟེ། ཡུལ་དེར་ཕམ་ཉེས་ཆེན་པོ་བྱུང་རྐྱེན་མི་ཚང་མ་ཕྱོགས་གཡས་གཡོན་བྲོས་བྲོལ་དུ་ཐལ་ཡང་། ཁོང་གཅིག་པུར་བླ་མའི་བཀའ་ལ་བརྟེན་ནས་མ་ཕེབས་པར་བཞུགས་པས། དགྲ་དམག་གིས་བཙུངས་ཏེ་ཁ་ཤས་ཀྱིས་འདི་བཙོན་པ་ཡིན་པ་འདྲ་ཞེས་ལྕགས་སྒྲོག་གཏོར་གྲབས་བྱས་པས་ཁོང་གིས་བླ་མའི་བཀའ་བཞིན་སྒྲུབ་པ་ཡིན་ཚུལ་སོགས་ནན་ཞུས་བྱས་འཐབ་མཐར་མ་གཏོར་ཙམ་བྱུང་། དེ་ནས་ཁོང་ཡུལ་དེར་བཞུགས་པའི་ཐུགས་རེ་བྲལ་ནས་དབེན་གནས་ཛམ་རྐྱང་པོ་

ཞེས་པའི་གནས་རིའི་རྩེར་ཕེབས་པའི་ལམ་བར་དུ་དཔལ་ཆུ་ཤིན་ཏུ་རྒྱས་ནས་ཕ་རོལ་བརྒལ་ཐབས་བྲལ་ཡང་། ཁོང་རླུང་དབུ་མར་ཚུད་པའི་སྟོབས་ཀྱིས་ཞལ་ནས་དབུགས་རྫུབ་མི་དགོས་སྐབས། ཆུ་འོག་ཏུ་འཛུལ་ཏེ་རྡོ་ལ་འཛུས་ནས་ཆུའི་ཕ་རོལ་ཏུ་ཕེབས་པའི་མཛད་པ་ངོ་མཚར་བསྟན། རྒྱུན་དུ་ཁྲ་དགོན་ནས་ཀུན་རིག་སྒྲུབ་ཁང་གི་བར་རླུང་བུམ་ཅན་ཚར་གཅིག་གིས་ཕེབས་ཐུབ་པ་དང་། མ་ཚད་ས་ཆ་གཞན་དུ་ཕེབས་སྐབས་ཀྱང་ཐད་ཀར་ཕེབས་པ་ལས་བྲག་རི་དང་ཆུ་སོགས་གང་ལ་ཡང་གཟུར་མི་མཛད་ཅིང་། ཐག་རིང་གང་འདྲ་ཡིན་ཡང་མྱུར་བར་ཕེབས་ཐུབ་པའི་གྲུབ་རྟགས་བསྟན། འོན་ཀྱང་མིའི་མདུན་ནས་དལ་པོའི་ངང་ཕེབས་ནས་སྦས་པའི་ཚུལ་མཛད། དེ་ནས་དབེན་གནས་ཛམ་རྐྱང་པོ་ཞེས་པའི་གནས་རི་མཐོན་པོ་དེའི་རྩེ་ལ་མི་སུ་ཡང་མི་ཐོན་ཀྱང་། ཁོང་ཉིད་བདེ་བླག་ངོས་ཕེབས་ཏེ་རྗེས་སུ་མི་རྣམས་ཀྱིས་གང་ལྟར་ཕེབས་མིན་བཀའ་འདྲི་ཞུ་སྐབས། ཁོང་གི་ཞལ་ནས་ཕྱག་མཛུབ་ཀྱིས་གནས་ལ་སྦྲར་ནས་སྐུ་སྨད་ཡར་འཕེན། ཡང་ཕྱག་ཞབས་ཀྱིས་སྦྲར་ནས་སྐུ་སྟོད་མདུན་དུ་འཕངས་པ་ཡིན་ཞེས་གསུངས་ཤིང་། མ་ཚད་ཁོང་གིས་གསུངས་ན། སྔོན་མའི་ཁ་གཏམ་ལ་ཛམ་རྐྱང་པོའི་དབུ་རྩེ་ཚང་མ་ཤེལ་གྱི་རང་བཞིན་ཡིན་པར་གསན་མྱོང་ཡང་། གནས་ལས་ཤེལ་མི་འདུག་ཅེས་ཀྱང་གསུངས། གནས་དེ་རུ་ཟླ་གཅིག་གི་བར་ཟས་སུ་ཏིང་འཛིན་དང་གོས་སུ་གཏུམ་མོ་ལ་བརྟེན་ནས་སྒྲུབ་པའི་དམ་བཅའ་མཐར་ཕྱིན་རྗེས་ཞབས་ཀྱི་ལྷུགས་སྒྲོགས་ཀྱང་གཏོར་མི་དགོས་པར་རང་ཞིག་ཏུ་སོང་། རེས་འགར་ཁོང་གི་ཞལ་ནས། རྒྱུན་དུ་སྤྱོད་ལམ་རྣམ་བཞིར་གང་བྱས་ཀྱང་འོད་གསལ་ལས་གཡོ་བ་མེད་ཕྱིར་ཉམས་ལེན་ཞེས་ལོགས་སུ་རྩོལ་བཅས་ཞིག་མི་དགོས་ཕྱིར་ན་བདེ་པོ་འདུག་གསུངས། སླར་སྨྲས་པ། །ཕ་བླ་མའི་བཀའ་ལུང་རིན་པོ་ཆེ། །ཡིད་མོས་གུས་འགྱུར་མེད་རྒྱལ་མཚན་རྩེར། །ཕྱག་དམ་བརྩོན་བརྟན་པོས་བསྒྲེངས་པའི་མཐུས། །འབྲས་བསྒྲུ

མེད་དགོས་འདོད་འབེབས་ལ་གསུས།། (༢) །རྫོགས་ཆེན་གྱི་རྣལ་འབྱོར་དྲི་མེད་འོད་ཟེར་ནི། འགྲོ་མགོན་ཕྱག་སྟོང་སྤྱན་སྟོང་གི་སྐྱུང་གནས། །འགྲོ་དྲུག་སྐྱེ་སྒོ་ཆོད་ངེས་ཀྱི་དགེ་སྦྱོར་ཾ། །འགྲོ་ལ་དམིགས་མེད་བརྩེ་བ་ཡིས་གཟིགས་ཾཔའི། །འགྲོ་བའི་སྐྱབས་མགོན་བྱ་བྲལ་ལ་ཾའདུད་དོ། །རྣལ་འབྱོར་དྲི་མེད་འོད་ཟེར་གྱི་ཡབ་ཾཡུལ་འགོ་ལོག་གསེར་ཏ་ནས་ཡིན་ཅིང་སྐུ་ཆུང་ངུའི་དུས་རབ་ཏུ་བྱུང་སྟེ་གནས་ངེས་མེད་དུ་བྱ་བྲལ་མཛད་ནས་ཕེབས་ཏེ་རིམ་པར་དྲིན་ཅན་བླ་མའི་ཡབ་ཡུལ་གྱི་ཡུལ་ལྷ་དགེ་རི་ཆོས་རྒྱལ་རྡོ་རྗེའི་སྒྲུབ་གནས། (དགེ་རི་ཆོས་རྒྱལ་རྡོ་རྗེ་ནི་༧རྒྱལ་དབང་བཅུ་བཞི་པ་ཐེག་མཆོག་རྡོ་རྗེའི་གཏེར་བཏོན་ཡིན་ཅིང་། ༧རྒྱལ་དབང་མཆོག་དང་གཏེར་བཏོན་རྣམ་གཉིས་ནས་ཨ་མྱེ་རྡོ་རྗེ་གཉན་རྒྱལ་གྱི་རི་མཚོ་གཉིས་ཀའི་གནས་སྒོ་ཕྱེས་ནས་སྒྲུབ་ཕུག་ནང་དུ་ཚོགས་འཁོར་མཛད་སྐབས་བྲག་ཞུ་ནས་བཀྲ་ཤིས་རྟག་བརྒྱད་དང་རྒྱལ་སྲིད་སྣ་བདུན་གྱི་གཟུགས་སུ་གྲོན་ཅིང་། ཤེལ་གྱི་ཆར་པ་ཡང་བབས། གཞན་ཡང་གཏེར་གཏོན་གྱིས་སྒྲུབ་ཕུག་དེ་ནས་ཧཱུྃ་དཀར་གཡང་སྐྱབས་དང་། གུ་རུ་མཐིང་ནག་གི་སྒྲུབ་ཐབས་སོགས་གཏེར་དུ་བཏོན་པ་མངལ་དུ་ཡོད་ཅིང་། མ་ཚད་བྲག་ཕུག་དེར་ཁོང་གི་ཞབས་རྗེས་མང་པོ་དང་སྐུ་རྗེས་ཀྱང་ཡོད། འོན་ཀྱང་ཡུལ་དེ་ཡིས་ཇི་བཞིན་མ་རྟོགས་པར་ཁོང་གིས་ཡུལ་གྱི་ས་གཡང་འཕྲོག་གི་འདུག་ཅེས་ལབ་ནས་ཡུལ་ཕྱུད་བྱས་པས། གཏེར་ལེན་སའི་སྒྲུབ་ཕུག་གི་ཁུང་བུ་སྟར་བཞིན་གསབ་མ་ཐུབ་པས་ཁུང་བུ་ཆེན་པོ་ཡོད་ཕྱིར་གཉན་རྒྱལ་གྱི་གྲོང་པ་སྐྱོ་པོ་ཡོད་པའི་རྒྱུ་མཚན་ཡང་དེ་ཡིན་ཟེར། མཆན།) ཨ་མྱེ་རྡོ་རྗེ་གཉན་རྒྱལ་གྱི་རྩེར་བྲག་ཕུག་ཆུང་ངུ་ཞིག་ནང་སྒྲུབ་པ་མཛད་ཅིང་བཞུགས་ཡོད་པ་དང་པོར་སུས་ཀྱང་ཤེས་རྟོགས་མ་བྱུང་། ཉིན་ཞིག་འབོ་རི་ཀཿརྣམ་རྒྱལ་ལུག་དེད་ནས་རི་རྩེར་འགྲོ་སྐབས། བྲག་ཕུག་དེ་རུ་གྲུ་ཆུང་ཞི་དུལ་སྤྱོད་པ་ཅན་ཞིག་མཉམ་བཞག་མཛད་ནས་བཞུགས་འདུག་པ་མངལ་ནས་ཁོའི་སེམས་ལ། འདི་རི་དེའི་ཡུལ་ལྷ་ཡིན་ནམ་སྙམ་ནས་ལེགས་པར་མངལ་སྐབས་སྤྱན་འཛུམ་པར་མཐོང་། དེ་ནས་ཁོ་རང་ཕྱི་ལོག་སུ་སོང་སྟེ་བརྟགས་པས་ས་ལ་མི་ཡི་རྗེས་མེད་སྟབས་ཡུལ་

ལྷ་ཡིན་པར་ཐག་ཆོད་སྐམ་ནས་ཡང་བསྐྱར་མཇལ་དུ་ཕྱིན་པས་སྔོན་བཞིན་བཞུགས་འདུག །དེ་ནས་རྒན་པོས་ཁྱེད་སུ་ཡིན་ཞུས་པས། ཁོང་གིས་ཕྲན་འགོ་ལོག་གི་གྲྭ་ཞིག་ཡིན་ཞིང་གནས་འདིར་སྨོན་ལམ་གྱི་སྟོབས་ཀྱིས་ངེས་པར་སྡོད་དགོས་ཡོད་པས་སུ་ལ་ཡང་མ་སྨྲ་ཞིག་གསུངས། རྒན་པོས་སྒྲུབ་ཕུག་ཕྱོགས་ཀུན་ཏུ་ཙུལ་ཡང་ཁོང་གི་མདུན་དུ་རྩམ་པ་ཕོར་པ་གང་ཙམ་ཞིག་ཁུག་མའི་ནང་དུ་འདུག ༑གཞན་དངོས་པོ་གང་ཡང་མ་རྙེད་སྐབས་ཁོས་ནོ་ཞིག་ཕུལ་བས་ཕྲུག་གིས་མཆོད་པ་ཞིག་དང་། ལྷགས་སྟེང་དུ་ཐིག་གཅིག་བཞེས་ཏེ་དེ་འཕྲོས་མར་གནང་བྱུང་། མི་རྒན་ཡང་དགའ་གྲུས་སྐྱེས་ནས་མི་སུ་ལ་ཡང་མ་སྨྲས་པར་ཟླ་བ་གཅིག་མཚམས་ཡང་བསྐྱར་མཇལ་དུ་སོང་བས་སྔོན་བཞིན་བཞུགས་འདུག་ཅིང་། རྩམ་པ་ཡང་སྔར་ལྟར་ལས་མ་བཞེས་པར་འདུག །ཡང་རྒན་པོས་སྔར་བཞིན་གསོལ་ནོ་ཕུལ་བས་ཁོང་གིས་མཆོད་པ་དང་ཐུར་མ་གང་ཙམ་བཞེས་ཏེ་ད་དུང་ཡང་གཞན་ལ་མ་སྨྲ་ཞིག་ཅེས་གདམས། ཟླ་གཅིག་གི་རྗེས་སུ་སྔོན་དུས་འཕེལ་ཞིང་དགུན་ལ་ཉེ་བའི་སྐབས་སླར་ཡང་མདུན་དུ་བཅར་བས། སྔར་བཞིན་བཞུགས་འདུག་ཅིང་སྔོན་མའི་རྩམ་ཁུག་དེ་བྲག་ངོས་སུ་ཤིང་ཕུར་ཞིག་བཏབ་ཏེ་དེའི་སྟེང་དུ་བཀལ་མཛད་འདུག །ད་གཟོད་ཁོང་གི་ཞལ་ནས། ཁྱེད་རང་གསང་མི་དགོས་པར་གཞན་ལ་སྨྲས་ཀྱང་ཆོག་ཞེས་བཀའ་འཁྲོལ་བས་མི་རྒན་ཤིན་ཏུ་དགའ་སྟེ་ཁོང་ལ་ཞུ་དོན། འདི་ནས་མི་རིང་བའི་སར་དགེ་རི་གཏེར་ཆེན་ཆོས་རྒྱལ་རྡོ་རྗེའི་སྒྲུབ་གནས་གཉན་རྒྱལ་ཕུག་རྒན་དུ་ཡུལ་འདིའི་བླ་མར་བཞུགས་རོགས་ཞུས་པས་ཁོང་གིས་ཀྱང་བཞུགས་པར་ཞལ་གྱིས་བཞེས། མི་རྒན་གྱིས་ཡུལ་མིར་སྨྲས་བརྟེན་ཀུན་དགའ་གྲུས་ཆེན་པོས་སྒྲུབ་ཕུག་ཙུང་ཟད་ཞིག་རལ་སོང་བ་གསོས་ཏེ་བཞུགས་གྲལ་བསྒྲིགས། ཇ་མི་བཅུ་གསུམ་ཙམ་བླ་མ་གདན་འདྲེན་ཆེད་རི་རྩེར་སོང་སྟེ་མཇལ་ནས་བྱིན་རླབས་ཞུས་ཤིང་། ད་རྗེ་ཆིབས་ནས་བྱོན་པར་ཞུས་པས། ཁོང་བཞེད་མོ་

མཛད་ཅིང་གློ་བུར་དུ་བཞེངས་ནས་བྲག་ངོས་ཀྱི་ཕྱུར་མ་བཅག་སྟེ་རྩམ་ཁྱུག་གཟན་འོག་ཏུ་བསྣམས་ནས་རྟ་ལ་ཆིབས་མ་མཛད་པར་ཞབས་ཐང་དུ་ཕེབས། རྗེས་སུ་མི་རྣམས་ཀྱིས་བླ་མས་ཤིང་བཅག་མཛད་པའི་ལྷག་མ་དད་རྟེན་དུ་ལེན་སྐབས་ཤིང་གི་རི་མོ་ཇི་བཞིན་བྲག་ལ་ཡང་ཡོད་ཅིང་། བྲག་ལ་གས་སྲུབས་མེད་པར་དཔེར་ན་མར་གྱི་ནང་དུ་ཞུར་པ་བཏབ་པ་བཞིན་མཐལ་བས་ཀུན་དད་པའི་གསོས་སུ་གྱུར་ཅིང་བླ་མ་ལ་གྲུབ་ཐོབ་དངོས་ཀྱི་འདུ་ཤེས་དང་མི་བྲལ་བར་གྱུར་ཏོ། །དེ་ནས་བཟུང་ཁོང་གིས་ལོ་རེ་བཞིན་སྨྱུང་གནས་ཚ་བརྒྱ་རེ་དང་རྒྱས་འགོགས་རྣམས་ལ་འཕོ་བ་བདུན་ཕྲག་རེ་གསུངས་སྐབས་ཀུན་ལ་རྟགས་ཐོན་ཞིང་། གཞན་གྱིས་འབུལ་དངོས་རྣམས་ཆུད་ཟོས་སུ་མི་གཏོང་བར་ཡིག་དྲུག་རྡོ་ལ་བརྐོ་བ་དང་མར་མེ་རྫ་དར་སོགས་མཆོད་སྦྱིན་གྱི་ལས་ལ་གཞོལ་ཞིང་སྐུ་ཚེ་གང་པོར་བྱ་བཏང་ཁོ་ན་མཛད། པེ་ནུ་སྟོད་ནས་པད་རྡོའི་གཏེར་བླངས་ནས་བཀའ་འགྱུར་ཚར་གཅིག་རྡོ་ལ་བརྐོས། སྤྱིར་ས་ཕྱོགས་དེར་པད་རྡོ་ཤིན་ཏུ་དཀོན་པས་བཀའ་འགྱུར་རྡོ་ལ་བརྐོ་རྒྱུའི་བཀའ་མོལ་གནང་སྐབས། ཡུལ་མི་རྣམས་ཀྱིས་དེ་འདྲའི་པད་རྡོ་ཞིག་ག་པར་ཐོབ་ཀྱི་རེད་ཅེས་ལབ་གླེང་སྣ་ཚོགས་བྱས་པས། ཁོང་ནས་ས་ཆ་འདི་བྲུས་དང་པད་རྡོ་འདིར་ཡོད་ཅེས་གསུངས་པ་བཞིན། དཔེར་ན་པོ་ཏིའི་ཤོག་ལྷེབ་བཞིན་པད་རྡོ་ལེན་རྒྱུ་བྱུང་ནས། རྡོ་བརྐོ་རྣམས་ཀྱིས་པད་རྡོ་ལེན་པའི་ཤུལ་དུ་བསྡད་ནས་ཉིན་མོར་རྡོ་བརྐོ་བ་དང་། མཚན་མོ་དོང་ཁ་ནུ་ཕྱུ་རའམ་རེ་ལྟེས་བཀབ་ནས་དེ་ནུ་ཉལ། རྡོ་བརྐོ་བརྒྱ་ཙམ་གྱིས་ལོ་གཉིས་ལ་བཀའ་འགྱུར་ཚར་གཅིག་རྫོགས་པར་གྲུབ་པའོ། །སྤྱིར་དམ་པ་འདི་ཉིད་ཐུགས་རྒྱུད་དུལ་ཞིང་སྐུ་བཙུན་པ་སོགས་དམ་པའི་ཡོན་ཏན་མངོན་ཞིང་། རྒྱུན་དུ་བྲག་ཕུག་དེའི་ནང་དུ་མུན་མཚམས་བཞུགས་ཤིང་དགུང་གྲངས་བདུན་ཅུ་ཙམ་བཞེས་སྐབས། གནམ་གཤིས་ཕུ་ཞེས་པའི་ས་ཆ་དེ་ནུ་ཁོང་གི་སློབ་མ་ཞིང་འབྲོག་གཉིས་ཀའི་ཡོན་བདག་རྣམས་ཤོག་ཅེས་གསུངས་ཏེ་སྨྱུང་

གནས་ཆ་བརྒྱད་མཛད། མི་ཤིན་ཏུ་མང་པོ་འདུས་ཤིང་སྙིང་གནས་སྨོན་ལུང་གི་སྐབས་གཟིམ་གུར་གྱི་མཐར་གྱེན་དུ་དཔྱངས་ཤིང་མི་ཐམས་ཅད་ཀྱིས་མཇལ་དུ་ཡོད་པ་མཛད། སྙིང་གནས་ཆ་བརྒྱད་ཀྱི་མཐའ་མར་དག་བཅད་ཀྱི་སྨོན་ལུང་གནང་སྐབས་དབུ་ཅུང་ཟད་གུག་པའི་ཚུལ་མཛད་ནས་ཕྱག་གིས་སྐྱོར་ཞིང་གསུངས་ཚིག་མཐོན་པོའི་ངང་ནས་སྨོན་ལུང་རྫོགས་པར་གྲུབ་རྗེས་སྐུ་ལུས་ཐད་ཀར་བསྲངས་ཤིང་མྱ་ངན་ལས་འདའ་སྐབས་གཞན་གྱིས་གཟིམ་གུར་གྱི་མཐར་ཕབས་པས། དེ་ནས་ཞིབ་པར་མཇལ་མ་སོང་ཞེས་རང་གི་ཕ་མེས་ཀྱི་བརྒྱུད་ནས་གོ་མྱོང་ཞིང་མ་ཚད་ཁོང་ནི་རང་གི་ཕ་མེས་ཀྱི་རྩ་བའི་བླ་མ་ཡང་ཡིན་ནོ་ཅེས་བླ་མས་གསུངས།། སླར་སྨྲས་པ། སྙིང༷་གནས་ཀྱི་ཕན་ཡོན་ཚད་མེད། །སྙིང༷་གནས་ལ་མ་འཛིགས་འགྲོ་རྣམས། །སྙིང༷་གནས་ལས་སྐྱོང་འགྱུར་སྡུག་བསྔལ། །སྙིང༷་གནས་གཅིག་བཞེས་ན་དག་གསུངས། །འདི༷་བགྱིས་ཀྱི་དགེ་བས། །འདི༷་དོན་བཞིན་རྟོགས་ནས། །འདི༷་འདྲ་བའི་ཉམས་ལེན། །འདི༷་ཕྱི་བའི་སྐྱབས་མཆོག། ༼༨༽ འབྲི་གུང་བཀའ་བརྒྱུད་ཨ་ཡང་དགོན་གྱི་གྲྭ་བླ་མ་ཐབས་མཁས་ནི། རྒྱལ་བས་བསྔགས་པའི་དབེན་གནས་སུ། །གུ་ཡངས་བློ་བདེའི་སྒྲུབ་མཛད་པས། །རེ་དོགས་མེད་པའི་གདེངས་ཤིག་རྙེད། །རྣལ་འབྱོར་ཁྱེད་ནི་ཕྱག་གི་ཡུལ། ཁོང་ནི་གཏེར་ཆེན་ཆོས་རྒྱལ་རྡོ་རྗེའི་ཡང་སྤྲུལ་ཡིན་པར་ལུང་བསྟན་ཡོད་ཅིང་། ཁོང་རབ་བྱུང་གི་དུས་སུ་དངོས་དང་ཉམས་སྣང་ལ་རང་གི་ཕ་ཡུལ་གྱི་ཡུལ་ལྷ་སྐྱོ་རྒྱལ་དང་མ་ཞེས་པའི་དབེན་གནས་དེར་ཉམས་ལེན་མཛད་ན་གྲུབ་པ་ཐོབ་པའི་རྟགས་མཚན་ཡོད་པར་བརྟེན། གསང་ཐབས་སུ་དབེན་གནས་དེར་བྱོན་ཏེ་སྒྲུབ་པ་གཙོ་བོ་ནཱ་རོ་ཆོས་དྲུག་གི་ཉམས་ལེན་ལོ་བཅུ་གཉིས་ལ་མཛད་ཀྱང་ཡོན་ཏན་ཆེར་མ་སྐྱེས། དེ་ནས་བཟུང་ཁོང་གི་སྙན་ལམ་དུ་བུད་མེད་སྐད་སྙན་མོ་ཞིག་གིས་སྙིང་རུས་བསྐྱེད་ཅེས་རྟག་པར་གསན་ཞིང་ཐུགས་རུས་ཆེར་བསྐྱེད་ཀྱང་ད་དུང་

དེ་བཞིན་གསན་པས། ཉིན་ཞིག་ཁོང་བྲག་སྟེང་དུ་སྒོམ་གདན་མེད་པར་འཁྲུལ་འཁོར་རྒྱབ་པས་སྐུ་ལུས་ཀུན་ཁྲག་དམར་ཙ་རེ་དོན་ཞིང་ན་ཚ་ཆེར་བྱུང་བས་དེ་ནས་སྐྱུ་ལུས་བསྒོམས་བརྟེན་སྐུ་ལུས་ལ་སྣང་བ་ཙུང་ཟད་ཀྱང་མེད་ཅིང་ཐུགས་ལ་རྟོགས་པ་ཁྱད་པར་ཅན་འཁྲུངས་ནས་གྲུབ་པ་ཐོབ། རྗེས་སུ་དགོས་པའི་དབང་གིས་ལྕམ་བཞེས་པའི་མཚན་ལ་སྒྲོལ་མ་ཞུ་ཞིང་། ཉིན་ཞིག་ལྕམ་གྱིས་འབྲི་བཞོ་བའི་སྐབས་སུ་སེར་བ་དྲག་པོ་བབས་ནས་ཐོག་འཕངས་པས་མོའི་དབུ་ལ་རས་ཞྭ་གྱོན་ཡོད་པའི་ཐོག་ཏུ་འཁེལ་བས་ཁྲོ་ཆུ་དབུ་ཞྭའི་སྟེང་དུ་འཁྱིལ་བ་ལས་གར་ཡང་མ་སྐྱོན་པས་མཚན་ལ་ཐོག་རྟགས་སྒྲོལ་མ་ཞེས་ཐོགས་སོ། །སླར་སྨྲས་པ། རྒྱན་ངན་ལམ་དུ་འཁྱེར་བའི་རྣལ་འབྱོར་ལ། །ནད་གདོན་བགེགས་རྣམས་སེམས་ཀྱི་རློས་གར་ཙམ། །ཕལ་པ་རྣམས་ལ་བདེན་གྲུབ་སྣང་བ་ཡང་། །ཀུན་རྫོབ་ངེས་ཚིག་ཇི་བཞིན་རང་མཚང་རྗེམས།། ༼༡༠༽ འབྲུག་པ་བཀའ་བརྒྱུད་ཀྱི་བླ་མ་འཁོར་རྫུ་སྟོབས་བཙུ་ནི། བསྐལ་མང༷་སྟོན་ནས་བྱང་ཆུབ་བརྙེས་གྱུར་ཀྱང་། །འགྲོ་མང༷་སྲིད་པའི་གནས་ལས་བསྒྲལ་བའི་ཕྱིར། །ཡོ་མང༷་དཀའ་ཐུབ་སྒྲུབ་པ་མཐར་ཕྱིན་མཛད། །རྣམ་མང༷་ལུས་ཀྱིས་མགོན་ཞབས་པསྐོར་འདུད། ཁོང་འབྲུག་དགོན་ཀྱི་གྲྭ་པ་ཡིན་ཞིང་འཁོར་བ་ལ་ངེས་འབྱུང་སྐྱེས་ནས་འབྲི་གུང་བཀའ་བརྒྱུད་ཀྱི་གྲུབ་ཐོབ། སློབ་དཔོན་པདྨའི་རྣམ་སྤྲུལ་ཇོ་སྐར་རྡོ་རྗེ་དྲག་པོ་ལ་བསྟེན་ཅིང་ཁྲིད་དང་གདམས་ངག་མ་ལུས་པར་ཞུས་ཏེ། ཇོ་ཁྱུང་ཞེས་པ་ཤིན་ཏུ་དབེན་ཞིང་བྲག་རི་མཐོན་པོ་ཡོད་པའི་མགུལ་དུ་ལུག་གི་མཆིན་པ་གཅིག་ལ་ལོ་གསུམ་གྱི་བཅུད་ལེན་མཛད་རྗེས་གྲུབ་པ་ཐོབ་ཅིང་ཁོང་ཉིད་མཉམ་མེད་བླ་འོད་གཞོན་ནུའི་ཡང་སྤྲུལ་ཡིན་པར་༸རྒྱལ་དབང་ཀརྨ་པ་མཁའ་ཁྱབ་རྡོ་རྗེས་ལུང་བསྟན་ཡོད། དེའི་ཚུལ་ཡང་ཕ་ཡུལ་ཡུལ་ཤུལ་ནས་ཡིན་པའི་ཡུལ་ཤུལ་ཁྲི་ཐོག་པདྨ་རྡོ་རྗེ་ནས་མི་

བདུན་ཙམ་བསད་རྗེས། ལྷ་ས་རུ་སྦྲིབ་སྦྱོང་ཆེད་གནས་སྐོར་སོང་ནས་༧རྒྱལ་དབང་མཁའ་ཁྱབ་རྡོ་རྗེ་མཇལ་ནས། ཁོ་རང་སྡིག་པོ་ཆེ་ཡིན་ཕྱིར་དེ་ལས་ཐར་བའི་ཐབས་ཞུས་པས། ཀརྨ་པའི་ཞལ་ནས། ཁྱོད་དང་ང་གཉིས་ལས་འབྲས་མེད་ཕྱིར་ང་ཡིས་མི་འདྲོངས་པར་འདུག་པས་ཁྱོད་རང་ཁམས་སུ་སོང་ནས། མཉམ་མེད་ཟླ་འོད་གཞོན་ནུའི་སྤྲུལ་པ་འབྲུག་པ་སྟོབས་བཅུ་དང་། རྒྱལ་བ་བྱམས་པའི་སྤྲུལ་པ་རབ་ཤུལ་གླུང་ཤོད་དགོན་གྱི་གྲྭ་ཡོན་ཏན་ཆོས་འཕེལ་གཉིས་ལ་བརྟེན་ནས་སྦྲིབ་སྦྱོང་གྱིས་གསུངས་པས། མཚམས་ལས་གྲོལ་རྗེས་ཁོང་གི་སྙན་པ་ཤིན་ཏུ་ཆེ་ཞིང་། ཡོན་བདག་མང་པོ་དང་། ཁྱད་པར་ཨ་ནེ་དགོན་པ་གསར་འཛུགས་གནང་ནས་ཨ་ནེ་སུམ་བརྒྱ་ལྷག་ཙམ་ཡོད། ཁོང་འདས་ཁར་ཁོང་གི་ཡང་སྲིད་ཁྲ་དགོན་གྲྭ་བན་ཁྲ་ཀརྨ་དམ་ཆོས་ཀྱི་ཡུམ་ལ་སང་གནང་ཁྱེད་ཚང་ཕེབས་ཀྱི་ཡིན་པས་གནས་ཚང་གཡར་རོགས་ཅེས་གསུངས་ནས་སྐུ་གཤེགས་རྗེས། དེའི་ཕྱི་ལོར་སྔར་གྱི་ཞལ་ཆེམས་བཞིན་སྐུ་འཁྲུངས་ནས་མཚན་ལ་ཀརྨ་དམ་ཆོས་ཅེས་བཏགས། (བན་ཁྲ་ནི་སའི་མིང་ཡིན་ཞིང་རུས་མིང་ལ་ཡང་བེད་སྤྱོད་ཕྱིར་བན་ཁྲ་ཚང་ཞེས་མཚན་ཐོགས་ཤིང་། དེ་ལའང་ཆེ་ཆུང་གཉིས་ཡོད་པ་ལས། ཁོང་བན་ཁྲ་ཆེ་ཚང་ལ་འཁྲུངས། སྐབས་རྗེ་ཁྲ་ལེབ་རིན་པོ་ཆེའི་སྐུ་ཕྲེང་བདུན་པ་ཀརྨ་རང་བྱུང་ཀུན་ཁྱབ་ཉི་མ་བན་ཁྲ་ཆེ་ཚང་ལ་འཁྲུངས་སྒོང་། མཆན།) སྐུ་ན་ཆུང་དུ་ནས་རང་བཞིན་གྱིས་ཐུགས་རྒྱུད་འཇམ་ཞིང་ཐུགས་ལ་སྙིང་རྗེ་ཚད་མེད་མངའ་མཐུས་ཀུན་གྱིས་ཡང་སྲིད་ལ་ཡིད་ཆེས་དང་། བྱང་སེམས་ཡིན་པར་གྲགས། དེའི་རྗེས་སྐྱབས་རྗེ་ཁྲ་འགུ་རིན་པོ་ཆེ་དང་། དྲིན་ཅན་བླ་མ་སོགས་དང་མཉམ་དུ་བཤད་གྲྭར་ལོ་ལྔ་བཞུགས་ནས་ཐོས་བསམ་དང་། དེའི་སྐབས་སུ་ལྷག་པར་དུ་ཕྱག་ཆེན་སོགས་སེམས་ཁྲིད་སྐོར་ཁྲིད་པ་ཙམ་གྱིས་ལམ་སེང་ངོ་འཕྲོད་ཐུབ་པའི་སྒོམ་བྱུང་གི་ཤེས་རབ་མངའ་ཞིང་། རིམ་བཞིན་ཁྲ་དགོན་གྱི་མཁན་པོ་མཛད་ནས་དབྱར་གནས་བཞུགས་བཞིན་པའི་

སྐབས་དུས་ཀྱི་དབང་གིས་དགོན་པ་གཏོར་ནས་བཙོན་དུ་བཟུང་། ཁོང་སོགས་མཁན་སྤྲུལ་མང་ཙམ་ཟི་ལིང་དུ་ཁྲིད་པའི་ལམ་དུ་རླངས་འཁོར་ཐོག་ནས་མཆོང་བས། དམག་མིས་མེ་མདའ་ཚར་གཉིས་རྒྱབ་ནས་བཀྲོངས། །འགྲོ་ལ་བརྩེ་བའི་བཙོས་མིན་སྙིང་རྗེ་དང་། །བླ་མ་མཉེས་པའི་བསླབ་གསུམ་རྣམ་དག་གིས། །ཚོགས་གཉིས་བཙན་ཐབས་རྫོགས་ནས་ཡེ་གནས་ཀྱི། །རང་བྱུང་ཡེ་ཤེས་རྗེན་པར་གཟིགས་མཆོག་རྒྱལ། ༼༡༡༽ དགེ་ལུགས་གླུང་ཤོད་དགོན་གྱི་གྲྭ་ཡོན་ཏན་ཆོས་འཕེལ་ནི། བཀའ་གདམས་སྐྱེས་བུའི་སྙིང་ནོར། །བློ་སྦྱོང་བྱང་ཆུབ་ལམ་བཟང་། །སྟོང་ཉིད་སྙིང་རྗེའི་རྟོགས་པ། །འབྲུལ་མེད་སྐྱེས་ལ་གྲུས་བཏུད། སྐུ་ཆུང་དུ་ནས་རབ་ཏུ་བྱུང་། སྐུ་ཤིན་ཏུ་བཙུན་ཞིང་ཁོང་ལྷ་ས་འབྲས་སྤུངས་དགོན་འདན་མ་ཁང་ཚན་དུ་ཞུགས་ཏེ་རིམ་པར་འབྲས་སྤུངས་ཚོགས་ཆེན་གྱི་ཆོས་ཁྲིམས་མཛད་ཅིང་མཐར་ཕྱིན་རྗེས་རང་ཡུལ་དུ་ཕེབས། དེ་ནས་དབེན་པའི་སྒྲུབ་ཁང་དུ་སྒྲུབ་པ་གཙོ་བོ་བྱང་ཆུབ་ལམ་རིམ་དང་བློ་སྦྱོང་ལ་མཛད་པ་དང་། སྙིང་རྗེ་ཚད་མེད་མངའ་ཞིང་། འགྲོ་བ་ཐམས་ཅད་ལ་བདེ་གཤེགས་སྙིང་པོ་ཡོད་པས་ཐམས་ཅད་སངས་རྒྱས་ཡིན་ཅེས་གསུངས་ནས་མི་སུ་མཐོང་ནའང་ལམ་སེང་བཞེངས་ནས་ཕྱག་གཉིས་ཐལ་མོ་སྦྱར་བ་དང་། མ་ཚད་བྱ་དང་བྱེའུ་སོགས་ལའང་དེ་བཞིན་མཛད། ཡོན་བདག་རྣམས་ཀྱིས་འབུལ་བ་རྣམས་ལས་གཙོ་བོ་བུ་རམ་དང་མར། ༼ཁམས་སྐད་དུ་སྤོ་ནེ་ཞེས་པ་སྟེ། འབྲོག་མོ་རྣམས་ཀྱིས་ལག་མགོ་ལ་ལག་དཀྲིས་ཀྱི་ཚུལ་དུ་བརྒྱན་པ་ཞིག་ལ་གོ མཆན།༽ །ཁོང་གིས་མར་བྲག་ངོ་ལ་བྱུག་ནས་དེའི་སྟེང་དུ་སྤོ་ནེ་རྣམས་ཀྱིས་བརྒྱན། བུ་རམ་རྫོག་པོར་བྱས་པ་རྣམས་ཀྱང་བཀྲམ། བྱི་བ་རྣམས་མར་དང་བུ་རམ་ཟ་ཞིང་སྤོ་ནེ་འཕྱེར་བ་ལ་དགའ་སྟབས། བྱི་བ་རྣམས་ལ་མཆོད་པ་ཕུལ་བ་ཡིན་གསུངས་ནས་གུས་གུས་མཛད། ཡོན་བདག་རྣམས་ཀྱིས་མཇལ་

སྐབས་ཀྱི་ཞུ་དོན་གང་ཡོད་ཐམས་ཅད་ཞུ་མི་དགོས་པར་མ་ནོར་བར་གསུངས་པ་སོགས་མཁྱེན་པ་ཚད་མེད་མངའ་ཞིང་། སྐུ་མྱུ་ངན་ལས་འདའ་སྐབས་ཐུགས་ལྷགས་རིང་བསྲེལ་མང་པོར་འཕྲུངས་པའི་ལོ་རྒྱུས་དང་། ཁོང་ཉིད་རྒྱལ་བ་བྱམས་པའི་རྣམ་འཕྲུལ་ཡིན་པའི་ལུང་བསྟན་༸རྒྱལ་དབང་ཀརྨ་པ་མཁའ་ཁྱབ་རྡོ་རྗེས་ཁྲི་ཐོག་པདྨ་རྡོ་རྗེ་ལ་གསུངས་པ་གོང་གི་འབྲུག་པ་སྟོབས་བཅུའི་རྣམ་ཐར་ལས་གསལ་བ་ལྟར་རོ།། ཀླུ་དངོས་གདུལ་སྐལ་རྫོགས་ཀྱང་། །ཐུགས་ལྷགས་རིང་བསྲེལ་རྣམ་པས། །འབྲེལ་ཚད་མ་རྣམས་རྒྱུད་ལ། །ཐར་པའི་ས་བོན་བཏབ་མཛད།།

༼༡༢༽ ཁྲ་དགོན་གྱི་སྒྲུབ་དཔོན་ཁ་བཏགས་ཨོ་རྒྱན་ཆོས་འཕེལ་ནི། སྲིད༷་པའི་བདེ་འགྱུར་ཕྱུགས་ཀྱང་མ་ཆགས་ཤིང་། །སྲིད༷་ན་བླ་བྲལ་དྲིན་ཅན་བླ་མའི་དྲུང་། །སྲིད༷་པའི་འཁོར་ལོ་གཅོད་པའི་ཐུགས་སྟོབས་ཅན། །སྲིད༷་མཐར་མ་སྟོངས་བར་དུ་གུས་པས་འདུད། ཁོང་གི་ཡབ་ཡུལ་རབ་ཤུལ་བོ་རོག་དང་། ཡབ་ནི་ཡུལ་དེའི་དཔོན་ཡིན་ཞིང་། དགུང་ལོ་ཉེར་གཉིས་སྐབས་སྐུ་མཆེད་དང་མཉམ་དུ་མནའ་མ་ཞིག་བསུས། ཁོང་གི་རིགས་རྒྱུད་ལ་དགུང་ལོ་ཉེར་ལྔ་སྐབས་སྐག་ཆེན་པོ་ཡོད་གཤིས་དེར་སོན་ལ་ཉེ་གྲབ་སྐབས། གཡོག་པོ་ཞིག་དང་མཉམ་དུ་འབྲུག་པ་བླ་མ་སྟོབས་བཅུའི་མདུན་བརྟགས་པ་ཞུ་བ་ལ་ཕེབས་ཤིང་ཞུས་པས། བླ་མའི་ཞལ་ནས་རབ་ཏུ་མ་བྱུང་ན་ཤི་ངེས་ཤིང་མ་ཚད་དམྱལ་བར་འགྲོ། རབ་ཏུ་བྱུང་ན་སྲོག་ལས་ཐར་བར་གསུངས་པས། ཁོང་གིས་དེ་སྐད་ཕ་མ་དང་ཉེ་འབྲེལ་དང་མཐུན་མིན་གྱིས་བསྐྱར་བྱ་བར་འགྲོ་བར་ཞུས་པས། བླ་མས་ད་ལྟ་ཉིད་ནས་གྱོན་གོས་བརྗེས་ལ་རབ་ཏུ་བྱུང་དགོས་པའི་བཀའ་གནང་ནས་ཕྱིང་པ་འདི་གྱོན་གསུངས་བཞིན་དང་དུ་བླང་ནས་སྤྱར་གྱི་རྒྱ་ཆེན་གྱི་གོས་དང་། མདའ་གྱི་བཞོན་པ་སོགས་ཚང་མ་གཡོག་པོ་ལ་ཕྱིར་སློག་སྐབས། གཡོག་པོ་དངངས་སྐྲག་དང་སྐྱོ་ནས་དེ་ལྟར་མི་བྱེད་པར་ཞུས་ཀྱང་མ་གནང་། དེ་ནས་བླ་མའི་ཞལ་ནས། ཁྱེད་རང་གི་སེམས་དེ་ཐོག་མེད་ནས་ད་བར་

རྣམ་གཡེང་དང་འདུ་འཛིས་བསླད་རྐྱེན་དང་བོར་ཞི་གནས་བསྒོམ་དགོས་གསུངས་ནས་ཞལ་ཁྲིད་མཛད་པ་བཞིན་ཟླ་གཅིག་བསྒོམས་རྗེས་ཁྲིམ་ལ་ལན་གཅིག་འགྲོ་བར་ཞུས་ཀྱང་བླ་མའི་བཀའ་མ་འཁྲོལ་བས། དེ་ནས་ཟླ་བཞི་ཞི་གནས་བསྒོམས་ནས་ཤིན་ཏུ་བརྟན་པར་ཡོད་སྐབས་བླ་མས་བརྟགས་པའི་ཕྱིར་སྐུ་ལ་ཁབ་བཙུགས་ཀྱང་མ་ཚོར་བས། ད་གཟོད་བླ་མས་ཞི་གནས་བརྟན་ཞིང་རང་མགོ་ཐོན་པར་ཞལ་གྱིས་བཞེས་ཤིང་། ཡུལ་དེའི་རྒྱབ་རི་དཀར་གདོང་རི་བོ་ཆེའི་སྒྲུབ་ཕུག་ཏུ་སྒོམས་དང་སྒྲུབ་རྟགས་འོང་བར་གསུངས་བཞིན་ལོ་གསུམ་རིང་སྒྲུབ་པ་རྩེ་གཅིག་ཏུ་གཞོལ་བས། ཉིན་ཞིག་བྱ་ཕོ་རོག་ཞིག་དང་བྱ་ཁྲ་གཉིས་མ་འཆམ་པར་འཛིངས་ནས་ཕོ་རོག་གིས་བྱ་ཁྲ་བསད་པར་གཟིགས་པ་ལས་གཞན་རྟགས་ཁྱད་པར་ཅན་གར་ཡང་མ་གཟིགས་ནས་དེ་བཞིན་བླ་མར་ཞུས་པས། བླ་མས་སྔར་གྱི་ཕོ་རོག་དེ་ནི་ཆོས་སྐྱོང་དང་བྱ་ཁྲ་ནི་ཁྱོད་ཀྱི་སྲོག་བདག་ཏུ་མཚོན་པས་ད་ནི་ཁྱོད་རང་བར་ཆད་ཀྱི་བདུད་ལས་རྒྱལ་བར་ཡིན་ནོ་གསུངས། དེ་ནས་ཁོང་གི་བླ་མ་ཞི་བར་གཤེགས་རྗེས་༧འཇམ་མགོན་སྐྱ་ཕྲེང་གཉིས་པ་དཔལ་ལྡན་མཁྱེན་བརྩེར་ལོ་གསུམ་དཔལ་སྤྱུང་དབེན་ཁྲོད་དུ་བརྟེན་པས། ལན་གཅིག་ཁོང་གི་ཉམས་ལ་ཆོས་ཐམས་ཅད་འཁྲུལ་ངོར་བདེན་གྲུབ་ལྟར་སྣང་བ་ལས་དོན་ལ་རྡུལ་གྱི་ཆ་ཤས་ཙམ་ཡང་མ་གྲུབ་པའི་ཐུཏ་ཉམས་ཞིག་ཤར་བས། ཕུག་པའི་ངོས་སུ་ཕྱག་གིས་རེག་སྐབས་ཕྱག་རྗེས་གསལ་པོར་བྱུང་ཞིང་ཐུགས་སྤྲོ་བའི་ངང་ནས་བླ་མར་ཞུས་པས། བླ་མའི་ཞལ་ནས། དེ་ལྟར་དངོས་སུ་འདུག་གམ་ཡང་བསྐྱར་བརྟགས་དང་གསུངས་བཞིན་བརྟགས་པས་ཕུག་པའི་ངོས་སུ་ཅི་ཡང་མི་འདུག་པས། བླ་མས་ཉམས་ལ་རྟོགས་པ་རྫུམ་འཁྲུལ་བར་སྙིང་རུས་བསྐྱེད་ནས་བསྒོམས་ཤིག་ཅེས་བཀའ་གནང་བ་བཞིན་ཉམས་གང་སྐྱེས་ཀྱང་ཞེན་པའི་འཆིང་བ་རྒྱབ་ཏུ་བསྐྱུར་ནས་བསྒོམས་པས་མཐར་བླ་མས་ཁོང་ཉིད་སྤྲོས་བྲལ་གྱི་རྟོགས་པ་ཐོབ་པར་ཞལ་གྱིས་བཞེས་ཤིང་གཟེང་བསྟོད་དང་དབུགས་དབྱུང་མཛད། དེ་རྗེས་ཁྲ་དགོན་

ཀུན་རིག་སྒྲུབ་ཁང་དུ་ལོ་ཤས་དང་། དམིགས་གསལ་དུ་ནཱ་རོའི་ཆོས་དྲུག་སྒྲུབ་ཁང་དུ་སྒྲུབ་དཔོན་ལོ་བཅུ་གཉིས་མཛད་ཅིང་། དེ་རྗེས་དུས་ཀྱི་འགྱུར་བ་ལ་བརྟེན་ནས་རྒྱ་གར་དུ་སྐྱབས་རྗེ་ཁྲ་འགུ་རིན་པོ་ཆེ་དང་དྲིན་ཅན་བླ་མ་སོགས་དཔོན་སློབ་རྣམས་ཆིབས་བསྐྱོད་མཛད་དགོས་བྱུང་ཞིང་། རྒྱ་གར་དུ་འབྱོར་སྐབས་སྒྲུབ་དཔོན་ཤིན་ཏུ་སྐྱུང་ཞིང་སྐུ་སྨད་ཡོངས་རྫོགས་སྐྲང་བས་ན་ཚ་བཟོད་དཀའ་བ་དང་། དྲིན་ཅན་བླ་མ་སོགས་གྲྭ་བཞིས་ཉལ་ཁེབས་སྟེང་དུ་བཞག་ནས་སྨན་ཁང་དུ་གདན་དྲངས་སྐབས། ཁོང་ལམ་སང་ཉལ་ཁེབས་ཀྱི་སྟེང་དུ་ཅོག་པུར་བཞེངས་ནས་སྔོན་སྒྲ་སྒྱུར་མར་པ་ལོ་ཙྪའི་གཟིམས་ལམ་དུ་མཁའ་འགྲོ་བཞིས་མདོ་ལི་ལ་བཏེགས་ནས་ལྷོ་ཕྱོགས་དཔལ་གྱི་རི་ལ་ཕེབས་ཏེ་གྲུབ་ཐོབ་ཆེན་པོ་ས་ར་ཧ་མཇལ་སྐབས་ཁོང་གིས་དོ་ཧ་རྫོ་རྗེའི་མགུར་གསུངས་པ་དེ་ཉིད་སྐད་གསང་མཐོན་པོས་གསུངས་ཤིང་ཐུགས་དགྱེས་པའི་ཉམས་མཛད། སྨན་ཁང་དུ་ཞག་གཉིས་བཞུགས་རྗེས་མཇལ་སྐབས། ཁོང་གི་ཞལ་ནས། མདང་ནུབ་རྨི་ལམ་དུ་སྦྲུལ་དཀར་པོ་ཞིག་གིས་རང་གི་མཐེ་བོང་ལ་སོ་རྒྱབ་ནས་ན་ཚ་ཚང་མ་གཞིབས་ཤིང་ཁྱེད་རང་མཐེ་བོང་ལ་རྨ་རྗེས་ཙུང་ཟད་ལས་གཞན་ལྷག་མེད་སྨྲ་བར་རྨིས་པས་ལྷོད་དང་གསུངས་བཞིན་མཇལ་སྐབས། དེ་བཞིན་མཐེ་བོང་ལ་རྨ་རྗེས་ཙུང་ཟད་ལས་ཡོངས་རྫོགས་དྲག་སྐྱེས་སོང་འདུག་ཕྱིར་དེ་ནས་སྨན་ཁང་ལ་བཞུགས་དགོས་མ་བྱུང་། དེའི་སྐབས་གདན་ས་ཁག་གི་གྲྭ་པ་སོགས་དགེ་འདུན་པ་ཤིན་ཏུ་མང་པོ་ཡོད་ཅིང་། ཁོང་གི་ཞལ་ནས། ཉིན་གྱི་སྐབས་སུ་བསྒོམས་ན་གཞན་གྱིས་མཐོང་ཤིང་ཚུལ་འཆོས་ལས་མ་འདས་གསུངས་ཤིང་ཉིན་མོའི་སྐབས། ཁོང་གྲྭ་པ་རྣམས་ཀྱི་གཟིམ་ཤག་ཏུ་སྐོར་ནས་ཕེབས་ཏེ་གང་ལ་ཞེན་པ་ཆེའི་དངོས་པོ་དེ་བསྡམས་ཤིང་ཉིན་ཁ་ཤས་རིང་ཁོང་གི་གཟིམ་ཆུང་དུ་བཞག་མཛད་ནས་ཕྱིར་གནང་མཛད། དེ་ནི་ཁོང་གིས་ཐབས་མཁས་ཀྱིས་བདག་འཛིན་སྐྱེ་བའི་ཡུལ་འཇོམས་པའི་ཆེད་ཡིན་གསུངས་བཞིན་ཕན་ཐོགས་ཀྱང་རྒྱ་ཆེར་བྱུང་བར་གྲགས།

མཚན་གྱི་སྐབས་དུས་ཚོད་བཅུ་གཉིས་ལ་ཅོག་ཕུར་བཞེངས་ནས་བླ་མར་རྒྱང་འབོད་ཀྱི་གདུང་དབྱངས་ཅུང་ཟད་མཛད་རྗེས་ཏིང་ངེ་འཛིན་ལ་མཉམ་པར་བཞག །སྔ་དྲོར་དུས་ཚོད་བདུན་པར་མཉམ་བཞག་ལས་ལྡངས་ནས་ཐུགས་ཤིན་ཏུ་དགྱེས་པའི་རྣམ་པས་ཆོས་བྲོ་འཁྲབ་པ་དང་། ཁོང་གི་སྨྱོང་བ་དང་བསྟུན་པའི་མགུར་སྟར་ཐོས་མ་སྨྱོང་བ་མང་པོ་རང་བཙོལ་དུ་གསུངས། མཐར་(༡༩༥༩)ལོའི་དགུན་ལོ་དོན་བརྒྱད་སྐབས་སྐུ་མྱ་ངན་ལས་འདས་ཤིང་ཞག་གསུམ་རིང་ཐུགས་དམ་ལ་བཞུགས། གདན་ས་ཁག་ཚང་མས་ཁོང་ལ་ཤིན་ཏུ་དད་ཅིང་སྐུ་མྱ་ངན་ལས་འདས་རྗེས་དབུ་སྐྲ་དང་ན་བཟའ་སོགས་ནན་ཏན་གྱིས་སྲུང་ཞིང་ཤིན་ཏུ་རྩ་ཆེན་མཛད་པ་སོགས་དམ་པའི་སྐྱེས་བུའི་རང་རྟགས་མངོན་སུམ་དུ་སྣང་ངོ༎ །སླར་སྨྲས་པ། རྣམ་དཀར་གྱི་ཤོག་བུའི་ངོས་སུ། །རྣམ་གྲངས་ཀྱི་ཚིག་ཚོགས་ཞུང་དུས། །རྣམ་ཐར་གྱི་ཆེ་བ་བརྗོད་དགེས། །རྣམ་འདྲེན་གྱི་བསྟན་པ་འཕེལ་ཤོག། (༡༣) རི་མའི་རྣལ་འབྱོར་མ་གྲོ་རིལ་ནི། སྙིང་རྗེའི་གཏེར་ཆེན་ལྷག་པའི་ལྷ་མཆོག་ལ། །སྙིང་ནས་དད་གུས་ཡིད་ཆེས་འགྱུར་མེད་དང་། །སྙིང་པོ་ཡིག་དྲུག་བཟླས་ནས་མཐར་ཐུག་གི །སྙིང་པོ་མངོན་གྱུར་རྣལ་འབྱོར་མ་ལ་འདུད། དེ་ཡང་ཡབ་ཡུལ་ཁམས་རི་དམར་ནས་ཡིན་པའི་རྣལ་འབྱོར་མའི་མཚན་ལ་གྲོ་རིལ་ཞུ་དགོས་དོན་ནི། ཁོང་གི་དབུ་སྐྲ་དུང་ལས་དཀར་ཞིང་དུས་རྒྱུན་ཕྱིང་གོས་དཀར་པོ་ཕྱི་ལོགས་ཏུ་མནབས་པས་མཚན་ལ་ཡང་དེ་སྐད་དུ་ཟུར་ཆག་གོ །ཁོང་ནི་རྟག་པར་ལུག་རྫི་ལ་ཕེབས་བརྟེན་ཡི་གེ་ཀ་ཁ་ཡང་ཀློག་མི་ཤེས་མོད། འོན་ཀྱང་དད་པ་དང་ཡིད་ཆེས་བརྟན་པོས་མ་ཎི་ཁ་ནར་འབད་པས། མ་ཎི་དུང་ཕྱུར་གསུམ་ལྷག་བགྲང་; ཁོང་གི་མིང་པོས་མ་ཎི་དུང་ཕྱུར་གཅིག་ཙམ་བགྲང་ཞིང་ཉམས་ལེན་ཡག་པོ་ཡོད། ལུག་རྫིར་ཕེབས་སྐབས་གནམ་གཤིས་གྲང་ན་ལུག་ཡོད་པའི་རི་མགོ་དེར་མ་ཎི་གསུངས་ཏེ་ལུག་གི་མཐར་སྐོར་དུ་དམིགས་ནས་ཞལ་ཕྱུ་མཛད། འཕགས་པ་སྤྱན་རས་གཟིགས་ཀྱི་ཐུགས་རྗེས་ད་ནི་

གང་ཡང་མི་སྐྱོན་གསུངས་ནས་ཉིན་གང་པོར་གཟིམས་དེ་ཐ་ན་གཟིཏ་ཙམ་ཡང་མི་མཛད་ན་ཡང་། ལུག་རྣམས་ནི་བྱིན་རླབས་མཛད་པའི་ས་ཆ་དེ་ལས་མི་འགྲོ་ཤིང་། དགོང་མོར་སྔར་བཞིན་མོ་རང་གི་ཕྱོགས་སུ་དགུག་པའི་དམིགས་པ་མཛད་སྐབས་ལུག་རྣམས་མོ་རང་གི་ཕྱི་བཞིན་དུ་འོང་། གནམ་གཤིས་ཡག་པོ་ཡོད་ན་མ་ཎི་གསུངས་ཞོར་རི་མགོར་ཕེབས་སྐོར་མཛད། དེའི་སྐབས་དྲིན་ཅན་བླ་མ་དགུང་ལོ་བཅུ་ཙམ་ཡིན་ཞིང་། རྟག་པར་མོ་རང་གི་མཉམ་དུ་ལུག་རྫི་ལ་ཕེབས་པ་ཤིན་ཏུ་ཐུགས་དགྱེས་གསུངས། གང་ཞེ་ན་མོ་རང་ནི་བྱམས་སྙིང་རྗེ་འབྱོངས་པའི་བྱང་ཆུབ་སེམས་མ་ཡིན་པའི་མཐུས་སྐྱེ་འགྲོ་ཀུན་དང་ཁོང་ལ་ཡང་བྱམས་པོ་མཛད་པ་དང་། ལུག་ལ་བྱིན་རླབས་མཛད་བརྟེན་སྐྱུང་ཀི་སོགས་གནོད་པ་ཀུན་ལས་བསྲུངས་ཤིང་ལུག་རྫི་ལ་ཕེབས་མི་དགོས་སྐབས་ཐུགས་འཕྲལ་མེད་པ་དང་། ཁོང་ལ་མནབས་གོས་ལྷག་སྐྱོབ་ཙམ་ལས་མེད་ཀྱང་མོ་རང་གི་ཕྱིང་ཁེབས་འོག་ཏུ་གཉིད་དུ་ཉལ་བཅུག་པ་སོགས་ཀྱིས་སོ། །མོ་རང་ཕྲེང་བ་བགྲང་ཆེ་བའི་སྐྱོན་གྱིས་ཕྲེང་ཐག་རྟག་པར་ཆད་འགྲོ་བརྟེན། ཁོང་གིས་ཕྲེང་ཐག་བལ་སྐྱུད་བཟོ་བའི་རིགས་རམ་མཛད་ཀྱི་ཡོད་གསུངས། མི་དང་དུད་འགྲོ་སོགས་མིག་ལོང་བ་རྣམས་ལ་ཞལ་ཕུ་མཛད་པ་ཙམ་གྱིས་དྲག་པ་སོགས་གཞན་ཕན་ཡང་མི་ཉུང་བ་མཛད། ཁྱད་པར་དུ་སྐྱུ་ན་ཤིན་ཏུ་བགྲེས་ཀྱང་མ་ཎི་དུང་ཕྱུར་འདོན་ན་དུང་སོ་སྐྱེས་རྒྱུ་ཡོད་པའི་ལོ་རྒྱུས་ཁུངས་ལྡན་བཞིན་ཞལ་དུ་ཡ་སོ་གསུམ་སྐྱེས་ཤིང་། དེ་ཡང་དུང་བཞིན་ཤིན་ཏུ་དྭངས་ཤིང་དཀར་བས་མཛལ་མ་ཐག་ངོ་མཚར་དང་དད་མོས་སྐྱེ་བའི་གནས་སུ་འགྱུར་ངེས་ཡོད། རྗེས་མར་ཁོང་ཞི་བར་གཤེགས་སྐབས་ཕྱག་གཉིས་ཐལ་མོ་སྦྱར་ཞིང་ཨོག་ཕྱུར་བཞུགས་ཡོད་པའི་ལོ་རྒྱུས་གཞན་ལས་ཐོས་སོ། །དེ་ཡང་དུས་སྙིགས་མའི་ཚེ་ཐུང་གི་སྐབས་འདིར་ཐོས་བསམ་རི་རབ་ཙམ་བྱེད་པ་ལས་བསོད་ནམས་མེ་སྟག་ཙམ་བསགས་པ་དགའ་གསུངས་བཞིན་བསོད་ནམས་བསགས་པ་ལ་ལྷ་གཅིག་འཕགས་པ་སྤྱན་རས་

གཟིགས་བསྒོམ་ཞིང་།   སྔགས་གཅིག་ཡི་གེ་དྲུག་མ་འདི་བཟླས་པ་ལས་བསོད་
ནམས་ཆེ་བར་མ་ཐོས་མོད།   འོན་ཀྱང་རང་འདྲའི་གང་ཟག་ཕལ་ཆེར་གྱིས་བསོད་
ནམས་བསགས་པ་ལ་གཙོ་བོ་མི་བྱ་བར་ལྟ་སྒོམ་སྤྱོད་གསུམ་ཞེས་སྟོང་སྐད་མཐོན་པོ་
ཞིག་བཤད་དེ་སྒོ་གསུམ་ཐ་མལ་དུ་ལུས་པ་ནི་འདི་ཕྱི་གཉིས་ཀར་མཚང་ཆེ་ཞིང་རང་
གཞན་ཀུན་ཕུང་ལ་སྦྱོར་བ་ཙམ་ལས་ཕན་ཡོན་ཁྱད་པར་ཅན་ཞིག་མ་མཐོང་ངོ་།
།སླར་སྨྲས་པ།   འདི་བགྱིས་དགེ་བས་མ་གྱུར་འགྲོ་དྲུག་རྣམས།   །སྔགས་ཀྱི་རྒྱལ་པོ་
ཡིག་དྲུག་ལ་བརྟེན་ནས།   །སྲིད་པའི་ཉེར་རྒྱུ་ཉོན་དྲུག་ཀུན་བྱང་སྟེ།   །དྲུག་པ་རྡོ་རྗེ་
འཆང་གི་སར་གནས་ཤོག།   ༼༡༨༽   ཁྲ་འགུ་བླ་ཆུན་ཆོ་མཚམས་ཀརྨ་བསྟན་
འཛིན་ནི།   གནས་ལུགས་རོ་ཡིས་མྱོས་པའི་སྨྱུག་ལྡན་གྱི་བླ་མས།   །གནས་ཁྲལ་
གདུང་བས་མནར་བའི་མགོན་མེད་ཀྱི་འགྲོ་ལ།   །གནས་མེད་འགྲོ་འོང་དཔེན་པའི་
དམིགས་མེད་ཀྱི་སྙིང་རྗེས།   །གནས་མཐར་བདེ་ལ་འགོད་མཛད་རྟོགས་ལྡན་ལ་
འདུད་དོ།   །ཁོང་གི་ཡབ་ཡུལ་ཁྲ་འགུ་འཕེལ་ནས་ཡིན་ཞིང་།   ནཱ་རོའི་ཆོས་དྲུག
སྒྲུབ་ཁང་དུ་ལོ་གསུམ་བཞུགས་རྗེས་འཕེལ་རྣམ་པར་སྣང་མཛད་སོགས་དཔེན་གནས
གང་སར་རྟག་ཏུ་མཚམས་ལ་བཞུགས་མཛད།   སྐབས་ཤིག་རོང་པོ་དཔོན་ཚང་གི་
ཕྱུགས་རྣམས་ལ་རྫོན་ནད་ཕོག་ནས་མང་ཙམ་ཤི་བས།   ཁོང་གདན་འདྲེན་ནས
ཞབས་ཕྱི་གྲྭ་པ་ཞིག་ཀྱང་མཉམ་དུ་ཕེབས།   དེ་ནས་དཔོན་ཚང་གིས་ནད་ཕོག་པའི་
ནོར་དང་།   མ་ཕོག་པའི་ནོར་གཉིས་ཁ་ཁ་ཕྱེས་རྗེས་བླ་ཆུན་གྱིས་གཟིགས་སྐོར་
མཛད་བཞིན།   ཞལ་ནས་སྙིང་རྗེ་ཡང་ཡང་གསུངས།   དེའི་ནུབ་མོ་ཁོང་གིས་གཙོད་
གསུངས་རྒྱུ་ཞལ་བཞེས་མཛད་པས་དཔོན་པོའི་འཁོར་གཡོག་གཙོས་མི་སུམ་ཅུ་ཙམ་
འདུས།   དེ་ནས་གཙོད་གསུངས་འགོ་ཚུགས་སྐབས།   སྒྲོན་མེ་གཉིས་བཏེགས་ཀྱང་
སྐབས་སྐབས་སུ་ཡི་གེ་མི་གཟིགས་པའི་ཚུལ་མཛད་པ་དང་།   སྐབས་སྐབས་སུ་དཔེ་
ཆ་གློག་མི་ཤེས་པའི་ཟློལ་མཛད་ནས་གློ་བུར་དུ་ཞབས་ཕྱི་ལ་ཅབ་ཛ་ཁྱེར་ཤོག་

གསུངས་པས། ཞབས་ཕྱི་ནི་ཤིན་ཏུ་ངོ་ཚ་ཡང་བཀའ་ལྡོག་མ་ཕོད་ནས་ཆབ་རྫ་ཕུལ་བས་བླ་ཆེན་གྱིས་ཆབ་བསིལ། དེར་འདུས་ཀྱི་དཔོན་འཁོར་ཚང་མ་ཞལ་སྐྱེམས་ཤིང་གད་མོ་ཤོར་གྲབས་བྱུང་ཡང་མ་ཕོད། དོན་ལ་ཁོང་གིས་གཅོད་ཀྱི་སྙིང་དོན་བདག་འཛིན་གཅོད་པ་དང་། བདུད་རྩི་འབེབས་སྦྱོང་མཛད་པ་ཡིན་པར་རྗེས་ནས་གསུངས། དེ་ནས་གཟིམས་སྐབས་ན་བཟའ་ཤམས་ཐབ་སོགས་ཚང་མ་ཕུད་དེ༑ ཞལ་ནས་ཨ་ཚ་ཚ་གསུངས་ཤིང་ཤིག་ཕྲུག་མཛད་པས་ཞབས་ཕྱི་ངོ་ཚ་ནས་ལམ་སེང་གཟིམས་གོས་སྙིང་དུ་བཀབ། ཕྱི་ཉིན་གསུར་འདོན་དགོས་གསུངས་ནས་གསུར་རྫས་བསྡུ་རུབ་གནང་། ཟན་གྱི་ཏྲ་དང་མི་དང་ར་དང་ནོར་སོགས་མང་པོ་བཅས་མཛད་དེ། ཟན་གྱི་མི་ཏྲ་སོགས་ལ་རེ་རེ་བཞིན་དུ་ཏྲ་ཡི་གོང་ཚད་དང་། མི་ཡི་བརྩི་ཐང་སོགས་ཀྱི་བཤད་པ་མང་པོ་མཛད་གནང་། དེ་ནས་གློ་བུར་དུ་དུད་འགྲོ་ཚང་མ་མངགས་ཤོག་གསུངས་པས། མི་རྣམས་ཧང་སང་ཡང་དེ་བཞིན་བྱེད་པ་ལས་བཀའ་དང་འགལ་མ་ཕོད། དེའི་ནུབ་ནམ་གཞུང་དུ་ཁོང་གྲོད་པ་བཤལ་ནས་སྨྱུང་བའི་ཚུལ་བསྟན་པས། གནས་ཚུལ་བཀའ་འདྲི་ཡང་ཡང་ཞུས་རྗེས་ཁོང་གིས་གཏོང་ལེན་གྱི་དམིགས་པ་མཛད་པའི་སྐོར་གསུངས། སྤྱིར་ཧོན་གྱི་ནད་ནི་དུད་འགྲོ་ལས་མི་ལ་ན་རྒྱུ་མེད་ཀྱང་ཁོང་གིས་སེམས་ཅན་གྱི་དོན་དུ་ན་ཚ་བཞེས་གནང་༑ ཕྱི་ཉིན་ཁོང་ཁྲ་དགོན་དུ་ཐེབས་རྗེས་དཔོན་ཚང་གི་ཕྱུགས་ཀྱི་ན་ཚ་ཚང་མ་གློ་བུར་དུ་ཆད་པས་དཔོན་འབངས་ཡོངས་རྫོགས་སློབ་འབངས་སུ་གྱུར། རྗེས་སུ་དྲིན་ཅན་བླ་མ་དགུང་ལོ་སུམ་ཅུ་ཙམ་གྱི་སྐབས་བླ་ཆེན་ངོ་མཚར་བའི་ལྟས་དང་བཅས་སྐུ་གཤེགས། སླར་སྨྲས་པ།

འཁོར༷་བའི་ཚ་བས་གདུང་བའི་སྐྱབས་མེད་ཀྱི་འགྲོ་རྣམས། །འཁོར༷་མེད་དྲིན་ལྡན་ཕ་མ་ཡིན་པ་བཞིན་རྟོགས་ནས། །འཁོར༷་གསུམ་དམིགས་མེད་སྙིང་རྗེའི་ཆུ་རྒྱུན་གྱི་བསིལ་བས༑ །འཁོར༷་འགྲོ་བདེ་ལ་འགོད་པའི་མཛད་རྣམ་བཞིན་འཁྱོང་སྨོན།།

(༡༥) གྲུབ་ཐོབ་ཨར་ཁམས་སེར་འབལ་ཡབ་ཡུམ། སྨྲས༷་དོན་ཆོས་ཉིད་ཟད་

སར་འཁྱོལ་ན་ཡང་། །སྤྲ༷ས་མེད་མངོན་སུམ་གཅོར་འཛིན་འགྲོ་ངོ་ཙྭ། །སྤྲ༷ས་པའི་གྲུབ་ཐོབ་མཛད་རྣམ་སྟོན་མཛད་པའི། །སྤྲ༷ས་པའི་རྣལ་འབྱོར་ཡབ་ཡུམ་རྒྱལ་གྱུར་ཅིག །ཨར་ཁམས་སེར་འབལ་ནི་བཀའ་བརྒྱུད་མཛོ་རྫི་དགོན་གྱི་ཆུ་ལེན་ཡིན་ཞིང། ཁོང་གི་གསང་ཡུམ་ཡང་དགོན་གྱི་མཛོ་རྫི་ཡིན། ཉིན་ཞིག་ཁོང་གཉིས་པོ་ཆུ་ལེན་ས་རུ་བཞུགས་ཤིང་གླིང་མོ་དང་། མི་མགོ་སྔོན་པའི་ཀཱ་པ་ལར་མི་ཡི་ཀླད་པ་བཀང་བ་ཞིག་མདུན་དུ་བཞག་ནས། ཕྱག་མཛུབ་ཀྱིས་བཞེས་བཞིན་བཞུགས་ཡོད་པར་དགོན་པའི་གྲྭ་ཞིག་གིས་མཐོང་བས། ཁོང་ཧ་ལས་ནས་དགོན་པར་ཞུས་པས། དགོན་པས་ཁོང་གཉིས་དང་། སྲས་དང་སྲས་མོ་གཉིས་དང་། ཁོང་གཉིས་ཀྱི་ར་དང་ཁྱི་བཅས་དགོན་ནས་ཕུད་དེ། ལུང་པ་དོག་པོ་ཞིག་གི་ནང་དུ་ཁྲིད་ནས་ཕྱོགས་གཡས་གཡོན་དང་། རྒྱབ་ཏུ་རི་བྲག་དོག་པོ་ཡོད་ཕྱིར་ཐར་ས་དང་བྲོས་ས་ཡང་མེད་ཅིང་། མ་ཚད་ཕྱོགས་གང་དུ་ཡང་འགྲོ་མི་ཆོག་པའི་བཀའ་གནང་། དེའི་ཕྱིར་སྲུང་བའི་ཆེད་དུ་རྟག་པར་མི་རྣམས་ཀྱིས་བལྟ་སྐོར་བྱེད་ཀྱི་ཡོད། རྒྱུན་དུ་མི་རྣམས་ཀྱིས་ལྐོག་ནས་བལྟ་སྐབས་ཁོང་གཉིས་ལྟོད་པོར་བཞུགས་ཡོད་ཅིང་། ཁོང་གཉིས་ཀྱིས་མི་རྣམས་ཚུར་མཐོང་ན་ལམ་སེང་ཕན་ཚུན་འཐབ་མོ་ཁོ་ནར་མཛད༑ ཞག་ཤས་རྗེས་སུ་ཁོང་གཉིས་འཁྲུགས་པ་ཆེན་པོ་མཛད་ནས་ལུང་པ་འུར་གྱིས་ཁེངས། མི་རྣམས་འདུ་ནས་བལྟས་པས། ཁོང་ཡབ་ཡུམ་གཉིས་འཐབ་ཆོག་རྒྱང་པ་མིན་པར་དངོས་སུ་འཁྲུགས་པ་མཛད་ཀྱི་ཡོད་ཅིང་། ཡབ་ནས་སྲས་མོ་འཛུས་ཏེ་ཡུམ་ལ་བརྡབ་མ་ཐག་ཡུམ་ལ་ཐིམ། དེ་ནས་ཡུམ་གྱི་ཞལ་ནས་ཁྱོད་ཀྱིས་ངའི་བུ་མོ་བཀྲོང་སོང་ཞེས་བཤུམས་འབོད་དང་བཅས། བུ་ལ་འཛུས་ནས་ཡབ་ལ་བརྡབ་མ་ཐག་ཡབ་ལ་ཐིམ། ཡབ་ཀྱིས་དེ་བཞིན་ངའི་བུ་ཁྱོད་ཀྱིས་བཀྲོང་སོང་ཞེས་འོ་དོད་དང་བཅས་ཡུམ་ལ་འཐབ་མོའི་ཚུལ་གྱིས་འཐམས་པས། ཡུམ་གྱིས་ཀྱང་ཡབ་ལ་འཐབ་མོའི་ཚུལ་གྱིས་འཐམས་མ་ཐག་ཕན་ཚུན་གཅིག་གིས་གཅིག་ལ་དབྱེར་མེད་དུ་ཐིམ་ནས། རིམ་

བཞིན་རྒྱབ་ཀྱི་བྲག་ངོས་ནས་ཡར་ཕེབས་པའི་ཐྲོལ་དང་བཅས་མཐར་མི་སྣང་བར་གྱུར་ཏོ། །དེ་བཞིན་ར་དང་ཁྲི་རྣམས་ཀྱང་སོ་སོའི་རང་སྐད་འདོན་བཞིན་བྲག་ལ་རིམ་བཞིན་འཛོགས་པའི་ཐྲོལ་བཅས་མཐར་མི་སྣང་བར་གྱུར་པས། དེར་འདུས་ཀྱི་མི་རྣམས་ཧ་ལས་ཧོན་ཐོར་གྱུར༑ ཛེས་མར་བྲག་གི་ངོས་སུ་མི་དང་ར་ལུག་གི་ཞབས་ཛེས་གསལ་པོར་མཇལ་རྒྱུ་འདུག །ལྷག་པར་དམ་པའི་ཡོན་ཏན་མ་མངོན་ནས་ཚུལ་མིན་གང་བྱུང་བྱས་པ་རྣམས་དྲན་ནས་དགོན་སྡེ་ཚང་མ་ད་གཟོད་འགྱོད་པའི་གནས་དང་། དད་པའི་གནས་སུ་བཀོད་དོ། །སླར་སྨྲས་པ། ༼ྃ་གསལ་བའི་རབ་རིབ་ངོ་ཙུ །༼ྃ་དག་པའི་སྐུ་སྐྱེ་སྟོན་ཡང་། །༼ྃ་བཙོས་པའི་གནས་ལུགས་རྟོགས་ཕྱིར། །༼ྃ་ལུས་པ་འཛའ་ལུས་གཤེགས་སྐབས། །༼ྃ་རིག་པའི་སྐྱེ་འགྲོ་ཀུན་གྱིས། །༼ྃ་ཤེས་པའི་རང་མཚང་མངོན་པས། །༼ྃ་བརྟགས་པའི་འོལ་ཚོད་མཛུབ་མོ། །༼ྃ་འོངས་པར་ནམ་ཡང་མ་ཚུགས། །༼ྃ་ལུས་པའི་དགེ་བ་གང་མཆིས། །༼ྃ་རྣན་རྣམས་བདེ་བའི་ཕྱིར་བསྔོ༑ ༼༡༥༽ ཞི་ཆེན་དགོན་གྱི་མཁན་པོ་གང་ཤར། །ཡེ་གནས་ཡེ་ཤེས་གཙང་མའི་བཞིན་རས། །ཀུན་གྱིས་མ་རྟོགས་དྲི་མས་གོས་ལ༑ །ཕྲག་རྫོགས་ཆུ་ཡིས་ཐད་ཀར་བཀྲུས་ནས། །སྐུ་གསུམ་རྒྱན་སྤྲས་མཛད་ལ་འདུད་དོ། མཁན་པོ་གང་ཤར་ཁམས་ཞི་ཆེན་དུ་སྐུ་འཁྲུངས་ཤིང་། ཁོང་གི་རིགས་བརྒྱུད་ནི་ཨ་དྲོ་སྒྲ་རབ་འབྲུམས་པ་ལས་བརྒྱུད་པ་ཡིན་ཞིང་། ཨ་དྲོ་སྒྲ་རིམ་ནི་སི་ཏུ་ཆོས་ཀྱི་འབྱུང་གནས་ཀྱི་སློབ་མ་ཡིན། སི་ཏུ་ཆོས་ཀྱི་ འབྱུང་གནས་ལ་བླ་བྲང་བཀྲ་ཤིས་འཁྱིལ་དགོན་པས་འབེ་ལོ་ཚེ་དབང་ཀུན་ཁྱབ་གཏོང་གནང་བར་ཞུས་པས། དེའི་ཚབ་ཏུ་ཨ་དྲོ་སྒྲ་རིམ་པ་གཏོང་གནང་། དེས་ན་བླ་བྲང་བཀྲ་ཤིས་འཁྱིལ་ལ་སི་ཏུའི་སུམ་རྟགས་འགྲེལ་ཆེན་གྱི་ཁྲིད་རྒྱུན་མ་ཉམས་པར་བཞུགས་ཡོད། ཨ་དྲོ་སྒྲ་རིམ་པ་ནི་སྟུག་ས་འཆང་ལས་རབ་བྱུང་མིན། དེ་ལས་རིམ་བཞིན་བརྒྱུད་དེ། ཞི་ཆེན་རྒྱལ་ཚབ་ཀྱི་སྐུ་ཚ་ནི་ཞི་ཆེན་མཁན་པོ་བློ་གྲོས་རབ་གསལ་དང་། མཁན་པོ་གང་

ཤར་ནི་མཁན་པོ་བློ་གྲོས་རབ་གསལ་གྱི་སྐུ་ཚ་ཡིན། ཁོང་གི་ཡབ་ཡུམ་གཉིས་ལ་སྲས་དང་སྲས་མོ་མང་པོ་ཡོད་ཀྱང་ཐམས་ཅད་གྲོངས་ཤོར། དེར་བརྟེན་ཁོང་འབྲུངས་ནས་ཞག་གཅིག་གི་རྗེས་སུ་ཡབ་ཀྱིས་ཉེ་འབྲེལ་ཞིག་ལ་སྤྲད། རྗེས་མར་ཞལ་གྲགས་ཤེས་ཙམ་ལ་སླེབས་སྐབས། ཡབ་ཀྱིས་ཉེ་འབྲེལ་ལ་སྤྲད་པ་དང་། དེའི་སྐབས་སུ་རི་གང་འདྲའི་བརྒྱུད་པ་དང་། ན་བཟའ་གང་འདྲ་མནབ་པ་སོགས་ཐུགས་ལ་གསལ་པོར་གསུངས་པ་སོགས་རྟགས་མཚན་དང་། ཉིན་ཞིག་ཁ་བ་ཆེན་པོ་བབས་ནས་བྱེའུ་མང་པོས་ཀྲུམ་བུ་འཐུ་ཞིང་ཡོད་པ་ལ། ཁོང་གི་གཟིམས་ཆུང་གི་ཐོག་ནས་རྡོ་ལེབ་ཞིག་འཕངས་པའི་འོག་ཏུ་བྱེའུ་མང་པོ་ཞིག་བསད་པས། མ་ཡུམ་གྱིས་བཀྱོན་པས། ཁོང་ལམ་སེང་ཕེབས་ནས་རྡོ་ཡར་བཀྲུག་མ་ཐག །བྱེའུ་ཚང་མ་འུར་གྱིས་འཕུར་སོང་བ་སོགས་སྐུ་ཆུང་དུ་ནས་མཛད་པ་ངོ་མཚར་ཅན་མང་པོ་བསྟན་གནང་། དེ་ནས་ཞེ་ཆེན་ལ་ཕེབས་ཏེ་མཁན་བློ་གྲོས་རབ་གསལ་མདུན་ནས་འབྲི་ཀློག་སོགས་བསླབས། ཀཿཐོག་བཤད་གྲྭ་རུ་ཕེབས་ཏེ་མཁན་པོ་ནུས་ལྡན་མདུན་ནས་གསན་བསམ་མཐར་ཕྱིན་པར་མཛད། ཁོང་ནི་ཐུགས་རྒྱུད་ཤིན་ཏུ་དུལ་ཞིང་། ཁྱད་པར་དུ་ཀུན་གྱིས་དཔེར་འོས་པའི་འདུལ་ཁྲིམས་ལ་ཤིན་ཏུ་གཅེས་སྲུང་སོགས་དམ་པའི་ཡོན་ཏན་མ་ལུས་པ་མངའ། དྲུང་པ་རིན་པོ་ཆེ་ཡང་ཞེ་ཆེན་ལ་ཕེབས་ནས་ཐོས་བསམ་མཛད་རྗེས་མཁན་པོ་བློ་གྲོས་རབ་གསལ་མདུན་དུ་ཕེབས་ཏེ་ཟུར་མང་དགོན་པ་ལ་བཤད་གྲྭའི་མཁན་པོ་མེད་པ་དང་། མཁན་པོ་གང་ཤར་གཏོང་དགོས་ཚུལ་ནན་ཞུས་ཆེན་པོ་མཛད་པས། མཁན་པོ་བློ་གྲོས་རབ་གསལ་གྱིས་མཁན་པོ་གང་ཤར་གཏོང་རྒྱུ་ཞལ་བཞེས། དྲུང་པ་རིན་པོ་ཆེ་དགུང་ལོ་བཅུ་བཞི་ཙམ་སོན་ཡོད་པ་ལ་བསྟན་པའི་དོན་དུ་ཐུགས་ཁུར་ཆེན་པོ་མཛད་པ་ངོ་མཚར་ཆེ་ཞེས་མཁན་པོ་བློ་གྲོས་རབ་གསལ་བཤུམས། དེ་ནས་མཁན་པོ་གང་ཤར་ཟུར་མང་དགོན་དུ་ཕེབས་ཏེ་ལོ་གཉིས་ཙམ་བཞུགས་རྗེས་ཤིན་ཏུ་སྟོང་ནས་ཞིང་དུ་ཕེབས། ཁོང་ཐུགས་དམ་ལ་

བཞུགས་ཡོད་ཅིང་། དྲུང་པ་རིན་པོ་ཆེ་ནས་སྐུ་གདུང་ཡོད་སའི་ཕྱོགས་ལ་ཡོལ་བས་བཅད་ཡོད་པ་དེ་ཉིད་བཀྲུག་ཙམ་བྱས་ནས་སྐུ་གདུང་ལ་མཇལ་བས། སྐུ་གདུང་དྲང་པོར་ཐུགས་དམ་ལ་བཞུགས་འདུག །ཡོལ་བ་བཀྲུག་པའི་རྐྱེན་གྱིས་རླུང་ནུར་ཙམ་ཞིག་ཞལ་རས་ལ་ཕོག་པས། སྤྱན་ཟུམ་ཟུམ་མཛད་ཅིང་ཐུགས་དམ་ལས་བཞེངས་; ཞལ་ནས་ང་རང་གི་ཚེ་ཡི་འཕེན་པ་ནི་རྫོགས་ཟིན་ཀྱང་། འཛམ་མགོན་ཀོང་སྤྲུལ་ཡོན་ཏན་རྒྱ་མཚོ་དང་། མཁྱེན་བརྩེ་དབང་པོ་གཉིས་མཇལ་ནས་ཁོང་གཉིས་ཀྱི་གདུལ་བྱ་ལྷག་མ་སྐྱོང་བའི་ཆེད་དུ་ཕྲན་ཡར་མངགས་གནང་ཞིང་། མ་ཚད་ཕྲན་ནི་གུ་རུ་རིན་པོ་ཆེས་ལུང་བསྟན་གནང་བའི་གཏེར་བཏོན་བརྒྱ་རྩ་བརྒྱད་ལས་མཐའ་མའི་སྤྲུལ་པ་ཡིན་ཅིང་། སྤྱིར་གཏེར་བཏོན་ཞེས་པའི་དོན་ནི། རི་བྲག་ལས་འདྲ་སྐུ་དང་། དཔེ་ཆ། ཕྱག་མཚན་སོགས་བཏོན་པ་ལ་གོ་ཡང་། རང་ནི་དེ་འདྲ་མིན་པར། ཀུན་གྱི་རྒྱུད་ལ་ཡོད་པའི་བདེ་གཤེགས་སྙིང་པོ་གཏེར་ལྟ་བུར་གནས་པ་དེ་ཉིད། གདམས་ངག་གིས་ཐད་ཀར་ངོ་སྤྲོད་ནས་སྐུ་གསུམ་གྱི་གཏེར་ལེན་དགོས། ད་ལྟ་དུས་ཚོད་འགྱུར་བ་འགྲོགས་པོར་འོང་བས། སྟོན་འགྲོ་ཉམས་ལེན་སོགས་བྱེད་ཁོམ་མེད་གསུངས་ནས་མི་སུ་ཐུག་ལ་ཕྱག་ཆེན་དང་རྫོགས་ཆེན་གྱི་སྒོ་ནས་ངོ་སྤྲོད་ཐད་ཀར་གནང་། དགོས་པའི་དབང་གིས་གསང་ཡུམ་ཡང་བཞེས། སྐབས་ཤིག་ཁོང་གིས་ཚོགས་འཁོར་ཆེན་པོ་ཞིག་གནང་ནས་ཚོགས་རྫས་ལ། རྒྱུད་ནས་གསུངས་པ་བཞིན་དགོས་གསུངས་ནས་ཉིན་ཞག་གསུམ་གྱི་ལམ་ནས་འཁྱེར་འོངས་པའི་བྱིས་པའི་རོ་ཞིག་ཡོད་པ་དེ་དང་། གཞན་ཡང་རྟུག་པ་སོགས་བསྟུ་མཛད། ཚོགས་རྫས་འདི་ཉིད་སུས་མྱོང་བ་དེ་ཉིད་ཚེ་འདིར་རྡོ་རྗེ་འཆང་གི་གོ་འཕང་འཐོབ་པར་གསུངས་པས། ཀུན་གྱིས་བླ་མའི་གསུངས་ལ་ཡིད་ཆེས་དང་། མོས་གུས་ཀྱིས་ཚོགས་ལ་རོལ་བས་དམན་པའི་འདུ་ཤེས་ལྟ་ཅི། དྲི་རོ་ཕུན་སུམ་ཚོགས་པ་དང་། ཚོགས་རྫས་ལ་རོལ་བའི་སྐྱེ་སེར་ཐམས་ཅད་འཇིག་རྟེན་ལ་ཞེན་པ་ཆུང་ཞིང་། སྒོམ་རྒྱུག་རྒྱུ་ཁོ་ནར་དགའ་

བ་དང་། མ་ཚོད་ཡུལ་ལ་ཡང་མི་ནད་ཕྱུགས་ནད་ཞི་བ་དང་། དཔལ་འབྱོར་རྒྱས་པ་སོགས་ངོ་མཚར་གྱི་ལྟས་ཁྱད་འཕགས་བྱུང་། ཁོང་ཕྱོགས་གང་སར་ཕེབས་ནས་སེམས་ཁྲིད་ཁོ་ནར་གནང་། ཁྲ་འགྲུ་ལ་ཕེབས་ནས་ཞག་གཉིས་བཞུགས་ཏེ་གྲྭ་ལྔ་བརྒྱ་ཙམ་ལ་སེམས་ཁྲིད་གནང་། ཁོང་མཇལ་མ་ཐག་ཏུ་དྲིན་ཅན་བླ་མའི་ཐུགས་ལ་ཡང་གྲུབ་ཐོབ་ཆེན་པོ་ཏི་ལོ་དང་ནཱ་རོ་སོགས་མཇལ་བ་ལྟ་བུའི་མོས་གུས་ཀྱི་ཚོར་བ་ཆེན་པོ་བྱུང་གསུངས། ཞལ་ནས་ཀྱང་། ཐམས་ཅད་ཀྱི་རྒྱུད་ལ་བདེ་གཤེགས་སྙིང་པོ་ཡོད་ཅིང་། ཕྱག་ཆེན་དང་རྫོགས་ཆེན་ལ་བརྟེན་ནས་སེམས་ངོ་ཐད་ཀར་བལྟ་དགོས་ཚུལ་དང་། སེམས་ངོ་བལྟ་བ་ཉིད་ཤིན་ཏུ་སྐྱབས་བདེ་ཞིང་། རྗེས་མར་དུས་ཀྱི་འགྱུར་བ་བྱུང་ནས་ངལ་ལས་སོགས་དགོས་པ་བྱུང་ནའང་སེམས་ངོ་བལྟ་བ་དེ་ཉིད་ཉམས་ལེན་གཞན་ལས་སླ་ཞིང་། དུས་ཀྱི་འགྱུར་བ་ཅི་འདྲ་བྱུང་ནའང་འཛིང་པ་སོགས་ཁ་གཏད་བྱ་མི་ཉན་སོགས་ནན་ཏན་གསུངས། ཁོང་གིས་མི་སུ་ཐུག་ལ་སེམས་ཁྲིད་གནང་ཞིང་། དང་པོར་མི་ལ་སྐྱོན་ཅི་ཡོད་ཐད་ཀར་གསུངས་པས། སྐྱོན་ཅི་ཡོད་མཁྱེན་པའི་སྟོབས་ཀྱིས་མི་ཐམས་ཅད་བཅོས་མིན་གྱི་མོས་གུས་སྐྱེ་ཞིང་། དེ་ནས་སེམས་ངོ་སྤྲོད་ཅིང་། མང་ཆེ་བར་ཐད་ཀར་གྲོལ་ཐུབ་པའི་ཐུགས་རྗེ་དང་བྱིན་རླབས་མངའ། ཁྲ་འགྲུ་སྒྲུབ་དཔོན་ལ་སེམས་ཁྲིད་གསུངས་པ། ཁྱེད་རང་ཀ་བ་འདི་ལ་དང་པོ་རྒྱབ་གཏད་པ་དང་། དེ་རྗེས་མདུན་གཏད། དེ་ནས་རྒྱབ་གཏད་གསུངས་པ་བཞིན་བྱས་ནས་གོ་འམ་གསུངས་པས༑ སྒྲུབ་དཔོན་གྱིས་གོ་ལགས་ཞུས། རྗེས་སུ་དྲིན་ཅན་བླ་མས་དེའི་དོན་གང་ཡིན་ཞུས་པས། སྒྲུབ་དཔོན་གྱིས། དེའི་དོན་སླ་པོ་ཡིན། ཀ་བ་ལ་རྒྱབ་གཏད་པའི་དོན་ནི། ཆོས་ཉིད་དང་ཆོས་ཅན་ཟུང་འཇུག་ཡིན་པར་མ་རྟོགས་ན། དེའི་དོན་རྟོགས་པ་ལ་རྒྱབ་ཀྱིས་ཕྱོགས་པ་དང། གཉིས་པར་ཀ་བ་ལ་མདུན་གཏད་པ་ནི། ཆོས་དང་ཆོས་ཉིད་ཟུང་འཇུག་ཡིན་པའི་བརྡ་དང་། གསུམ་པར་ཀ་བ་ལ་རྒྱབ་གཏད་པ་ནི། ཟུང་འཇུག་དེ་ཉིད་ཚུལ་

བཞིན་དུ་རྟོགས་ན་འཁོར་བ་ལ་རྒྱབ་ཀྱིས་ཕྱོགས་པའི་བརྡ་ཡིན་གསུངས། དེ་འདྲའི་ཐབས་མཁས་ཀྱི་ངོ་སྤྲོད་གཞན་ལ་ཡང་མང་པོ་གནང་། ལོ་གཅིག་ལྷག་ཙམ་ལ་དེ་ལྟ་བུའི་སྤྲོད་པ་མཛད་རྗེས། གསང་ཡུམ་ཡང་མར་གཏོང་གནང་ཞིང་། ཁོང་ཞེ་ཆེན་ལ་ཕེབས་ནས་སྔར་བཞིན་སྤྲོད་ལམ་དུལ་ཞིང་འདུལ་ཁྲིམས་ལ་གནས་པ་སོགས་གནང་། དེ་ནས་དུས་ཀྱི་འགྱུར་བ་རྗེས་སུ་ཁོང་དང་། མཁན་པོ་བློ་གྲོས་རབ་གསལ། ཞེ་ཆེན་གོང་སྤྲུལ་སོགས་དང་རྒྱ་མདོའི་བཙོན་ཁང་དུ་བཞུགས་དགོས་བྱུང་ནས་དེ་རུ་ཞིང་ལ་གཤེགས་པ་འདྲའོ། །སྣང་སྲིད་སེམས་སུ་རྟོགས་པའི་རྣལ་འབྱོར་རྣམས། །སྐྱེ་འཆི་སྒྱུ་མའི་གར་ལ་ཅི་དགའ་རོལ། །དེ་ཡང་རྟོགས་ལྡན་བླ་མའི་བྱིན་རླབས་དང་། །རང་གི་བཙོས་མིན་མོས་གུས་མཆོ་ལས་འཁྲུངས།།

༼༡༧༽ བཀའ་བརྒྱུད་ཁྲ་འགུ་དགོན་གྱི་གྲྭ་འབོ་རི་སྒྲུབ་དཔོན་ཀརྨ་དར་རྒྱས༑

སྣང་སྲིད་ཆོས་རྣམས་སྒྱུ་མའི་རོལ་གར། །དམ་པས་རྟོགས་ནས་ཅི་དགར་དབང་བསྒྱུར། །གྲུབ་གྲུབ་བདེན་འཛིན་བཅིངས་པ་བདག་རྣམས། ། ཚེ་འདིར་འཛིན་མེད་རྟོགས་པའི་གྲོགས་མཛོད། འབོ་རི་ཀརྨ་དར་རྒྱས་ནི་རོང་པོ་སྟོད་ལ་འཁྲུངས་ཤིང་། སྐུ་ཆུང་དུ་དུས་ནས་ཁྲ་དགོན་ལ་རབ་ཏུ་བྱུང་ཞིང་། སྒྲུབ་ཁང་དུ་བཞུགས་སྐབས། ཁོང་གི་གཟིམས་ཤག་སྒྲུབ་དཔོན་གྱི་གཟིམས་ཆུང་འགྲམ་དུ་ཡོད་ཅིང་། ཉམས་ལེན་ལ་བརྩོན་འགྲུས་དང་། གཟུངས་སྔགས་བགྲང་སྐབས་སྐད་མཐོན་པོ་དང་སྒྲ་དག་པོ་གསུངས་ཤིང་། སྐབས་སྐབས་སུ་གཟུངས་བགྲང་ཞོར་སྒྲུབ་ཁང་ལ་སྐོར་བ་བྱེད་ནས་ཕེབས་ཀྱི་ཡོད་པར་སྒྲུབ་དཔོན་གྱིས་གསན་པས༑ སྒྲུབ་ཁང་སྒོ་ཆེན་ལ་སྒོ་ལྕགས་རྒྱབ་ཡོད་ན་གང་ཡིན་དགོངས་ནས་ཕྱི་རུ་ཕེབས་ནས་གཟིགས་སྐབས། ཁོང་རང་གི་གཟིམས་ཆུང་ལས་སྔར་བཞིན་སྔགས་བགྲང་ཞིང་བཞུགས་ཡོད། དེ་ལྟར་སྒྲུབ་དཔོན་གྱིས་ཐེངས་མང་པོར་གསན་ཞིང་། ཁོང་ནི་སྒྱུ་ལུས་ཀྱི་ཉམས་ལེན་བརྟན་པ་ཐོབ་པར་དགོངས། རྗེས་མར་སྒྲུབ་ཁང་གྲོལ་རྗེས་ཁོང་གི་གཟིམས་ཤག

ཏུ་བཞུགས་སྐབས། སྐབས་སྐབས་སུ་ཀྱང་གིས་མི་སྒྲིབ་པར་ཕྱི་རུ་ཕེབས་པ་མང་པོས་མཐོང་ངོ། །བླ་མ་གཏྣ་ཆུང་ངུའི་སྐབས་སུ། འཕོ་རི་སྤྲུལ་དཔོན་ཁོང་གི་དགེ་རྒན་མཛད་ཅིང་། སྐབས་སྐབས་སུ་སྤྲུལ་དཔོན་གཟིམས་ཚར་རྗེས་ཡར་བཞེངས་ནས་དགོང་མོའི་ཞལ་ལག་ཟ་དགོས་གསུངས་ནས་ཉིན་རེ་ལ་དགོང་ཟས་ཐེངས་གཉིས་བཞེས། འཕོ་རི་སྤྲུལ་དཔོན་ནི་བླ་མ་གཏྣའི་སྤྲུལ་དཔོན་ཨོ་རྒྱན་གྱི་སྤྲུལ་དཔོན་ཡིན། ཉིན་ཞིག་སྤྲུལ་དཔོན་ཨོ་རྒྱན་གྱིས་སྤྲུལ་ཁང་ནང་ནས་འདུག་པ་ཙུང་ཟད་རྐྱེད་ནས་མི་ལ་རས་པའི་རྐུ་བརྙན་ཞིག་བཟོས་ནས་མདུན་ལྕོག་སྟེང་དུ་བཞག་ནས་ཐུན་གྱི་སྐབས་སུ་གཟིགས་གནང་སྐབས། གློ་བུར་དུ་འཕོ་རི་སྤྲུལ་དཔོན་གྱིས་སྒོ་ཕྱེས་ནས་ནང་དུ་ཕེབས་ནས་འདུག་སྐུ་ས་ཐོག་ཏུ་འཕངས་པས། དགོད་མི་ལའི་སྐུ་ཡིན་པར་གཟིགས་ནས་མགྱོགས་པར་ཡར་བསྣམས་ནས་དབུ་ཐོག་ཏུ་བཞག་རྗེས་ཕྱི་ལོགས་ཏུ་འཕངས། ཕྱི་ཉིན་ཚོགས་པ་འཚོགས་སྐབས། སྤྲུལ་དཔོན་གྱིས། ཁ་སང་ཨོ་རྒྱན་གྱིས་ཐུན་འཁྲོ་བརླག་བྱས་པ་མ་ཚད་ང་ལ་མི་ལ་རས་པ་གྲོངས་བཅུག་སོང་ཞེས་བཀྱོན་མཛད། ཁོང་སྤྲུལ་དཔོན་མཛད་སྐབས། སྤྲུལ་ཁང་གི་སྒྲིག་ལམ་ཡང་མཐོ་དམའ་མང་པོ་མཛད་ཅིང་། ཉིན་ཞིག་ཁོང་ཕྱི་རུ་ཕེབས་དགོས་པས་ཕེབས་སོང་། སྤྲུལ་གྲྭ་རྣམས་གསོ་སྦྱོང་ཚོགས་བཞིན་པའི་སྐབས། སྤྲུལ་གཡོག་གི་སྒོ་འགྲམ་ནས་ཐག་པའི་སྣེ་མོ་འཐེན་འཐེན་མཛད་ཅིང་འདུག །དེ་ནས་སྤྲུལ་དཔོན་ཡང་ཡར་ཕེབས་འདུག་ཅིང་། འབྲི་ཞིག་ཁྲིད་མཛད་དེ་ཞལ་ནས༑ ངས་འབྲི་འདི་སྒྲོག་བསླུ་བྱས་པ་ཡིན་པས་ཁྱེད་རྣམས་རྗེས་སུ་ཡི་རང་ངམ་གསུངས་པས། ཐམས་ཅད་ཀྱིས་རྗེས་སུ་ཡི་རང་ཞུས་པས། དངོས་གནས་རྗེས་སུ་ཡི་རང་ངམ་ཞེས་བསྐྱར་དུ་གསུངས། ཐམས་ཅད་ཀྱིས་དངོས་གནས་དེ་ལྟར་རྗེས་སུ་ཡི་རངས་ཞུས་པས། འོ་ན་ཚང་མས་འབྲིའི་རིན་དུ་འབྲུ་བསྡུ་དགོས་གསུངས། གྲྭ་གཅིག་གིས་ཁྲ་ལེབ་རིན་པོ་ཆེའི་རྣམ་ཐར་ཤིང་སྤར་བཟོ་རྒྱུའི་སྦྱིན་བདག་བྱེད་ཀྱི་ཡོད་

པས་འབྲུ་ཡིས་མི་འདང་ཞུས་པས། འོ་ན་ང་ལ་ཐོད་པ་གཏུགས་གནང་གསུངས་ནས་དབུ་ཐོད་གནང་། ཞལ་ནས། ད་ཁྱེད་རང་གིས་ང་ཐུད་སོང་ཟེར་ནས་ཐོད་པ་གཏུགས་པས་ད་ང་འགྲོ་གི་ཡིན་གསུངས་ནས་ཕེབས་གྲབ་མཛད་པས། ཐམས་ཅད་ཀྱིས་ཞུ་བ་དང་། ལྷག་པར་གྲྭ་དེས་འབྲུ་བསྡུ་བར་ཞུས། ཡང་མཉན་པ་རབ་རྒྱས་ཞེས་པའི་གྲྭ་རྒན་ཞིག་ཡོད་ཅིང་། ཁོང་ཞབས་ཞར་ཟིན་ཀྱང་། ནཱ་རོ་ཆོས་དྲུག་སྒྲུབ་ཁང་ནང་ནས་འཁྲུལ་འཁོར་དྲག་ཤོས་ཡིན། ཉིན་ཞིག་ཁོང་གི་ཞབས་ཞུ་ཀརྨ་བསོད་ནམས་ལ། སང་ཉིན་ང་རང་ཤི་ངེས་རེད། ཁྱེད་ཀྱིས་འཁོ་རི་ཀརྨ་དར་རྒྱས་འདི་རུ་གདན་འདྲོངས་ཤིག་གསུངས་བཞིན་གདན་དྲངས་པས། དུས་ཚོད་གང་འཚམས་ཤིག་ལ་བཀའ་མོལ་གནང་རྗེས་འཁོ་རི་སྒྲུབ་དཔོན་ཕེབས་སོང་། དགེ་རྒན་རབ་རྒྱས་ཀྱི་ཞལ་ནས། འཁོ་རི་སྒྲུབ་དཔོན་ལ་རྟོགས་པ་ཡོད་པར་གྲགས་བཞིན་རང་ལ་ཡང་ཕན་པོ་བྱུང་། དོ་ནུབ་ཀརྨ་བསོད་ནམས་ཁྱེད་ཀྱིས་རང་ལ་དགོང་ཟས་བཟོ་བ་ལས་སང་ཉིན་ང་རང་ཤི་ཚར་བས་ཞོགས་ཇ་བཟོ་མི་དགོས་གསུངས། ཞབས་ཞུ་ནས་ལགས་སོ་ཞུས་ཀྱང་ཡིད་ཆེས་གཏན་པོར་མ་བྱུང་། སང་ཉིན་སྔ་མོར་བྱ་བོས་སྐད་རྒྱག་སྐབས། དགེ་རྒན་གློ་ལུ་མཛད་པ་གོ་བས། ཁོང་འདས་འགྲོ་གསུངས་པ་ལས་དངོས་སུ་ཞིང་གཤེགས་མི་འདུག་བསམ་མ་ཐག །དགེ་རྒན་གྱི་ཞལ་ནས། ཀརྨ་བསོད་ནམས་བྱ་བོས་སྐད་རྒྱག་སོང་ངམ་གསུངས། སྐད་རྒྱག་སོང་ཞུས་པས། འོ་ད་ཡག་པོ་རེད་སོང་གསུངས་ནས་ཅུང་ཟད་འཛམ་ཧྲིང་ངེར་སོང་བས། གང་ཡིན་ནམ་བསམ་ནས་མཛལ་སྐབས། ཁོང་གི་དབུ་ལ་ཞྭ་ཁྲ་དང་། སྐུ་ལ་ཆོས་གོས་མནབས་ནས་ཅོག་པུར་ཐུགས་དམ་ལ་བཞུགས་ནས་གྲོངས་འདུག་གོ། སེམས་ཉིད་གསལ་བའི་མེ་ལོང་ངོས། །ཕྱི་ནང་ཡུལ་གྱི་གཟུགས་རིས་ཤར། །སོ་སྐྱེ་འཁྲུལ་པའི་དྭ་བར་ཆུད། །འཕགས་པས་བདེན་མེད་སྒྱུ་མར་རྟོགས། །གཟུང་འཛིན་འཁྲུལ་པའི་དྭ་བ་འདི། །རྟོགས་པའི་སྦྱུ་གྲིས་ཆོད་པར་ཤོག། ༼༡༨༽

ཁྲ་དགོན་གྱི་གྲྭ་གཙོད་པ་ཤ་རྒོད། གཟུང་བ་ཡུལ་གྱི་འཆིང་བ་ཆོད། །འཛིན་པ་ནང་གི་ཉོན་མོངས་ཆོད། །གཙང་རྨེ་བྲལ་བ་རྟོགས་པའི་གདེངས། །རྣལ་འབྱོར་ཁྲིད་ནི་ཕྱུག་གི་ཡུལ། ཁོང་དགུང་ལོ་ཉི་ཤུ་ཙམ་ལ་སླེབས་སྐབས་ཁོང་གི་ཨ་ཁྱུས་ཁལ་ཞིག་བསད་དུ་བཙུག་པས། ཁལ་དེ་ཡུན་རིང་ཤི་མ་ཐུབ་པར་མིག་ནས་མཆི་མ་ཤོར་བ་སོགས་མཐོང་རྐྱེན་དེ་ནས་བཟུང་འཇིག་རྟེན་གྱི་ལས་རྣམས་སྤངས་ནས་རབ་ཏུ་བྱུང་། ཀུན་རིག་སྒྲུབ་ཁང་དུ་ལོ་གཅིག་དང་ནཱ་རོ་ཆོས་དྲུག་སྒྲུབ་ཁང་དུ་ལོ་གསུམ་བཞུགས། ཁོང་གིས་གཙོད་ག་དུས་གསུངས་ནའང་ཉམས་མཛད། ཕྱོགས་ལས་རྣམ་རྒྱལ་གྱི་སྤྱོད་པ་མཛད་ཆེད། སྐུ་ལ་ཨང་རག་གསོལ་ཞིང་དབུ་སྐྲ་རལ་པ་ཉི་ལེ་བ་དང་། སྐུ་གཅེར་བུ་དང་བཅས་མི་རྐང་འབུད་བཞིན་དགོན་སྐོར་དུ་ཕེབས་སྐབས། དྲིན་ཅན་བླ་མ་དེའི་སྐབས་དགུང་ལོ་བཅུ་གཅིག་ཙམ་ཡིན་ཞིང་ཆུ་ལེན་ལ་ཕེབས་ལམ་ནས་མཇལ་བས་འཇིགས་ནས་རྡོ་ཆེན་པོ་ཞིག་གི་ཕག་ཏུ་གབ། སྐྱེ་དམན་མཚན་ལྡན་ཞིག་གིས་ཆབ་གསང་གནང་བཞིན་པ་ལ། མོས་ཀྱང་གཙོད་པ་མཇལ་མ་ཐག་དངངས་སྐྲག་གིས་ཙ་ཙོ་དང་བཅས་བྲོས་པས། གཙོད་པ་ནས་འཛེམས་བག་མེད་པར་དྲི་ཆེན་ལྷངས་པ་དང་བཅས་ཞལ་ལ་གསོལ་ནས་ཕྱོགས་ལས་རྣམ་རྒྱལ་གྱི་སྤྱོད་པའི་རྟེན་འབྲེལ་ཚུལ་བཞིན་འགྲིག་གོ། བསྐལ་མང་གོམས་པའི་ངེས་འབྱུང་གི་བག་ཆགས། །རྒྱུ་རྐྱེན་ཚུང་དུས་སྐད་ཅིག་ལ་སད་ནས། །རི་དྭགས་མེད་པའི་ལམ་མཆོག་ལ་ཞུགས་ཏེ། །ཞི་བའི་གོ་འཕང་བགྲོད་པ་ལ་ཡི་རངས།།

༼༡༨༽ འཇུ་མི་ཕམ་འཇམ་དབྱངས་རྣམ་རྒྱལ་རྒྱ་མཚོ། སྤྲངས་རྟོགས་ཡོན་ཏན་རིན་ཆེན་རྒྱན་གྱིས་མཛེས། །མཁས་བཙུན་བཟང་པོའི་སྣན་པ་ཐ་གྲུར་ཁྱབ། །གངས་ཅན་མཁས་གྲུབ་ཡོངས་ཀྱི་གཙུག་རྒྱན་མཆོག །འཇམ་པའི་དབྱངས་དངོས་མི་ཕམ་མཆོག་ལ་འདུད། འཇམ་དབྱངས་མཁྱེན་གོང་གཉིས་ཀྱི་དངོས་སློབ་འཇུ་མི་ཕམ་རྣམ་རྒྱལ་རྒྱ་མཚོ་མཆོག་གི་རྣམ་ཐར་རྒྱས་པ་ལོགས་སུ་

གསལ་བ་ལྟར་ལ། ད་ལམ་ལོ་ལྔའི་རིང་ལ་སྨན་ཡུལ་བདེ་མཆོག་ཕོ་བྲང་སྟེ། ཁྲ་འགྱུ་བཀྲ་ཤིས་ཆོས་གླིང་གི་ད་ལྟ་ཀུན་རིག་སྒྲུབ་ཁང་ཡོད་པའི་གནས་སུ་བཞུགས་པའི་སྐོར་མདོར་ཙམ་སྨོས་ན། ཁོང་ཕོག་མར་དེར་ཕེབས་མ་ཐག་གཟིམས་ཆུང་གི་གྱང་ངོས་སུ་འཇམ་དབྱངས་མཚོན་བྱེད་རལ་གྲི་ཞིག་དང་། ལོ་ཙཱ་བ་མཚོན་བྱེད་བྱ་མགོ་གཉིས་ཅན་ཞིག་བྲིས་མཛད་ཅིང་དེ་གཉིས་པོ་རྙིང་མའི་ཁ་རྟགས་ཀྱང་ཡིན། ཁོང་གིས་དབེན་གནས་དེར་ས་དཔེ་ཡག་པོ་དང་། ཉམས་རྟོགས་ཤིན་ཏུ་འཕེལ་བར་འདུག་གསུངས་ཤིང་མཚན་ལ་ཡང་དབེན་བདེ་མཆོག་ཕོ་བྲང་ཞེས་གནང་མཛད། ཁོང་ནི་ཁྲ་དགོན་གྱི་གྲྭ་ཚོ་མཚམས་པ་ཀརྨ་བཀྲ་ཤིས་སོགས་ཀྱིས་མཇལ་སྐྱོང་ཞིང་། སྐུ་གཟུགས་རིང་པོ་དང་། སྐུ་མདོག་དམར་སྨུག་ཅན་ཤིན་ཏུ་རྗིད་པོ་ཞིག་ཡོད། ཁོང་དེར་བཞུགས་རིང་མཁས་འཇུག་དང་དུས་འཁོར་འགྲེལ་བ་སོགས་བརྩམས་མཛད། མ་ཚད་དེའི་སྐབས་སུ་བརྒལ་ལན་དང་རབ་ལན་རྣམས་ཀྱང་བརྩམས་མཛད་དེ། ཉིན་ཞིག་ཨ་མདོ་འདྲ་བའི་མི་ཞིག་གིས་པོ་ཏི་ཁ་ཤས་ཁྱེར་ནས་ཁོང་ལ་ཕུལ་ཏེ། འདིའི་ལན་ཟླ་གཅིག་ཙམ་གྱི་རྗེས་སུ་དགོས་ཞུས་པས། མི་ཕམ་རིན་པོ་ཆེས་པོ་ཏི་རྣམས་དབུ་ཕོག་ཏུ་བཞག་ཙམ་རེ་མཛད་རྗེས་ལོགས་ཤིག་ཏུ་བཞག །དེ་ནས་ཟླ་གཅིག་ཙམ་གྱི་རྗེས་སུ་མི་དེ་སླེབས་ནས་པོ་ཏི་ཚུར་ལ་གནང་དགོས་ཞུས་པས། པོ་ཏི་རྣམས་ནི་འགྱུལ་ཙམ་ཡང་མ་མཛད་པར་སྔར་དང་པོ་བཞག་ས་དེ་རུ་འདུག་ཅིང་ཐལ་བས་ཅུང་ཟད་གོས་འདུག །མི་ཕམ་གྱི་ཞལ་ནས། ད་དེ་རིང་ཙམ་སྒྲུག་རོགས་གནང་ཞེས་པོ་ཏི་རྣམས་ཞལ་ཕྱེས་ནས་བཞད་མོ་ཅུང་ཟད་རེ་མཛད་བཞིན་གང་སར་མཆན་བྲིས་ཅུང་ཟད་རེ་མཛད་ནས་གནང་བས། མགྲོན་པོའི་སེམས་ལ། པོ་ཏི་འདི་རྣམས་ནི་དཔལ་རིས་བློ་བཟང་རབ་གསལ་སོགས་མཁས་པ་མང་པོས། ཟླ་མང་པོའི་རིང་ལ་བགྲོ་གླེང་མཛད་ནས་བརྩམས་པ་ཡིན་པས། མི་ཕམ་ཁོ་རང་གིས་ཞག་གཅིག་ཙམ་གྱི་རིང་ལ་མཆན་བྲིས་མཛད་པ་ལ་ལན་ཞིག་ག་པར་ཐོག་ཡོད་

བསམ་ཤོར་ཡོག ༑དེ་ནས་བླ་བྲང་བཀྲ་ཤིས་དགོན་ལ་འབྱོར་ནས་པོ་ཏི་རྣམས་དཔལ་རིས་བློ་བཟང་རབ་གསལ་ལ་ཕུལ་བས། ཁོང་གིས་ལམ་སེང་དབུ་ལ་བཞག་རྗེས། ཁོང་གི་སློབ་མ་ཡོངས་རྫོགས་ལ་པོ་ཏིས་བྱིན་བརླབ་གནང་ཏེ་ཞལ་ནས། ང་ཚོ་ཚོ་ཕྱི་མར་ཁམས་གསུམ་ཆོས་ཀྱི་རྒྱལ་པོ་མི་ཕམ་རིན་པོ་ཆེའི་ཞལ་སློབ་ཏུ་འགྱུར་བའི་སྨོན་ལམ་འདེབས་དགོས་ཅེས་གསུངས། འདི་གསུངས་སྐབས་དྲིན་ཅན་བླ་མ་མཆོག་ཀུང་སྤྱན་ཆབ་ཁྲ་ཉིལ་ཙམ་བྱུང་། འཇམ་མགོན་མི་ཕམ་དང་ཉེ་གནས་འོད་གསལ་གཉིས་ལ་མཇོ་ཁ་ཤས་ཡོད་ཅིང་། དེའི་རྗེ་བོ་ལ་ཁྲ་དགོན་གྱི་གྲྭ་བན་ཀྲབ་ཧ་ར་ཞེས་པ་དེ་ཡིན་ཞིང་། འཇམ་མགོན་མི་ཕམ་མཆོག་དང་པོར་ཁྲ་དགོན་ཕེབས་སྐབས། ཁྲ་དགོན་གྱིས་དགེ་བསྙེན་གསོལ་ཀ་གསུངས་པར་གཟིགས་པས། ཐུགས་ལ་དགོན་པ་འདིས་ཀུང་དྲིགས་པ་ཞིག་སྒྲུབ་ཀྱི་འདུག་དགོངས། ཉིན་ཞིག་གྲྭ་ཆུང་མང་པོ་ཤུགས་པ་འཐུ་རུ་ཕེབས་སྐབས། རུ་ཤོག་གཟར་ས་ནས་དགེ་བསྙེན་ཕྲུག་གིས་གྲྭ་ཆུང་རེ་རེ་བཞིན་སྐྱོར་བར་གཟིགས་པས། མཛོ་རྫི་ལ། ཁྱོད་ཚོའི་གནས་བདག་གི་མཚན་ལ་གང་ཞུ་རེད་དྲིས་པས། རྡོ་རྗེ་རྒྱལ་མཚན་ཞུ་རེད་ཞུས། འཇམ་མགོན་གྱིས་ཕྲིན་བཅོལ་འདི་བརྩམས་མཛད།

ཧྲཱིཿ གནས་ཀྱི་བདག་པོ་མཐུ་སྟོབས་རྩལ་ལྡན་པ། །དགེ་བསྙེན་ཆེན་པོ་རྡོ་རྗེ་རྒྱལ་མཚན་ཞེས། །ཉེར་བདག་ཚུལ་འཆང་དགྱེས་ཡུམ་ཀླུ་མོར་བཅས། །འདིར་བྱོན་གཙང་སྤྲུར་གཏོར་མ་སྐྱེམས་ཕུད་དང་། །བརྟན་ཆས་འདོད་ཡོན་སྤྲིན་ཕུང་རྒྱ་མཚོས་མཆོད། །ཁྱེད་ཐུགས་དགྱེས་པ་རབ་ཏུ་བསྐང་གྱུར་ཅིག ༑རྟག་ཏུ་བུ་བཞིན་མགོན་སྐྱབས་སྐྱོང་གྲོགས་མཛོད། །དགྲ་དང་ཉེར་འཚེ་ཀུན་ལས་སྲུང་བ་དང་། །ལྷ་གཡག་ཞོལ་དཀར་སྤྲུལ་ཆེན་འཛིགས་རུང་བ། །ཆུ་སྲིན་ཞོན་པའི་ཀླུ་བདུད་དྲག་པོ་སོགས། །སྣ་ཚོགས་རྫུ་འཕྲུལ་འདོད་རྒྱུར་བསྒྱུར་བ་ཡི། །རང་གི་ཕྱོགས་སྲུང་ཕ་རོལ་ཆམ་ལ་འབེབས། །མཐུ་ལྡན་ཁྱེད་ལ་མཆོད་ཅིང་མངོན་བསྟོད་ན། །སྒྲུབ་བརྒྱུད་བསྟན་པ་སྤྱི་

དང་ཆོས་སྡེ་འདི། །དགེ་འདུན་སྡེ་དང་འབྲུ་ནོར་འབྱོར་པར་སྤེལ། །མཐོན་པར་མཐོ་བའི་དོན་ཀུན་འགྲུབ་པར་མཛོད། ཅེས་སོ། ཧྲག་པར་འཇམ་མགོན་གྱིས་མཛོ་ཛྲི་བན་རྒྱབ་ཧྲ་ར་ལ། ཁྱོད་ལ་ཟ་རྒྱུ་གང་ཡོད་རྣམས་སེར་སྣ་མ་བྱེད་པར་ཟོ་ཞིག་ཅེས་གསུངས་པས། མཛོ་ཛྲིའི་སེམས་ལ༑ ང་རང་གིས་ཟ་འཐུང་གང་ལེགས་བྱེད་ཅིང་། སེར་སྣ་གཏན་ནས་བྱེད་ཀྱི་མེད་ན། འདིས་ག་རེ་གསུངས་པ་ཡིན་ནམ་ཞེས་ཡྭ་མང་པོ་ལ་ལབ། རྗེས་སུ་མཛོ་ཛྲི་བགྲེས་སོང་ཀྱུར་སྐབས། ཁྲ་དགོན་ཚོགས་པའི་སྐབས་སུ་དྲངས་པའི་མར་སོགས་ཟ་མ་བྲ་བར་གསོག་འཇོག་ཁོ་ནར་བྱེད་ཅིང་། ཁོ་རང་མདོག་དང་གོས་སྐྱོ་པོ་མནབས་པས། གྲོངས་སྐབས་མར་བསགས་པ་རྣམས་རུལ་ནས་མདོག་སྔོན་པོ་ཀྱུར་འདུག་པས་ད་གཟོད་འཇམ་མགོན་གྱི་ཞལ་ལུང་འཁྲུལ་མེད་ལུང་བསྟན་མཛོན་ནོ། །ཉིན་ཞིག་སྐྱབས་རྗེ་ཁྲ་སྤྲུལ་རིན་པོ་ཆེའི་སྐུ་གོང་མ་མཆོག་ཚེ་མཚམས་ཀརྨ་བཀྲ་ཤིས་ཀྱིས་ཞབས་ཞུ་བྱས་ནས་ཆིབས་པར་ཆིབས་ཏེ་བདེ་མཆོག་ཕོ་བྲང་དུ་འཇུ་མི་ཕམ་རིན་པོ་ཆེ་ཕེབས་ཁར་ཐུག་ཡོད་པར་མཇལ་དུ་ཕེབས་ཤིང་། ཁོང་གིས་མཆོད་འབུལ་མང་ཙམ་དང་། གཞན་ཡང་སྣག་བུམ། བྲིས་སྨྱུག །ཡི་གེ་འབྲི་ས་ཤོག་སྟོང་ཁ་ཁ་ཤས་བཅས་ཕུལ་ནས་ཞུ་དོན། མཁས་གྲུབ་མཆོག་འདིར་ཕེབས་ནས་ལོ་ཤས་བཞུགས་ཀྱང་། རང་ནི་ལོན་རྒྱས་ཤིང་ན་རྒྱུ་མང་བ་དང་། ཡུལ་སྡེ་ཁག་ལ་གྲོང་ཚོག་བྱ་བ་སོགས་ཀྱི་རྐྱེན་ལ་བརྟེན། ཉིད་ཀྱི་མདུན་ནས་སློབ་སྦྱོང་སོགས་གང་ཡང་མ་ཐུབ་པས་ཤིན་ཏུ་འགྱོད་ཅིང་། མ་ཚད་བསྟན་པ་ལ་ཡང་རང་བློ་ཁེངས་པའི་ཞབས་ཞུ་གང་ཡང་མ་ཐུབ་པས་སྐྱེ་བ་རྗེས་མར་བསྟན་ལ་ཞབས་ཞུ་དང་། མ་ཚད་ཉིད་ཀྱི་ཆོས་བརྒྱུད་གཙང་མར་འཛིན་ཐུབ་པ་ཞིག་ཐུགས་རྗེས་འཛིན་པར་ཞུ་ཅེས་ཞུས་ནས་ན་བཟའ་ལ་འཇུས་ཏེ་བཤུམས་པས། འཇམ་མགོན་མི་ཕམ་ཤིན་ཏུ་དགྱེས་ཉམས་བཅས་ཞལ་ནས། ཨོ་ཚོག་གི །ཁྱེད་ཀྱིས་སྣག་བུམ་དང་བྲིས་སྨྱུག །ཤོག་གྲུ་ཕུལ་བ་རྣམས་ནི་རྟེན་འབྲེལ་ཤིན་ཏུ་

ལེགས་པས། ཉི་མ་ནུབ་ལ་ཁད་ལ། ཉི་མ་གནམ་གྱི་དཀྱིལ་དུ་མར་འཕེན་ཐུབ་པའི་ངས་རོགས་རམ་བྱ་ཞེས་གསུངས་ཀྱང་དེའི་སྐབས་སུ་གོ་དོན་ཅི་ཡིན་མ་རྟོགས་མོད། རྗེས་མར་སྐུ་ཕྲེང་འདི་ལ་དཔགས་ན། བཀའ་བརྒྱུད་ཀྱི་བསྟན་པ་ཤིན་ཏུ་ཉམས་དམས་པ་ལ། དམ་པ་འདི་ཉིད་ཀྱིས་བཤད་སྒྲུབ་ལས་གསུམ་གྱི་སྒོ་ནས་སྤྱིར་རྒྱལ་བསྟན་དང་། ལྷག་པར་བཀའ་བརྒྱུད་བསྟན་པ་འཛིན་སྐྱོང་སྤེལ་གསུམ་གྱི་ཕྲིན་ལས་འགྲན་ཟླ་བྲལ་བར་མཛད་པ་ལ། གོང་གི་འཇམ་མགོན་མི་ཕམ་གྱི་ཞལ་གསུང་ངམ་ལུང་བསྟན་ཤིན་ཏུ་གསལ་བར་གདའ། རྗེས་མར་མཁས་དབང་མི་ཕམ་ཞིང་དུ་ཕེབས་ཁར། ཁྲ་འགུ་རིན་པོ་ཆེ་ལ་ཁོང་གི་སྐུ་རུས་དུམ་བུ་ཞིག་ཕུལ་དགོས་པར་ཉེ་གནས་འོད་གསལ་ལ་གདམས་པ་བཞིན་ཕྱག་ཏུ་འབྱོར་ཞིང་། དུམ་བུ་གཅིག་ཁོང་གི་གཟིམས་ཤུང་ནང་དུ་མཆོད་རྟེན་ཞིག་བཞེངས་ནས་དེའི་ནང་དུ་བཙུག །དུམ་བུ་གཅིག་རིན་པོ་ཆེ་མཆོག་གི་མགུལ་གའི་ནང་དུ་ད་ལྟ་ཡང་བཞུགས་ཡོད་དོ། སྣ་ཡུལ་ཡང་དབེན་བདེ་མཆོག་ཕོ་བྲང་དུ། །འཇམ་དཔལ་དབྱངས་དངོས་མི་ཕམ་རིན་པོ་ཆེ། །འཇམ་དཔལ་དགྱེས་པའི་རྡོ་རྗེ་གང་དེ་ཉིད། །གསང་གསུམ་འོད་གསལ་འདྲའ་བའི་བྱིན་རླབས་མཛད།། ༼༢༠༽ ཞེ་ཆེན་དགོན་གྱི་མཁན་པོ་བློ་གྲོས་རབ་གསལ། མཁས་བཙུན་གྲུབ་པའི་གངས་རི་མཐོན་པོའི་རྩེར། །ལུང་རིགས་མན་ངག་སྨྲ་བའི་ང་རོའི་སྒྲས། །ཕས་རྒོལ་ཤ་སྐྱེས་ཞུམ་པའི་སྨག་ལ་གབ། །རིས་མེད་རྒྱལ་བསྟན་སྤེལ་མཛད་གང་དེར་འདུད། དེ་ཡང་ཞེ་ཆེན་མཁན་པོ་བློ་གྲོས་རབ་གསལ་ནི་ཨ་དྲོ་སྒྲ་རིམ་གྱི་རིགས་ལ་ཞེ་ཆེན་དུ་སྐུ་འཁྲུངས། ཁོང་ལ་ལྕམ་སྲིང་ཨ་ནི་ཞིག་ཡོད་པ་དེ་ཉིད་ཞེ་ཆེན་རྒྱལ་ཚབ་དང་སྤྲུལ་སྐུ་གཉིས་ཀྱི་གཉེར་པ་ཡིན། འཇམ་མགོན་ཀོང་སྤྲུལ་བློ་གྲོས་མཐའ་ཡས་དང་འཇུ་མི་ཕམ་འཇམ་དབྱངས་རྣམ་རྒྱལ་རྒྱ་མཚོའི་གཉིས་ཀྱི་དངོས་སློབ་ཞེ་ཆེན་རྒྱལ་ཚབ་འགྱུར་མེད་པདྨ་རྣམ་རྒྱལ་ནི་ཁོང་གི་ཁུ་བོ་དང་བླ་མ་ཡིན། སྐབས་ཤིག་ཁོང་དང་ལྕམ་སྲིང་ཨ་ནི་

གཙོས་གནས་སྐོར་བ་སུམ་ཅུ་ལྷག་ཙམ་ལྷ་ལྡན་དང་བསམ་ཡས་སོགས་ལ་གནས་སྐོར་ཕེབས་སྐབས། ཁོང་དྭགས་ལྷ་སྒམ་པོ་ལ་མ་ཕེབས་ན་འགྲིག་གི་མེད་ཅེས་གསུངས་པས། གནས་སྐོར་བ་ཚང་མ་སྙིང་མ་ཡིན་པས་ཁོང་ཚོ་འགྲོ་གི་མིན་ཟེར་ན་འགྲོར་མ་གཅུབ་པས། ཁོང་དང་ལྕམ་སྲིང་ཨ་ནི་གཉིས་ཕེབས་ནས་གནས་མཇལ་ཞིབ་པར་མཛད་པས། ཁོང་མིང་སྲིང་གཉིས་ཀྱིས་སྒམ་པོ་པའི་སྐུ་འདྲ་མཇལ་སྐབས་སྤྱན་ཧྲིལ་གྱིས་མཁན་པོ་ལ་གཟིགས་སོང་ཞེས་ཨ་ནིས་གསུངས། རྗེས་མར་མཁན་པོ་ཁྲ་འགུ་ལ་བཞུགས་རིང་དྭགས་པོ་རིན་པོ་ཆེའི་ཞལ་ལན་གསུམ་གཟིགས་སོང་གསུངས། ལན་གཅིག་མཁན་སློབ་རྣམས་བཤད་གྲྭ་རུ་མགུར་མཆོ་གསུངས་སྐབས། གློ་བུར་དུ་མཁན་པོའི་སྤྱན་ནམ་མཁར་གཟིགས་ནས་ཕྱག་དཔེ་ཡང་སེ་ལ་འཐོར་སོང་ཞིང་། ཅུང་ཞིག་མཉམ་པར་བཞག་རྗེས་ཧ་ལས་པ་ལྟ་བུ་མཛད་དེ། ང་སྐྱོ་བ་ནང་བཞིན་ག་རེ་བྱུས་སོང་གསུངས། སྒམ་པོ་པས་ཞལ་གཅིག་དེ་དུས་གཟིགས་ཡོད་པ་འདྲ། སྐབས་ཤིག་ལྷ་གཉེར་ཞིག་ཡོད་པ་བཤད་གྲྭ་རུ་འགྲོ་སྐབས་མཁན་པོ་སྤྱན་ནམ་མཁར་གཟིགས་བཞིན་འཚམ་འཁྲབ་བཞིན་འདུག་པ་དང་འཕྲད་པས་ཡར་མར་གར་ཡང་གཟུར་མ་ཐུབ་པས། མཁན་པོས་གཟིགས་མ་ཐག་ཚུར་ཕེབས་ནས་དབུ་ཐོད་ཞིག་གནང་ནས་ཕེབས་སོང་བས་དེ་དུས་སྒམ་པོ་པ་ཞལ་མཇལ་བ་འདྲ་གསུངས། སྐབས་ཤིག་འབྲི་གུང་གཏེར་སྟོན་གྱི་ཞལ་ནས། གྲུབ་མཐའ་གཞན་གྱིས་མི་ཕམ་ཆོས་བརྒྱུད་ལ་ཤིན་ཏུ་སྡང་བས། ཁྲ་འགུ་བཤད་གྲྭས་མཁན་པོའི་མདུན་ནས་མི་ཕམ་བཀའ་འབུམ་ལ་ཐོས་བསམ་བྱེད་ཀྱི་ཡོད་སྐབས། མཐུའི་བྱད་ཁ་ཆེན་པོ་འདུག་གསུངས་བཞིན་གཏེར་སྟོན་གདན་དྲངས་པས། གཏེར་སྟོན་ཐུགས་ཀ་ལ་མེ་ལོང་ཞིག་བཏགས་གནང་འདུག །དེ་ནས་བཀའ་བསྒོ་ཞུས་པས། ཁོང་གིས་རུམ་ནས་དཔེ་ཆ་ཞིག་བླངས་ནས་བཀའ་བསྒོ་གསུངས་པར་བརྩམས་ཀྱང་། ཡི་གེ་ཡག་པོ་ཀློག་མི་ཤེས་པའི་ཚུལ་དང་། གསུང་སྐད་འཛེར་བ་སོགས་མཐོང་ན་བཀའ་བསྒོ་

གསུང་མ་ཤེས་པས། མཁན་པོ་བློ་གྲོས་རབ་གསལ་གྱི་ཐུགས་ལ་གཏེར་སྟོན་རྫུན་པའམ་རྫོག་གེ་བ་ཅིག་འདུག་དགོངས་མ་ཐག །གཏེར་སྟོན་གྱི་ཡི་གེ་རུམ་དུ་བཅུག་ནས་མེ་ལོང་ལ་ཕྱག་གིས་ཡར་འཕྱུར་མ་འཕྱུར་མཛད་ནས། མཁན་པོ་དང་གཏེར་སྟོན་རྣམ་གཉིས་སྐྱེ་བ་མང་པོར་བླ་མ་དང་སློབ་མ་ཡིན་ཚུལ་ངོ་མཚར་བ་མང་པོ་ཐོགས་མེད་དུ་གསུངས་ཀྱང་། དེའི་སྐབས་སུ་སྦྲ་ཐག་འཁོར་ལོ་དང་ཡི་གེ་འབྲི་ས་མེད་རྐྱེན་ཡིག་ཐོག་ཏུ་འགོད་མ་ཐུབ་མོད། དེའི་ནང་ནས་དྲིན་ཅན་བླ་མས་ཐུགས་དྲན་གསོས་པ་གཅིག་ལ། གཏེར་སྟོན་གྱིས་མཁན་པོ་བློ་གྲོས་རབ་གསལ་མཆོག་དྭགས་པོ་བཀྲ་ཤིས་རྣམ་རྒྱལ་གྱི་སྐུ་སྐྱེ་ཡིན་པར་གསུངས་པ་དེ་ནི་གསལ་པོ་འདུག་གསུངས། དུས་རྒྱུན་མཁན་པོའི་ཞལ་ནས་ཀྱང་། ང་རང་སྐྱེ་བ་སྔོན་མར་བཀའ་བརྒྱུད་ཀྱི་བླ་གྲན་ཞིག་གི་སྐྱེ་བ་ཡིན་པར་ཐག་ཆོད་གསུངས། འབྲི་གུང་གཏེར་སྟོན་ཁྲ་དགོན་ལ་ཤིན་ཏུ་འདྲིས་ཆེ་ཞིང་། ལྷག་པར་དུ་ཁྲ་ལེབ་རིན་པོ་ཆེ་དང་ཐུགས་ཡིད་གཅིག་འདྲིས་ལྷ་བུར་ཡོད། ཁོང་གིས་ཁྲ་འགྲུ་དགོན་པ་མ་འོངས་པར་ཤིན་ཏུ་དར་ནས། དགྲ་བཀྱལ་ཆུ་མགོ་ནས་ཚུར་ལ་གཟིགས་སྐབས་ལྷ་ཁང་གི་གསེར་ཐོག་མཛལ་སོང་གསུངས་བཞིན། རྗེས་མར་དྲིན་ཅན་བླ་མ་དགྲ་བཀྱལ་ཆུ་མགོར་ཕེབས་ནས་མཛལ་སྐབས། ད་ལྟ་ཁྲ་དགོན་གྱི་གསེར་ཏོག་མཛལ་གྱི་འདུག་གསུངས། ཁྲ་ལེབ་རིན་པོ་ཆེ་ཞིང་དུ་གཤེགས་སྐབས། འཇམ་མགོན་དཔལ་ལྡན་མཁྱེན་བརྩེ་གདན་དྲངས་ནས་ཟླ་གཅིག་རིང་དགོངས་རྫོགས་མཛད། འཇམ་མགོན་ཞལ་ནས། ཁྲ་ལེབ་རིན་པོ་ཆེ་ད་ལྟ་གུ་རུ་རིན་པོ་ཆེ་དང་མཉམ་དུ་ཟངས་མདོག་དཔལ་རིར་སྐུག་ཀྱི་ལེར་བཞུགས་འདུག་ཅིང་། ང་རང་འདི་ན་སྐྱ་རིལ་ལེ་ལུས་པ་ལ་གསོན་ཡང་དགའ་རྒྱུ་མི་འདུག །ང་རང་ཡང་དེ་རུ་འགྲོ་གི་ཡིན་གསུངས་ནས་ཟླ་གཅིག་གི་དགོངས་རྫོགས་གྲུབ་མཚམས། ཡང་དབེན་བདེ་མཆོག་ཕོ་བྲང་ཏུ་ཞིང་ལ་གཤེགས། གདུང་བཞུ་སྐབས་ནམ་མཁའ་གཡའ་དག་པ་ལ། དུ་བ་ནམ་མཁའ་འཕྱུར་བ་རྣམས་

རིམ་བཞིན་འཇའ་འོད་ཀྱི་གུར་ཕུབ་པ་ལྷ་བུར་གྱུར་པ་དྲིན་ཅན་བླ་མ་སོགས་སྐྱ་སེར་ཡོངས་ཀྱིས་མཇལ། གདུང་བཞུ་སའི་སྒོར་ལ་རིང་བསྲེལ་མང་པོ་འཁྲུངས། སྐུ་གདུང་མཆོད་རྟེན་བཞེངས། བཤད་གྲྭ་མཁན་སློབ་རྣམས་ཀྱིས་མགུར་མཆོ་གསུངས་སྐབས། གློ་བུར་དུ་མཁན་པོ་བློ་གྲོས་རབ་གསལ་གྱིས་ཐལ་མོ་སྙིང་གར་སྦྱར་ཞིང་ཞལ་ནས། ཨ་ཕྱུག་ཚོ། རྫོགས་པའི་སངས་རྒྱས་དངོས་སུ་བྱོན་བྱུང་བས་སློན་ལམ་ཅི་བཏབ་འགྲུབ་པར་ངེས་པས་སློན་ལམ་ཐོབ་ཅིག་གསུངས། དེ་རྗེས་བཀའ་འདྲི་ནར་མར་ཞུ་སྐབས། འཇམ་མགོན་དཔལ་ལྡན་མཁྱེན་བརྩེ་དངོས་སུ་ཕེབས་བྱུང་གསུངས། རྗེས་མར་དུས་ཀྱི་འགྱུར་བ་བྱུང་རྗེས། ཞི་ཆེན་གོང་སྤྲུལ། མཁན་པོ་གང་ཤར། ཞི་ཆེན་བློ་གྲོས་རབ་གསལ་བཅས་དམག་མིས་བཟུང་སོང་བས། རྗེས་མར་དར་རྩེ་མདོ་ནས་གྲྭ་ཞིག་གིས་མཇལ། ཞི་ཆེན་བློ་གྲོས་རབ་གསལ་ཁོང་འདས་ཁར་ཁྲ་འགྱུ་དགོན་ལ་ཡར་བསྐྱལ་རོགས་ཞེས་ཞུས་ཀྱང་རོགས་པ་མ་ཐུབ། ཕལ་ཆེར་དར་རྩེ་མདོའི་བཙོན་ཁང་དུ་གྲོངས་པ་འདྲ་གསུངས། ཞི་ཆེན་གོང་སྤྲུལ་གྱི་ཞལ་ནས། སྔོན་མར་མཁན་པོ་བློ་གྲོས་རབ་གསལ་འདི་ཉིད་རིགས་པ་ཤིན་ཏུ་ཟོ་ཞིང་། རྟོག་གེ་རིག་གཞུང་ལ་མཁས་པ་ཙམ་ལས་རྟོགས་པ་གང་ཡང་མེད་ཀྱང་། སྣ་སྟོད་བཀྲ་ཤིས་ཆོས་གླིང་ནས་ཚུར་ཕེབས་རྗེས་མཁས་པ་ཙམ་མ་ཟད་རྟོགས་པའི་དབང་ཕྱུག་ཆེན་པོར་གྱུར་འདུག་པས། སྣ་སྟོད་བཀྲ་ཤིས་ཆོས་གླིང་འདི་གཞན་དང་མི་འདྲ་བའི་གནས་བྱིན་རླབས་ཅན་རེད་འདུག་གསུངས། སངས་རྒྱས་ཕྲིན་ལས་ཀརྨ་པ་ཞེས་གྲགས་པས། གསང་གསུམ་བྱིན་གྱིས་བརླབས་པའི་སྣ་ཡུལ་གནས་མཆོག །སྣ་སྟོད་བཀྲ་ཤིས་ཆོས་གླིང་ཡང་དབེན་དགོན་པ། །གནས་འདིར་མཇལ་བ་ཙམ་གྱིས་ཐར་པའི་ལམ་འདྲེན།། ༼༢༡༽ ཁྲ་འགྱུ་དགོན་གྱི་གྲྭ་མགོན་བླ་དགོངས་ཕན། རྒྱལ་བའི་ཕྲིན་ལས་རྣམ་རོལ་ཆོས་སྐྱོང་པེར། །མཆོད་བསྟོད་དང་པས་སྒྲུབ་ལ་དངོས་གྲུབ་སྟེར། །ཕྱིར་སྣང་གཟུགས་སྐུ་གྲྭ་སྤྲང་གར་བསྒྱུར་ཡང་།

།ནང་གི་ཡེ་ཤེས་ཆོས་སྐྱོང་དངོས་སྣང་འདུད། ཁོང་ནི་གྲྭ་སྒྲུང་རྒྱུ་རྫས་ཅི་ཡང་མེད་པ་རྟག་པར་མགོན་ཁང་དུ་བཞུགས་པ་དང་། འབྲུག་གློག་ཐོག་སེར་བྱུང་ན་རག་མ་བུ་འཁྱུར་སྟོད་སྟོད་གསུངས་ཤིང་། ཁོང་གི་འོག་ལ་མནན་ཡོད་གསུངས་ལྟར་ཁོང་བཞུགས་རིང་ཞིང་སེར་བས་བཏུང་མ་མྱོང་། མཚན་མོ་ཆབ་གསང་ཕེབས་སྐབས། ཞུར་ཐག་ཚག་སྒྲ་དང་བཅས་འཕེན་མཛད་ནས་དམྱལ་བའི་ཟངས་ལ་ཞུར་རྡོ་འཕེན་ཞིང་ཡོད་གསུངས་པས། མི་རྣམས་ཡིད་ཆེས་མེད་པར་བླ་རྒན་གྱིས་སྨྱུག་པ་ལ་ཞུར་འཚག་མཛད་ཀྱི་འདུག་ཅེས་འཕྱ་སྨོད་བྱེད། སྐུ་འདའ་ཁར་ཞལ་ནས། འདི་ཟླའི་ཚེས་བཅོ་ལྔ་ལ་ང་རང་ཤི་གི་རེད། གྲྭ་དགོན་འདི་རང་ལ་བཀའ་དྲིན་ཆེ་བས་རང་ལ་འབུལ་དངོས་གང་ཡང་མ་མཆིས་ཀྱང་། ཐོད་པ་འདི་བཞག་གི་ཡིན་པས་ངའི་རོ་བསྲེགས་དགོས། ཐོད་པ་ལ་ཡག་མཆོད་རྟེན་ནང་དུ་བཞག་ན་ཕན་ཐོགས་ཆེ། འོན་ཀྱང་རང་ལ་བསྲེགས་བྱེད་ཤིང་སོགས་དངོས་པོ་གང་ཡང་མེད་པས་གནས་ཚང་བྱ་འདབས་སྡེ་ཁག་གིས་རོགས་རམ་དགོས་ཞེས་གསུངས་བཞིན་ཞིང་དུ་གཤེགས། དབུ་ཐོད་མ་འཚིག་པར་བཞུགས་པས་ཁོང་གི་ཞལ་ཆེམས་བཞིན་ལ་ཡག་མཆོད་རྟེན་ནང་དུ་བཞུགས་སུ་བཙུག་གོ། མ༷་རྒན་འགྲོ་རྣམས་ཆེད་དུ། །མ༷་མགོན་ཆོས་སྐྱོང་འགྲུབ་པས། །མ༷་དག་དམྱལ་ཁམས་སེམས་ཅན། །མ༷་ལུས་ཐར་ལམ་འདྲེན་མཛད།། ༼༢༢༽ ས་སྐྱ་སླང་ཆེན་དགོན་གྱི་གྲྭ་ཤེས་རབ་རྒྱལ་མཚན། ཤེས༷་རབ༷་མཐར་ཕྱུག་གཉུག་མའི་གནས་ལུགས་རྟོགས། །ཤེས༷་རབ༷་ཆེན་པོས་ས་ལམ་ཚེ་གཅིག་བགྲོད། །ཐར་པའི་རྒྱལ༷་མཚན༷་འཛིན་མའི་ཁྲོན་ན་བགྲེངས། །སྙན་པའི་རྒྱལ༷་མཚན༷་སྲིད་རྩེར་ཁྱབ་ལ་འདུད། ཁོང་དང་པོར་ས་སྐྱ་སྐྱེ་རྒྱུ་དགོན་གྱི་གྲྭ་ཡིན་ཞིང་། དགོན་པའི་གཉེར་པ་མཛད་པས་བྱ་བ་ལམ་ལ་མ་སོང་ནས་དགོན་པས་མཐར་བུད་བཏང་། དེ་ནས་ས་སྐྱ་དར་རྗེ་དགོན་པར་ཕེབས་ནས་སླར་ཡང་གཉེར་པ་མཛད་པས། སྔོན་བཞིན་གཉེར་པའི་ལས་ཀ་མ་འཛིན་པས་མཐར་བུད་བཏང་།

དེ་ནས་ས་སྐྱ་གླང་ཆེན་དགོན་པར་ཕེབས་ནས་དེ་རུ་བཞུགས། སྲིད་གཞུང་ལ་ངོ་
འགྲོས་ཆེ་བའི་རྒན་མོ་ཞིག་ཡོད་པས། དེས་ཁོང་ལ་ཕྱུག་རིགས་ཞུས་པས་དུས་ཀྱི་
འགྱུར་བ་བྱུང་སྐབས་ཚད་པ་མ་ཐོག །སྐུ་འདས་ཁར་ཞལ་ཆེམས་ལ། གླང་ཆེན་
དགོན་པ་འདི་རང་ལ་ཤིན་ཏུ་སྐུ་དྲིན་ཆེ་བས། རང་གི་རོ་བསྲེགས་ལ་ཐོད་པ་འདི་
ཉིད་དགོན་པར་རྟེན་བཞག་དགོས་གསུངས་ནས་རྒན་མོར་གདམས། ཞིང་དུ་
གཤེགས་སྐབས་ཆོས་གོས་མནབས་ཡོད་པས། དེ་ནས་རྒན་མོས་མེ་ཤིང་བསྡུས་ནས་
ཁོང་གི་ཞལ་ཆེམས་བཞིན་གདུང་བཞུས་པས། ཆོས་གོས་མེ་ཡིས་གཏན་ནས་མ་
འཚིག །ཆོས་གོས་མར་བཤུས་ནས་རྡོ་ཐོག་ལ་བཞག་སྟེ་གདུང་བཞུས་པས།
དབུ་ཐོད་མ་འཚིག་པར་བཞུགས། གདུང་བཞུས་ཚར་རྗེས་ཆོས་གོས་ཀྱང་མི་སྣང་
བར་གྱུར། རིང་བསྲེལ་དཔག་ཏུ་མེད་པ་འཁྲུངས་པས། དད་མཇལ་རྣམས་ལ་
འདོད་པ་བཞིན་གནང་། རྗེས་མར་རིང་བསྲེལ་སྟེར་མང་ཆེ་གི་འདུག་ཅེས་བགྲོས་
ནས། རིང་བསྲེལ་ལ་དངུལ་ཙུང་ཟད་བླངས་ནས་བཟུང་སྟེ་དེ་ཙམ་མི་འཕེལ་བར་
གྱུར། ཁ་ཤས་ཀྱིས་རིང་བསྲེལ་ཤོག་གུའི་ནང་དུ་བསྒྲིལ་སྐབས་མི་སྣང་བར་གྱུར་
པ་སོགས་ཀྱང་བྱུང་བར་གྲགས་སོ།། དག་པའི་ས་ལམ་གསང་བས་བགྲོད།
།དག་པ་ཡེ་གནས་མངོན་དུ་གྱུར། །དག་པའི་གདུང་དང་རིང་བསྲེལ་འཁྲུངས།
།དག་པ་དམ་པའི་དགེ་བ་བསྔོ།། ༼༢༣༽ རྡོ་རྗེ་ཕག་མོའི་རྣམ་སྤྲུལ་འགར་མོ།
མཆོག་ཏུ་མི་འགྱུར་བདེ་བ་ཆེན་པོ་ཉིད། །འགྲོ་བའི་དོན་དུ་གཟུགས་སྐུ་ཅིར་ཡང་སྟོན།
།དག་དང་མ་དག་འགྲོ་རྣམས་འདུལ་བར་མཛད། །རྒྱལ་བའི་ཡུམ་གྱུར་དེ་ལ་གུས་པས་
བསྟོད། གཙང་ས་སྐྱའི་ཡུལ་དུ་འགར་བ་བཟའ་མི་གཉིས་ཡོད་ཅིང་། འགར་བའི་
རིགས་དམའ་ཤོས་ཡིན་པས་གཞན་གྱིས་བརྙས་བཀུར་ཆུང་། ཁྱད་པར་དུ་འགར་མོ་ལ་
མི་སུ་ཡང་མི་དགའ། ལུང་པའི་ཕུ་དེ་ན་རྣལ་འབྱོར་པ་དཔོན་སློབ་གཉིས་མཚམས་ལ་
བཞུགས་ཡོད་ཅིང་། བླ་མས་ཚོགས་འཁོར་བསྐོར་སྐབས་སློབ་མས་རྟག་པར་བྱུང་མེད་

ཀྱི་སྐད་སྙན་པོ་རྒྱག་པར་ཐོས་ཀྱང་དངོས་སུ་མ་མཐོང་བས། བླ་མ་ལ་དངོས་སུ་མཐོང་འདོད་ཡོད་པར་ཞུས་པས། བླ་མས་དེ་ནི་མཁའ་འགྲོ་མ་ཡིན་པས། དངོས་སུ་མཇལ་བ་ལ་རྟོགས་པ་ཅུང་ཟད་དགོས་གསུངས། སློབ་མས་ནན་ཏན་གྱིས་མཇལ་འདོད་ཡོད་ཚུལ་བསྐྱར་ནས་ཞུས་པས། བླ་མས་འོ་ན་དེ་རིང་གྲོང་དུ་སོང་ལ། ལམ་དུ་སུ་ཐུག་ན་ཡང་ཐེ་ཚོམ་མི་བྱ་བར་ཕྱག་ཕུལ་དང་དངོས་གྲུབ་ཕྲན་བུ་འཐོབ་འོང་གསུངས་པ་བཞིན་སོང་བས། ལམ་དུ་མགར་མོ་སྨྱོད་གོས་མར་ཕུད་ནས་ནུ་མ་གཉིས་ལྷུག་གེར་བྱས་ཤིང་། ལག་ཏུ་ལ་ཕུག་ཁ་ཤས་ཁྱེར་ནས་འོངས་པ་དང་ཐུག་པས། ལམ་སེང་ཕྱག་ཕུལ་བས། མོས་མི་དགའ་བའི་རྣམ་འགྱུར་དང་བཅས། སེར་སྣམ་ཁྱོད་ཀྱིས་ང་ལ་ཕྱག་ཕུལ་ནས་གང་བྱེད་ཅེས་སྐད་ཅོར་རྒྱག་བཞིན་ལ་ཕུག་དུམ་བུ་ཞིག་ནུ་མ་གཉིས་ཀྱི་མགོ་ལ་ཕུར་ཕུར་བྱས་ཏེ་དེ་ཁྱེར་ཅིག་གསུངས་ནས་འཕངས་བྱུང་། སློབ་མ་ཡར་བླ་མའི་མདུན་དུ་ལོག་ནས་དེ་བཞིན་ཞུས་པས། དངོས་གྲུབ་ལ་ཕུག་དུམ་བུ་ཐོབ་པ་དེ་ཡིན་གསུངས། སླར་ཡང་སློབ་མས་མཁའ་འགྲོ་མ་མཇལ་འདོད་ཡོད་པའི་ནན་བསྐུལ་ཞུས་པས། བླ་མས་འོ་ན་དོ་ནུབ་མར་མགར་ཚང་དུ་སོང་ནས་ཕག་ཚང་དུ་ཕག་དང་མཉམ་དུ་ཉོལ་ཅིག །སུ་བྱུང་ནའང་རྣམ་རྟོག་མ་མང་བར་དད་པ་བསྐྱེད་ཅིག་གསུངས་བཞིན་སློབ་མ་མགར་ཁང་གི་ཕག་ཚང་དུ་ཉལ། ནམ་གཞུང་ཙམ་ལ་ཕག་རྣམས་སྐད་ཅོར་ཆེན་པོ་བྱས་ནས་བྲོས་པས། ལམ་སེང་སློབ་མ་ཡར་ལངས་ནས་བལྟས་པས། ཕག་རྣམས་ཀྱི་མགོ་ལ་མེ་འབར་ཞིང་འདུག །གློ་བུར་དུ་བུད་མེད་གཅེར་བུ། སྐྲ་གྱེན་དུ་བརྫེས་པ་སོགས་རྡོར་ཕག་དངོས་སུ་ཕེབས་བྱུང་། ཁོ་ཤིན་ཏུ་སྐྲག་ནས་མིག་ལག་པས་བཀབ་པས། ཡུད་ཙམ་གྱི་རྗེས་སུ་བལྟས་པས་གར་ཡང་མི་སྣང་། བླ་མ་ལ་དེ་བཞིན་ཞུས་པས། བླ་མ་ཐུགས་མ་དགྱེས་པའི་ཉམས་དང་བཅས། ཨ་ཁ་དམ་ལེགས། རྡོར་ཕག་དངོས་སུ་ཕེབས་པ་ལ། ཁྱེད་དད་པ་མ་སྐྱེས་པའི་སྟེང་དུ་སྐྲག་སྣང་བྱས་ནས་དམ་ཚིག་ལ་ཉམས་ཆག་སོང་བས་རྟེན་འབྲེལ་མ་ལེགས། ད་ནི་

རྡོ་རྗེ་ཕག་མོ་ཞིང་དུ་གཤེགས་འོང་། སང་ཉིན་ཁྱེད་རང་དུར་ཁྲོད་དུ་སོང་ནས་མཇལ་ཞིག་གསུངས་པས། བླ་མའི་གསུངས་བཞིན་དུར་ཁྲོད་དུ་སོང་བས། ཕྱི་ཉིན་མགར་མོ་གྲོངས་ཤིང་རོ་དུར་ཁྲོད་དུ་བསྐྱལ་ནས་བྱ་རྒོད་རྣམས་ཀྱིས་ཟ་ཞིང་འདུག །ཁོ་དེར་སླེབས་སྐབས་བྱ་རྒོད་རྣམས་དཔའ་བོ་དཔའ་མོའི་རང་བཞིན་དུ་འདུག་པ་ལ། ཁོང་ཚོས་ཁོ་ལ་འཁར་མོའི་རྒྱུབ་མ་དུམ་ཞིག་འཕངས་ནས། འདི་ཉིད་དམ་ཉམས་ཁྱེད་ཀྱི་སྐལ་བ་ཡིན་གསུངས་བྱུང་ངོ།། ས་ལམ་རྫོགས་པའི་རྣལ་འབྱོར་ཕོ་མོ་ཡིས། །དག་དང་མ་དག་ཐབས་མཁས་སྒྱུ་རྩལ་གྱིས། །གདུལ་བྱ་དབང་རིམ་ཐར་ལམ་འགོད་མཛད་ལ། །འགྱུར་མེད་དད་གུས་ཆེན་པོས་རྗེས་ཡི་རངས། །ཅེས་སོ།།

(༢༩) ཁྲ་འགུ་དགོན་གྱི་བཀའ་སྲུང་དགེ་བསྙེན་རྡོ་རྗེ་རྒྱལ་མཚན། རྒྱལ་བ་གཉིས་པ་གུ་རུ་པདྨ་འབྱུང་། །གསལ་སྟོང་མཆོག་སྤྲུལ་ཉི་མ་འགྱུར་མེད་སོགས། །མཁས་གྲུབ་ཀུན་གྱིས་རྒྱལ་བསྟན་སྲུང་ལ་བཀུར། །དགེ་བསྙེན་ཆེན་པོའི་ཞབས་ལ་གུས་པས་འདུད། ཁྲ་འགུ་དགེ་བསྙེན་ནི་གུ་རུ་རིན་པོ་ཆེས་བཀའ་བསྒོ་གནང་བའི་དགེ་བསྙེན་ཉེར་གཅིག་གི་གྲལ་ནས་གཅིག་ཡིན་ཞིང་། དེ་ཡང་ཁྲ་ལེབ་སྣ་ཕྲེང་གཉིས་པ་ཉི་མ་འགྱུར་མེད་སོག་ལྕུག་ཟམ་སྟེང་ནས་ཕེབས་ཏུ་མ་བཅུག་པར་ས་གཡོ་བ་དང་། འབྲུག་གློག་ཐོག་སེར་སོགས་ཀྱི་ཆོ་འཕྲུལ་བྱས་པས། རིན་པོ་ཆེའི་སྣར་པ་ཞག་གཅིག་དེ་རུ་བཞུགས་ཤིང་ཁོང་གིས་དམ་ལ་བཏགས་ནས་ཁྱི་ལྷར་ཁྲིད་དེ་ཁྲ་དགོན་གྱི་བཀའ་སྲུང་དུ་བསྐོས། གྲུབ་ཐོབ་ཐང་སྟོང་རྒྱལ་པོས་ལྕུག་ཟམ་འདི་བཞེངས་སྐབས་ཡུལ་ལྷ་རྣམས་ཀྱིས་ཕྲག་དོག་བྱས་ནས་བཞེངས་ཏུ་མ་བཅུག་པས། ཁོང་གིས་བོད་ཀྱི་ལྷ་མོ་ཞབས་བྲོ་གསར་བརྩམས་གནང་ནས་འཁྲབས་པས། ཡུལ་ལྷ་ཐམས་ཅད་ཧ་ལས་ནས་དེ་ལ་ཡིངས་པའི་རིང་ལྕུག་ཟམ་བཞེངས་པའི་ལོ་རྒྱུས་ཡོད། ཙན་དན་དགོན་པ་ཞེས་པའི་དགེ་ལུགས་པའི་དགོན་པ་ཆེན་པོ་ཞིག་ཡོད་པའི་ས་གནས་ཡིན། འཛུ་མི་མི་

ཕམ་མཆོག་དང་པོར་ཁྲ་དགོན་ཕེབས་སྐབས། ཁྲ་དགོན་གྱིས་དགེ་བསྙེན་གསོལ་ཀ་གསུངས་པར་གཟིགས་པས། ཐུགས་ལ་དགོན་པ་འདིས་ཀྱང་དྲེགས་པ་ཞིག་སྒྲུབ་ཀྱི་འདུག་དགོངས། ཉིན་ཞིག་གྲྭ་ཚུང་མང་པོར་ཤུགས་པ་འཐུ་རུ་ཕེབས་སྐབས། རུ་ཤོག་གཟར་ས་ནས་དགེ་བསྙེན་ཕྱུག་གིས་གྲྭ་ཚུང་རེ་རེ་བཞིན་སྐྱོར་བར་གཟིགས་པས། མཛོ་ཛྷི་བན་ཐབ་ཧ་ར་ལ། ཁྱེད་ཚོའི་གནས་བདག་གི་མཚན་ལ་གང་ཞུ་རེད་དྲིས་པས། རྡོ་རྗེ་རྒྱལ་མཚན་ཞུ་རེད་ཞུས་པས། འཇམ་མགོན་གྱིས་ཕྲིན་བཅོལ་འདི་བརྩམས་མཛད། ཧཱུྃ༔ གནས་ཀྱི་བདག་པོ་མཐུ་སྟོབས་རྩལ་ལྡན་པ། །དགེ་བསྙེན་ཆེན་པོ་རྡོ་རྗེ་རྒྱལ་མཚན་ཞེས། །ནོར་བདག་ཚུལ་འཆང་དགྱེས་ཡུམ་ཀླུ་མོར་བཅས། །འདིར་བྱོན་གཙང་སྦྲུར་གཏོར་མ་སྐྱེམས་ཕུད་དང་། །བརྟན་ཆས་འདོད་ཡོན་སྤྲིན་ཕུང་རྒྱ་མཚོས་མཆོད། །ཁྱེད་ཐུགས་དགྱེས་པ་རབ་ཏུ་བསྐང་གྱུར་ཅིག །རྟག་ཏུ་བུ་བཞིན་མགོན་སྐྱབས་སྐྱོང་གྲོགས་མཛོད། །དགྲ་དང་ཉེར་འཚེ་ཀུན་ལས་སྲུང་བ་དང་། །ལྷ་གཡག་ཞོལ་དཀར་སྤྲུལ་ཆེན་འཇིགས་རུང་བ། །ཆུ་སྲིན་ཞོན་པའི་ཀླུ་བདུད་དྲག་པོ་སོགས། །སྣ་ཚོགས་རྫུ་འཕྲུལ་འདོད་རྒྱུར་བསྒྱུར་བ་ཡི། །རང་གི་ཕྱོགས་སྲུང་ཕ་རོལ་ཆམ་ལ་འབེབས། །མཐུ་ལྡན་ཁྱེད་ལ་མཆོད་ཅིང་མངོན་བསྟོད་ན། །སྒྲུབ་བརྒྱུད་བསྟན་པ་སྤྱི་དང་ཆོས་སྡེ་འདི། །དགེ་འདུན་སྡེ་དང་འབྲུ་ནོར་འབྱོར་བར་སྤེལ། །མངོན་པར་མཐོ་བའི་དོན་ཀུན་འགྲུབ་པར་མཛོད། །ཅེས་སོ།

བོད་ལ་དུས་ཀྱི་འགྱུར་བ་བྱུང་ནས་བླ་གྲྭ་རྣམས་མ་ཕེབས་པའི་སྔོན་དུ། ཁྲ་དགོན་གྲྭ་ཐན་གྲོང་སྨད་ཆོས་ལྡན་གྱི་གཟིམས་ལམ་དུ་དགེ་བསྙེན་བྱུང་ནས། ཁྱེད་ཚོས་བླ་མ་རྣམས་གདན་དྲངས་ལ་བྲོས་ཤོག །ང་རང་གནས་སྐབས་རྒྱ་ནག་ཏུ་སྡོད་དགོས་བྱུང་གསུངས་ནས། བུམ་པས་ཁྲུས་བྱས་ནས་བྱིན་བརླབས་བྱས་པར་རྨིས་པས། རྒྱ་གར་དུ་བླ་གྲྭ་རྣམས་དབུ་ཐོན་བྱུང་། རྗེས་མར་སྐབས་རྗེ་ཁྲ་འགུ་རིན་པོ་ཆེས་བལ་ཡུལ་སྟག་མོ་ལུས་སྦྱིན་དུ་བཤད་གྲྭར་བཞེངས་སྐབས་ཕྱུག་ལས་རྣམས་ལམ་ལ་མི་འགྲོ་བ

མང་པོ་བྱུང་བས། བླ་མ་ཀུན་གྲགས་ནས་འདྲེ་མཐོང་བ་དང་ཉམས་འཕར་བ་སོགས་རང་བྱུང་དུ་ཡོད་པས། སྐབས་ཤིག་ཁོང་གི་གཟིམས་ལམ་མམ་ཉམས་སྣང་ལ། རིན་པོ་ཆེ་རྒྱ་གར་དུ་ཕེབས་རྗེས་ང་ལ་གསོལ་ཀ་གསུངས་བ་ལྷ་ཅི། ཐུགས་ལ་དྲན་ཙམ་ཡང་མཛད་ཀྱི་མི་འདུག་ཅེས་སྟོན་མར་བསྟེན་པའི་བཀའ་སྲུང་རྣམས་ཐུགས་ཁྲེལ་བ་ལྟ་བུ་འདུག་ཞུས་པས། སྟོན་མར་རིན་པོ་ཆེ་མཆོག་ནས་དགེ་བསྙེན་དང་རྒྱལ་པོ་སྐུ་ལྔའི་གསོལ་ཀ་གསུངས་པ་བཞིན། དེ་ནས་བཟུང་སྟེ་བླ་གྲྭ་རྣམས་ནས་དགེ་བསྙེན་དང་རྒྱལ་པོ་སྐུ་ལྔའི་གསོལ་ཀ་ཉིན་ལྟར་ཆགས་མེད་གསུངས་པས། ལམ་སེང་ཕྲུག་ལས་རྣམས་གེགས་མེད་དུ་འགྲུབ་ཐུབ་པ་བྱུང་ངོ་། །བོད་དུ་དུས་ཀྱི་འགྱུར་བས་ལྷ་ཁང་ཞིག་རལ་སོང་བ་རྣམས་སླར་ཡང་ད་ར་ཀརྨ་རིན་ཆེན། བན་ཁྲ་མཐུ་སྟོབས། བན་ཁྲ་ཀརྨ་ཆོས་འཕེལ། རྒྱ་ར་བདུད་འདུལ། རིན་ཆེན་ནོར་བུ་གཙོས་གཞིས་ལུས་ཀྱི་དགེ་རྒན་རྣམས་གཙོ་བོར་གྱུར་པའི་གྲྭ་རྣམས་ཀྱིས་ཐུགས་རྩོལ་ཆེན་པོས་བཞེངས་སྐབས། ལྷ་ཁང་གི་ཤིང་ཆ་རྣམས་གཅོད་པ་ལ་ད་ར་ཀརྨ་རིན་ཆེན་སོགས་གྲྭ་གསར་རྣམས་ཟུར་མང་དུ་ཕེབས། ཤིང་གཅོད་རིང་དེ་རུ་གྱུར་སྐར་བྱུས་ནས་བཞུགས་པས། ཡུལ་དེའི་མི་རྣམས་ཀྱིས། ཁྱེད་ཚོའི་གྲུར་འགྲམ་དུ་ལྷ་གཡག་ཁམས་གྭ་ཞིག་རྟག་པར་ཉལ་བ་དང་། གྲུར་སྐོར་ནས་ངར་སྒྲ་བྱེད་པ་དང་། སྐོར་འཁྲོས་སོགས་བྱེད་ཀྱི་འདུག་ཟེར། ཉིན་ཞིག་མི་རྣམས་ཀྱིས། དེ་རིང་ཁྱེད་ཚོ་གཟབ་གཟབ་གྱིས་མ་གཏོགས། ལྷ་གཡག་དེས་ངར་སྒྲ་བྱས་པ་དང་། རྭ་གཉིས་ས་ལ་རྡེབ་ཅིང་འཚུབ་ཆ་ཆེན་པོ་བྱེད་ཀྱི་འདུག་ཅེས་ཟེར། དེའི་སྐབས་སུ་ཤིང་གཅོད་ཟིན་པ་རྣམས་ཤིང་ཁྲི་རྣམས་ཀྱིས་དགོན་དུ་སྒྲོ་ཞིང་ཡོད་ལ། དེའི་ཉིན་ཤིང་ཁྲི་གཅིག་ཤིང་གི་ལྡིད་ཚད་མ་སྙོམས་པར་གཞོགས་གཡས་བཙུགས་ནས་ཡོ་སོང་། འོན་ཀྱང་ཡོ་བ་ཙམ་ལས་གཞོགས་མང་པོ་མ་བརྗེས་པས། ཁ་ལོ་བ་དང་གྲྭ་སུ་ལའང་སླས་སྐྱོན་མ་བྱུང་། ཡུལ་མི་རྣམས་ཀྱིས་ཤིང་ཁྲི་ཡོ་བ་མཐོང་ཞིང་། མ་ཚད་

སྔོན་མར་མཐོང་བའི་ལྷ་གཡག །ཁམས་གྭ་དེས་ཤིང་ཁྲི་སྐྱོར་བས་ཁྱེད་རྣམས་སྐྱོབས་སོང་ཟེར་གྱི་འདུག །ཡུལ་མི་རྣམས་ནས་ཐད་ཀར་མཐོང་གི་འདུག་མོད། རང་གྲྭ་རྣམས་ནས་སུས་ཀྱང་མ་མཐོང་ངོ་། སྣ་སྟོད་བཀྲ་ཤིས་ཆོས་གླིང་། །མཁས་གྲུབ་བྱེ་བའི་འབྱུང་གནས། །བསྟན་སྲུང་དགེ་བསྙེན་ཆེན་པོ། །སྒྲུབ་བསྟན་སྲུང་བའི་མགོན་གཅིག ༼༢༥༽ བཀའ་བརྒྱུད་ཁྲ་འགུ་དགོན་གྱི་ཆོ་མཚམས་བླ་མ་ཚོགས་གཉིས་དང་མི་ཡུལ་ཆེ་མཚམས། གཞི༷་འཁོར་བའི་ཆོས་ལ་ངེས་འབྱུང་ཆེ། །ལམ༷་ཚོགས་གཉིས་བསགས་ལ་སྙིང་སྟོབས་ཆེ། །འབྲས༷་སྐུ་གཉིས་ཐོབ་ལ་མཚན་སྙན་ཆེ། །ཁྱེད་རྟོགས་ལྡན་རྣལ་འབྱོར་ཕྱུག་གི་ཡུལ། ཁོང་གི་སྐུ་ཡུལ་སྡེ་དགེ་སྐུ་ཆེ་ནས་ཡིན་ཞིང་མི་ཚང་དབུལ་པོ་ཞིག་ལ་འཁྲུངས། དེ་ནས་རིམ་བཞིན་སྡེ་དགེ་ཚོང་པ་ཀརྨ་བཟོད་པའི་དྲིལ་གཡོག་མཛད་ནས་ཚོང་པ་དང་མཉམ་དུ་སྐྱེ་རྒྱུ་བརྒྱུད་དེ་ཁྲ་དགོན་ལ་འཁོར་ནས་ཁོང་རབ་ཏུ་བྱུང་། ཞལ་གདན་ནས་བཟུང་རྒྱུ་མེད་པའི་རྐྱེན་གྱིས་ངན་མིང་ལ་པ་ར་ཁ་ཞེས་ཐོགས། དེ་ནས་ཁོང་ནཱ་རོའི་ཆོས་དྲུག་སྒྲུབ་ཁང་དུ་བཞུགས་རྒྱུ་འཁེལ་བས་ཚོང་པ་ཀརྨ་བཟོད་པ་ཡང་འོངས་ནས་དགུན་ཁའི་ཟ་རྒྱུ་ཁལ་ཞིག་ཀྱང་ཉོས་ནས་ཕུལ། ཕྱི་ཉིན་སྔ་དྲོར་ཐུན་ཟ་བཏང་ཞིང་ཐུན་བསྐུལ་དབྱངས་པ་ལ་བརྟེན་ནས་ངེས་འབྱུང་སྐྱེས་ཏེ། ཚོང་པ་ལ་ཁལ་དེ་ཆེ་ཐར་གཏོང་རྒྱུ་དང་། ཤ་ཡང་གཅོད་མཛད། སྒྲུབ་ཁང་གྲོལ་རྗེས་ཆེ་མཚམས་ལ་བཞུགས། ཁོང་གི་སྙུང་གནས་ཆ་སྟོང་ཕྲག་གཅིག་ཉམས་སུ་བཞེས། དེའི་བསོད་ནམས་ཀྱི་སྟོབས་ཀྱིས་འབུལ་བ་མང་པོ་བྱུང་བ་རྣམས་ཀྱིས་ཁྲ་དགོན་འདུ་ཁང་གསར་པའི་ནང་དུ་ཐང་ག་བརྒྱད་བཅུ་བཞེངས་པའི་སྦྱིན་བདག་མཛད། ཀ་ཤོད་ནས་ལྷ་བཟོ་གདན་དྲངས་ནས་ལོ་གསུམ་གྱི་རིང་སྐུ་ཐང་རྫོགས་པར་གྲུབ། སྐུ་ཐང་རེ་ལ་གསེར་སྲང་གསུམ་རེ་འགྲོ་གྲོན་གནང་། སྐུ་ཐང་རེའི་ཚད་ལ་ལྷ་ཁང་གི་ཀ་བ་རེའི་ཚད་ཡོད་ཅིང་འཆར་གཞི་ཡང་ལྷ་ཁང་གི་ཀ་བ་རེ་ལ་སྐུ་ཐང་རེ་རེ་བཤམས་རྒྱུ་མཛད། འོན་ཀྱང་དུས་ཀྱི་འགྱུར་བ་ལ་བརྟེན་

ནས་སྐུ་ཐང་རྣམས་བཞམས་པའི་སྐལ་བ་མ་ཐོབ། ཚེ་མཚམས་མཆོག་ཀྱང་བཙོན་ཁང་དུ་གྲོངས་པའོ། དེའི་ཡང་སྲིད་བལ་ཡུལ་ནུབ་རིར་འཁྲུངས་ནས་སྐྱབས་རྗེ་ཁྲ་འགུ་རིན་པོ་ཆེ་ཡིས་ངོས་འཛིན་གནང་བ་འདི་ཡིན། དེ་ཡང་ཁོང་ཞལ་གྲགས་ཐུབ་ཙམ་ནས་ཁྲ་དགོན་དུ་ཕེབས་ཀྱི་ཡིན་ཞེས་རྟག་པར་གསུངས་བརྟེན་ཡུམ་ གྱིས་སྐྱབས་རྗེ་ཁྲ་སྤྲུལ་མདུན་ཁྲིད་ནས་རབ་ཏུ་བྱུང་སྐེ་ཉར་ཚགས་གནང་བར་ཞུས་པས། དེའི་སྐབས་སུ་སྐྱབས་རྗེ་རིན་པོ་ཆེ་བལ་ཡུལ་ཕེབས་མ་ཐག་ཡིན་ཕྱིར་མཐུན་རྐྱེན་གང་ཡང་མེད་བརྟེན། ཁོང་གིས་ད་ལྟ་མཐུན་རྐྱེན་སོགས་འཛོམས་པར་དཀའ་འདུག་སོགས་གསུངས་པས། ཉིན་ཁ་ཤས་ཀྱི་རྗེས་སུ་ཡང་ཡུམ་གྱིས་ཁྲིད་གནང་ནས་ནན་ཞུས་བྱས་པས། ཐེངས་གཉིས་པའི་སྐབས་སྐྱབས་རྗེ་རིན་པོ་ཆེ་ནས་སྔར་བཞིན་ཁོང་ལ་མཐུན་རྐྱེན་མེད་ཅེས་གསུངས་པས། ཡང་སྲིད་སྐུ་ན་ཤིན་ཏུ་ཆུང་ཡང་། བྱིས་པ་གཞན་ལས་བརྒྱལ་བའི་སྤྱོད་པ་ནི། ལམ་སེང་རིན་པོ་ཆེའི་ཞབས་ལ་དབུ་གཏུགས་གནང་ཞིང་བཤུམས་ནས་རབ་ཏུ་བྱུང་བ་ཞུས་པས། ད་གཟོད་རིན་པོ་ཆེ་ནས་དེ་བཞིན་གནང་བར་ཞལ་གྱིས་བཞེས་ནས་མཚན་ལ་ཀརྨ་དམ་ཆོས་གནང་། དེ་ནས་རིམ་བཞིན་སློབ་སྦྱོང་དང་། རྒྱུར་བཙོན་ཆེན་པོས་རིན་པོ་ཆེའི་ཞབས་ཞུ་ལོ་མང་མཛད་ནས(༡༩༩༨)ལོར་བལ་ཡུལ་ཁྲ་དགོན་བཀྲ་ཤིས་ཆོས་གླིང་དུ་སྐྱབས་རྗེ་བློ་གྲོས་ཉི་མ་རིན་པོ་ཆེ་དང་མཉམ་དུ་གསེར་ཁྲི་མངའ་གསོལ་མཛད་རྗེས། ད་ལྟ་གནས་མཆོག་ཝཱ་ར་ཎ་སིའི་མཐོ་རིམ་སློབ་གྲྭ་རུ་གསན་སྦྱོང་མཐར་ཕྱིན་ནས། ནཱ་རོ་ཆོས་དྲུག་སྒྲུབ་ཁང་དུ་བཞུགས་ཡོད། རྣམ་ཐར་རྒྱས་པ་ཁོང་གི་སྐོར་རྒྱུས་ཡོད་པ་རྣམས་ཀྱི་ཞལ་ལས་གསན་པར་བྱའོ།།

གཟུགས་སྐུ་བཀོད་པ་ཆུང་ཡང་། །ཡེ་ཤེས་ཐུགས་ལ་འགྲིབ་མེད། །རེ་ཞིག་ཆོས་དབྱིངས་གཤེགས་ཀྱང་། །ཐུགས་རྗེ་ཕྲིན་ལས་མཐའ་མེད།། །མི་ཡུལ་ཚེ་མཚམས་ནི། གྲུབ་གནས་བདེ་མཆོག་ཕོ་བྲང་། །དཔའ་བོ་མཁའ་འགྲོ་འབྲལ་

མེད། །རྟོགས་ལྡན་ཕོ་མོ་རྣམས་ལ༔ །ཞལ་གཟིགས་ལུང་བསྟན་ཚད་མེད། དམ་པ་འདི་ཉིད་སྐུ་སྟན་ཤིན་ཏུ་ཆེ་ཡང་། སྐུ་ཆེའི་རྣམ་ཐར་ཞིབ་ཕྲ་བདག་གི་མི་ཤེས་ལ། ཁྲ་འགྲུ་ལྷ་རྗེ་དཔག་བསམ་བཀྲ་ཤིས་སོགས་ལ་བཀའ་འདྲི་ཞུས་ནས་འགོད་པར་བྱ། དེ་ཡང་རྣམ་སྣང་ལྷ་གཉེར་བསོད་ནམས་ཡོན་འཕེལ་ལས་བདག་གིས་ཇི་ལྟར་ཐོས་པ་འགོད་ན༔ བསོད་ནམས་ཡོན་འཕེལ་ཁོང་དང་མི་ཡུལ་ཚེ་མཚམས་གཉིས་ཡང་དཔེན་བདེ་མཆོག་ཕོ་བྲང་དུ་མཚམས་ཁང་ཁ་ཁ་མཛད་ནས་མཚམས་བཞུགས་པ་ལ། ཉིན་ཞིག་དུས་མཆོད་ལ་འཕེལ་ནས་ཚོགས་འཁོར་བསྐོར། བསོད་ནམས་ཡོན་འཕེལ་གྱིས་ཚོགས་སྐལ་ཞིག་བསྣམས་ནས་ཚེ་མཚམས་ལ་འབུལ་བར་སོང་བས། གཟིམས་སྒོ་ཉེ་སར་སླེབས་སྐབས། ནང་ནས་མགུར་སྟན་པོ་ཞིག་འཐེན་པའི་སྒྲ་དང་། དེ་ཡང་སྐྱེ་དམན་གྱི་སྐད་གདངས་ཡོད་པར་གོ་བས། སྐྱེ་དམན་ཞིག་ཡོད་པར་ཐག་ཆོད་སྣམ་པའི་ལོག་རྟོག་སྐྱེས་ནས་སྒོ་རྡར་གྱིས་ཕྱེས་པས། ཚེ་མཚམས་ཀྱི་མདུན་དུ་ཤོག་གུ་སྐྱ་ཉི་ལེ་འདུག་ཅིང་། ཁོང་གིས་ཕྱག་བྲིས་མཛད་བཞིན་པ་ལ་འཕེལ་བས། སྤྱན་ནམ་མཁར་གཟིགས་ཤིང་ཞལ་ནས། ཨ་ཁ་མཆེད་གྲོགས་འདིར་ཙུང་ཟད་ཕེབས་ཉན་ལེ་མིན་ཅེས་གསུངས་ནས། སྔར་བྲིས་ཟིན་པའི་ཤོག་ལྷེབ་ཚང་མ་མེ་ལ་བསྲེགས་མཛད། དེ་དུས་མཁའ་འགྲོའི་ལུང་བསྟན་གནང་ཡོད་ངེས་འདུག་ཀྱང་ང་རང་ལོག་རྟོག་གི་དབང་གིས་རྟེན་འབྲེལ་མ་འགྲིག་ཅེས་གསུངས་ནས་ཐུགས་འགྱོད་མཛད་གསུངས།། མ་བཅོས་རང་ཞལ་མཇལ་བས། །མ་དང་མཁའ་འགྲོའི་ལུང་བསྟན། །མ་དག་རྟོག་ཚོགས་སྐྱོན་གྱིས༔ །མ་འགྲིག་རྟེན་འབྲེལ་ཉེས་སོང་།། ༼༢༥༽ དགེ་ལུགས་འབུམ་སྣང་དགོན་གྱི་སྒོ་བརྒྱུད་ཨ་སྐུ་རིན་པོ་ཆེ། མཚན་དཔེའི་ཟླ་ཞལ་བཞད་མ་ཐག །མཚན་མ་རྟེན་འབྲེལ་རང་བྱུང་ཤར། །མཚན་སྟན་ལྷ་མིའི་ཡུལ་དུ་ཁྱབ། །མཚན་བཅས་དྲི་བྲལ་མཆོག་ལ་འདུད། དེ་ཡང་དྲིན་ཅན་བླ་མ་དགུང་ལོ༼༡༧༽ལ་སླེབས་སྐབས། ཁོང་གི་ཚ་མོ་རྒྱ

མཆོ་དབང་མོའི་ཕྲུག་གུ་བཙའ་བ་ལ་ཟླ་གཅིག་ཙམ་ཡོད་རེད་ཅེས་ལབ་པར་གསན། དེ་ཡང་ཡང་སྲིད་སྐྱེ་འཕྲུངས་ཡུལ་གྱི་མིང་ལ་པད་ལུང་ནང་ཟེར༑ ཡུམ་གྱིས་ལུག་བཞོ་བཞིན་པའི་སྐབས་སུ་འཕྲུངས་རྩིས་བྱུས་པས། ཡུམ་གྱི་ཕྲུག་ཏུ་འོམ་རྫེའུ་གང་བསྣམས་ཡོད་པ་དང་མཉམ་དུ་མགྱོགས་པོར་ཁྱིམ་དུ་ཕེབས་ནས་འོམ་རྫེའུ་གང་དེ་ཐབ་སྟེ་ལ་བཞག་གནང་། དེ་ནས་ཡུམ་ལ་གནོད་པ་མེད་པར་སྐྱེ་འཕྲུངས། རྗེས་མར་རྫེའུ་ནང་གི་འོམ་དེ་ཉིད་ཞོ་རུ་འགྱུར་འདུག་གསུངས། རྗེ་བོ་དང་མི་མང་པོས་སྨྲ་ཡི་ཐོག་ཏུ་འཛའ་གུར་ཕུབ་འདུག་ཅེས་རྗེས་སུ་ལབ་ཀྱི་འདུག་ཀྱང་ཁྱིམ་མིས་མ་མཐོང་གསུངས། དེ་ནས་འབུམ་དགོན་གྲྭ་རྒན་ཞིག་གིས་ཕྲུག་གུ་འདི་ཕལ་པ་ཞིག་མིན་པར་ཐག་ཆོད་དགོངས་ནས་ཁོང་གིས་བདག་གཉེར་གང་ལེགས་མཛད། ཉིན་ཞིག་ཁྱིམ་ཚང་རུབ་མཆེར་ས་གསར་པ་ཐོག་ཏུ་སྤོས་པས། ཕྲུག་གུ་ཞལ་ཕར་བསྒོར་ནས་ཕྱག་གཉིས་རུབ་རུབ་མཛད་ཀྱི་འདུག །དགེ་རྒན་གྱི་ཐུགས་ལ། འབུ་གསོད་ཀྱི་ཡོད་པ་འདྲ། འོན་ཀྱང་འཛམ་པོར་མ་བྱུས་ན་ཐུགས་སྐྲག་བཞེས་འགྲོ་དགོངས་ནས་ག་ལེར་གཟིགས་པས། ཡང་སྲིད་ཀྱི་ཕྱག་ཏུ་རྡོ་ཞིག་བསྣམས་ནས་རིལ་རིལ་དང་ལེབ་ལེབ་ནར་ནར་སོགས་ཅི་བདེར་མཛད་ཅིང་འདུག །དེ་ནས་དགེ་རྒན་གྱིས། ཁྱེད་ཀྱིས་རྡོ་དེ་རིལ་རིལ་མཛད་ནས་ང་ལ་གནང་རོགས་ཞུས་པས། ཁོང་གིས་རིལ་རིལ་མཛད་ནས་གནང་བྱུང་། ཡང་དགེ་རྒན་གྱིས་ཕུར་རྡོ་ལེབ་ལེབ་ཞིག་གཟིགས་པ་དེ་བསྣམས་ནས་ཞབས་ལྷམ་གཉིས་ཕུད་དེ། རྡོ་ཐོག་ཏུ་ཞབས་གཉིས་བཞག་ཙམ་མཛད་ནས་ཁྱེད་ཀྱིས་ཀྱང་དེ་ལྟར་གྱིས་དང་ཞུས་པས། ཡང་སྲིད་བཞེད་མོ་དང་བཅས་ཁོང་གི་ཞབས་ལྷམ་གཉིས་ཀྱང་ཕུད་མཛད་ནས་རྡོ་ལེབ་ཐོག་ཏུ་ཞབས་གཉིས་བཞག་པས། རྡོ་ལེབ་ཐོག་ཏུ་ཞབས་རྗེས་གསལ་པོ་བཞག་མཛད་དོ། །དགུང་ལོ་བཅོ་བརྒྱད་ལ་སླེབས་སྐབས། དུས་ཀྱི་འགྱུར་བ་བྱུང་ནས་སྲིད་གཞུང་གིས་མི་ཚང་མ་ལ་ཕྱི་བ་གསོད་དགོས་པར་བཀའ་ཕབ་ཀྱང་ཁོང་གིས་

མ་བསད་པས། གལ་སྲིད་ཕྱི་བ་མ་བསད་ན་ཉེས་ཆད་གཅོད་ཀྱི་ཡིན་ཅེས་ཞུས་པས། ཞལ་ནས་འགྲིག་གི་འདུག །སང་ཉིན་ངས་ཕྱི་བ་ཆེ་ཤོས་དེ་གསོད་ཀྱི་ཡིན་གསུངས་ནས་དེའི་ནུབ་མོ་གཞུང་དཔོན་དེ་ལ་གྲི་བརྒྱབ་ཏེ་སླས་ནས་བྲོས་མཛད་པས། དམག་མིས་རྗེས་ཟིན་ནས་བསྒྲོངས་ཏེ་སྐུ་གདུང་དེ་རུ་བསྒྱུར་ནས་སོང་ངོ་། །དེའི་གནས་ཚུལ་ཡུམ་ནས་གོ་བས་སྡུག་བསྔལ་ཆེན་པོས་སྐུ་གདུང་འཚོལ་དུ་ཕྱིན་པས། ཁོང་གིས་ན་བཟའ་རྣམས་ཆག་ཆག་ཡག་པོ་མཛད་ནས་ཇོ་ཕ་ཕྱང་ཞིག་གི་སྟེང་ལ་བཞག །ཕྱག་མཉམ་བཞག་དང་ཞབས་རྗོར་དཀྱིལ། སྐུ་དྲང་པོར་བསྲངས་ནས་སྒྲོངས་འདུག་པ་ཡུམ་གྱིས་མཇལ་བས། མཇལ་མ་ཐག་ཏུ་སྡུག་བསྔལ་གཏན་ནས་མེད་ཅིང་སེམས་ལ་དད་མོས་དང་དགའ་སྤྲོ་ཡིས་ཁེངས་སོང་ཅེས་དྲིན་ཅན་བླ་མ་ལ་ཞུས་པའོ།། སྣང༷་བཅས་འཁྲུལ་པའི་སྣང༷་ངོ་རུ། །གཏུ༷མ་དྲག་སྤྱོད་པས་གཏུ༷མ་པོ་བསྒྲལ། །འདུ༷ས་དང་བསད་ལས་འདུ༷ས་པའི་ཕྱིར། །འོ༷ད་གསལ་ཆོས་སྐུའི་འོ༷ད་ཀློང་གྱུར།། (༡༧) དགེ་ལུགས་སྔ་ར་ཉག་དགོན་གྱི་ཁོ་འཛོ་གྲུབ་ཐོབ་བམ་རི་གྱུར་གསེར་གྱི་རྡོ་རྗེ། རྒྱལ་བ་གཉིས་པ་ཙོང་ཁ་པའི། །ལུང་རྟོགས་བསྟན་པ་སྤེལ་མཛད་པའི། །དཔལ་ལྡན་ར་ཉག་དགོན་པ་ཡི། །གྲུབ་ཐོབ་གསེར་གྱི་རྡོ་རྗེར་འདུད། དཔལ་ལྡན་ར་ཉག་དགོན་པའི་གྲུབ་ཆེན་ཁོ་འཛོ་སྤྲུལ་སྐུའི་རྣམ་ཐར་རྒྱས་པ་མ་མཇལ་ཡང་ཡོད་ངེས་ལ། ཁོང་ནི་ལྷ་ལུང་དཔལ་གྱི་རྡོ་རྗེའི་སྤྲུལ་པ་ཡིན་པར་གྲགས་ཤིང་། དེ་ཡང་རི་གྱུར་ཞེས་པའི་དོན་ནི། ཡབ་ཡུལ་གང་ཡིན་མི་ཤེས་ཤིང་། དགུང་ལོ་ལྔ་ཙམ་གྱི་སྟེང་ནས་མ་ཡུམ་འདས། ཡབ་ཀྱིས་ཁྲིམ་ཐབ་གསར་པ་བཞེས་པས། དེས་ཁོང་ལ་རྟག་པར་བརྡུང་ཡང་ཁོང་ལ་ཆུང་ཆུང་ནས་སྟོན་གནས་རྗེས་དྲན་ཡོད་པ་ལ་སྐྱོན་གང་ཡང་མ་བྱུང་མོད། འོན་ཀྱང་ཉིན་ཞིག་མོ་རང་གི་ལྷམ་ལག་པ་གཡོན་དུ་བཟུང་ནས་དབུ་ལ་ལན་དགུ་བྲབ་པས་གྲིབ་ཀྱིས་བསྒྲིབས་ནས་སྔར་བཞིན་སྟོན་གནས་རྗེས་དྲན་མི་གསལ་བར་གྱུར་པས། ད་ནི་ཡུན་རིང་བསྡད་ན་ཕན་ཐོགས་མི་འདུག་

དགོངས་ཏེ་ཁྲིམ་ནས་བྲོས། རི་ལ་སྒོམ་རྒྱག་བཞིན་ནུབ་མོ་ལྷུམ་པའི་ཡོ་མ་གཉིས་སྐྱུ་རྒྱབ་ཏུ་མནབས་ནས་གཟིམས་པས་ཕོ་རོག་གཉིས་བྱུང་ནས། ཁོང་དེ་གཉིས་ཀྱི་གཤོག་པས་བཀབ་ནས་གཟིམས། དེ་ནས་སྒོམ་རྒྱག་ཞོར་ཕོ་རོག་གཉིས་ཀྱི་རྗེས་སུ་འབྲངས་ནས་ཕེབས་པས། རི་ལ་བཞུགས་ཤིང་ཡུལ་གྱུར་ནས་ཕེབས་པ་ལ་རི་གྱུར་ཞེས་མཚན་ཐོགས་ཚུལ་ཁ་རྒྱུན་དུ་གནས་སོ། །མཐར་དགེ་རྒྱས་ཡུལ་ཤུལ་དུ་སླེབས་ནས་ཨ་མ་རྒན་མོའི་ཞིག་གི་བུ་ཁྲལ་མཛད། ཉིན་ལྷར་ལུག་རྫི་ལ་ཕེབས་ཞོར་སྒོམ་རྒྱག་གནང་། ཉིན་ཞིག་རྒན་མོ་ཤི་ནས་བླ་གྲྭ་མང་པོ་གདན་དྲངས་བྱུང་། ཐུགས་ལ་འདི་ཆོས་ཤི་བོ་རྣམ་ཤེས་ལ་ཅི་ཙམ་ཕན་ཐུབ་བམ་དགོངས་ནས་ཉམས་སད་པའི་ཕྱིར་གཟིགས་པས། བླ་གྲྭ་དེ་རྣམས་ཀྱིས་ཆོ་གའི་དབྱངས་དང་རྔ་རོལ་སོགས་གཟི་བརྗིད་ཆེན་པོ་མཛད་ཀྱི་འདུག་ཅིང་། ཁོང་རྣམས་ལ་གསུང་སྐད་དང་འདོན་འགྲིག་དཔེ་སྐན་པོ་ཡོད་མཐུས། ཐུགས་ལ་ཡང་ང་རྒྱལ་དང་བཅས་འདོན་བཞིན་འདུག །གྲལ་མཐར་རྩུ་ཁོང་རྣམས་ཀྱི་ཧ་རྗེ་མཛད་པའི་གྲྭ་པ་ཞིག་བཞུགས་ཤིང་། གྲྭ་དེའི་སེམས་ལ། ཁོང་ཆོས་ཆོ་ག་དང་འདོན་པ་སོགས་རྒྱས་པར་མཛད་ཀྱི་འདུག །ང་རང་གིས་ཅི་ཡང་མི་ཤེས་པས་ཚེ་འདས་དོན་དུ་བསྔོ་གང་ནུས་འདོན་བསམ་ནས་འདོན་ཞིང་འདུག །ཚེ་འདས་རྣམ་ཤེས་དེ་འབུ་ཞིག་ལ་སྤྲུལ་ནས་ལྡིང་སྐོར་བྱེད་ཀྱི་འདུག་ཀྱང་། བླ་གྲྭ་གཞན་པས་གཟིགས་ཙམ་ཡང་མི་མཛད། ཧ་རྗེའི་སེམས་ལ། འབུ་འདི་ཉིད་ཚེ་འདས་ཀྱི་རྣམ་ཤེས་ཡིན་པའང་སྲིད་སྙམ་ནས་སྨོན་ལམ་འདེབས་བཞིན་ཞལ་ཕྱུ་མཛད་པས་ཕན་པ་ཆེན་པོ་བྱུང་། དེ་ནས་གྲུབ་ཐོབ་ཀྱི་ཐུགས་ལ་བླ་མ་འདིའི་ང་རྒྱལ་ཅུང་ཟད་བཅག་དགོས་ཀྱི་འདུག་དགོངས། ཞལ་ལག་ལ་ཐུག་པས། བླ་མའི་བཞེས་དཀར་གྱི་ནང་དུ་འབྲས་ཕུལ་ནས། བཞེས་དཀར་གྱི་ཁ་རུབ་མཛད་པས། བླ་མའི་ང་རྒྱལ་ཡོངས་སུ་ཞི་སྟེ་ཞལ་ནས། བཞེས་དཀར་གྱི་ཁ་ཕྱེ་རོགས་ཅེས་པའི་བརྫ་བྱེད་ཅིང་འདུག་པས་གྲུབ་ཐོབ་ཀྱིས་བཞེས་

དཀར་ཁ་ཕྱེས་ནས་སྟར་བཞིན་རང་མལ་བཞག །འོན་ཀྱང་གྲྭ་གཞན་གྱིས་གང་ཡང་མ་ཤེས་སོ། །གཞན་ཡང་ཁྲ་འགྲུ་དགོན་དང་ཐུགས་འབྲེལ་ཟབ་པའི་ཚུལ་ཙུང་ཟད་བརྗོད་ན། ཁྲ་ལེབ་ལྷ་པ་ཕྲིན་ལས་ཉི་མའི་དུས་ལ་ལྷ་ཁང་ཀ་བ་བརྒྱད་བཅུ་ཅན་འབྱུང་བཞི་གེགས་མེད་བདུད་ལས་རྣམ་རྒྱལ་བཞེངས་སྐབས། ཁོ་འཛིན་གྲུབ་ཐོབ་མཆོག་ནས་ལྷ་ཁང་ལ་ཆོས་དམར་གསོལ་རྒྱུའི་སྦྱིན་བདག་མཛད་པར་ཞལ་གྱིས་བཞེས། ལྷ་ཁང་གྲུབ་རྗེས་ཁྲ་དགོན་གཉེར་པ་མདུན་དུ་བཅར་ནས་ཆོས་དམར་གནང་བར་ཞུས་པས། རེའུ་ལུག་གང་གནང་བས། གཉེར་པས་སྐུ་ཉིད་ལ་འདི་ལས་མེད་པ་སྟར་ནས་གསུངས་ན་ང་ཚོས་ལོན་ཐབས་བྱེད་དེས་ལ། འདིས་ལྷ་ཁང་ཆེན་པོ་ལ་ག་པར་འདང་གི་རེད་ཅེས་ཞུས་པས། གྲུབ་ཐོབ་ཀྱི་ཞལ་ནས། འདིས་ལྷ་ཁང་ཚང་མ་མ་ཚད་གས་སྦུབ་རྣམས་ལའང་ཞལ་ཞལ་བྱེད་ཆོག་གི་རེད་ཅེས་གསུངས། ཁོང་གི་གསུངས་བཞིན་ཚང་མ་འདང་པ་མ་ཚད་དེའི་དུས་སུ་འཕྲུལ་ཆས་སོགས་མེད་པའི་རྐྱེན་གྱིས་ལྷ་ཁང་གི་ཀ་བ་རྣམས་ལ་གས་སྦུབས་དང་མཐོ་དམན་ཡོད་པ་རྣམས་ཆོས་དམར་གྱིས་ཞལ་བ་བྱས་ནས་ངོས་སྙོམས་པོ་བྱས་འདུག །རྗེས་མར་དུས་ཀྱི་དབང་གིས་ལྷ་ཁང་ཞིག་རལ་སོང་བས། མི་རྣམས་ཀྱིས་ལྷ་ཁང་ཀ་བའི་གས་སྦུབས་ལས་ཆོས་དམར་བཏོན་ནས་ཡི་གེ་འབྲི་བྱེད་བེད་སྤྱོད་བྱེད་ཀྱི་འདུག །ཡང་སྐབས་ཤིག་བྱ་ཆུ་ལ་ཟམ་པ་ཇི་ལྟར་འཛུགས་ཀྱང་རྡག་པར་ཆུས་འཁྱེར་བ་ལ། ཁོ་འཛིན་གྲུབ་ཐོབ་གདན་དྲངས་ནས་ཁྲ་ལེབ་ཕྲིན་ལས་ཉི་མ་དང་མཉམ་དུ་མར་མགོ་སྟགས་ཁང་དུ་ཕེབས། སྟགས་ཁང་ཕྱི་ནས་བསྐོར་བ་ལ་ཕེབས་ཞོར་དུ་བ་འཐེན་བཞིན་ཕེབས། སྟགས་ཁང་ཤར་དུ་ཕེབས་ནས་ཤར་གྱི་རི་སོགས་ཀྱི་མིང་གང་ཡིན་གསུངས། ཁྲ་ལེབ་རིན་པོ་ཆེ་ནས་རི་མིང་སོགས་གསུངས་མཛད། དུ་ཚག་གང་གི་ཐལ་བ་དེར་བླུགས་མཛད། དེ་བཞིན་ལྷོ་དང་། ནུབ་དང་། བྱང་གི་ཕྱོགས་སུ་ཡང་དེ་བཞིན་མཛད་ནས་ཕེབས་སོང་། ཁྲ་ལེབ་གཉེར་པས།

ང་ཚོས་སྦྱིན་སྲེག་གི་རྫས་ཆ་ཚང་གྲ་བསྒྲིགས་བྱས་ཀྱང་། གྲུབ་ཐོབ་ནས་འདོན་པ་ཚིག་གཅིག་གསུངས་མ་སོང་བས་གང་དགོས་སམ་ཅེས་ཁྲ་ལེབ་རིན་པོ་ཆེ་ལ་ཞུས་པས། རིན་པོ་ཆེའི་ཞལ་ནས། གྲུབ་ཐོབ་ཀྱིས་ཤར་ལྷོ་ནུབ་བྱང་བཞི་ལ་ཞི་རྒྱས་དབང་དྲག་གི་སྦྱིན་སྲེག་མཛད་སོང་བས། དེ་ལས་ལྷག་པའི་སྦྱིན་སྲེག་ཞིག་ག་པར་དགོས་ཞེས་གསུངས། དེའི་ནུབ་སེར་བ་དྲག་པོ་བབས་ནས་འབྲུག་གྲགས། ཐོག་ཁ་ཤས་འཕངས་པས་བྱ་རྒྱུ་ཕ་རི་དང་རྩུར་རིའི་བྲག་སྐྱིལ་ནས་ཟམ་པའི་ཀ་བ་སོགས་བཙུགས་སའི་ཁྲུང་བུ་ཡང་བྲག་ལ་རང་བྱུང་དུ་བྱུང་ནས། ཟམ་པ་གསར་རྒྱག་བྱས་པས་ཆུས་གནོད་པ་མེད་པར་གྱུར་ཏོ། ། རྒྱུན་དུ་སྐྱུ་ཆས་མཛད་ཅིང་། ན་བཟའ་ཡག་པོ་མནབས་ཤིང་། སྐེད་གྱི་རིང་པོ་སྐྲ་སྐེད་ལ་དྲངས། མི་འདྲའི་སྟེ་ཕྲུག་བོས་ཞིག་ཁོང་གི་ཞབས་ཕྱི་ལ་འཁྱུར་བཙུག་ནས་རྣམ་ཀུན་འཁྲིག་ཡུལ་དུ་ཕེབས་སྐབས། དད་ལྡན་རྣམས་ཀྱིས་རེ་ཞུ་བཞིན་ནོར་ལུག་རྣམས་ལ་བྱིན་རླབས་ཆེད་ཕྲུག་བོས་གནང་རྗེས། ལོ་གཅིག་ལ་སྤྱང་གིས་གནོད་པ་གཏན་ནས་མེད། དད་ལྡན་རྣམས་ཀྱིས་ཁོང་ལ་མདའ་རྫས་ཕུལ་སྐབས། ཕུལ་བའི་མདའ་རྫས་དང་མང་ཉུང་མཉམ་པའི་ཁོང་གི་ཕྲུག་བོས་ཀྱི་རྫས་གནང་ཞིང་། དད་ལྡན་རྣམས་ཀྱིས་བདུག་པ་དང་མཉམ་དུ་བསྲེ་ནས་དགོང་མོ་རྟག་པར་ཕྱུགས་ལ་བདུག་སྤྲོལ་ཡོད། དྲིན་ཅན་བླ་མ་དགུང་ལོ་ཆུང་དུའི་སྐབས་སུ། ཁོང་གི་ཡབ་རྒན་ལའང་བདུག་རྫས་ཡོད་པས། ཉིན་ལྟར་ཕྱུགས་ལྷས་ལ་བསྐོར་བ་བྱས་ནས་བདུག་རྫས་བདུག་སྤྲོལ་དང་། བདུག་རྫས་མེ་ལ་བསྲེགས་སྐབས་ཚག་སྒྲ་ཡོད་པས། ཁོང་རྟག་པར་བདུག་རྫས་བསྐུར་ནས་མངགས་ཀྱི་ཡོད་པས་ཤིན་ཏུ་ཐུགས་དགྱེས་ཀྱི་ཡོད་གསུངས། གྲུབ་ཐོབ་ཀྱིས་གསུངས་པའི་མགུར་མང་པོ་ཡོད་པར་ཐོས་ལ། དྲིན་ཅན་བླ་མ་མཆོག་དགུང་ལོ་བཞི་ལྔའི་སྐབས་སུ། ཁོང་རྨོ་མོ་སྐྱེ་ཨ་ཡས་ཀྱི་རུམ་དུ་ཉལ་ཞིང་། རྨོ་མོ་ནས་རྟག་པར་རི་གྱུར་གསེར་གྱི་དོ་རྗེ་མཁྱེན་

ཞེས་གསོལ་འདེབས་བྱེད་པ་དང་། གཞན་ཡང་མགུར་ནི། རྗེ་འགྲན་གྱི་དོ་མེད་
ཐོས་པ་དགའ། །སྤྱིར་འགྲོ་བ་ཡོངས་ཀྱི་དཔལ་དུ་ཆེ། །སྤྲང་མགོན་མེད་བདག་ལ་
སྐྱབས་གཅིག་པུ། །ཁྱེད་རྒྱང་ནས་འབོད་དོ་ཐུགས་རྗེས་གཟིགས། །མི་བདག་ལ་
བློ་གཏད་ཀྱི་བུ་སློབ་རྣམས། །ཡིད་མ་ཡེངས་རྣ་བའི་དབང་པོ་གཏོད། །སྟོན་
བསགས་ཀྱི་དགེ་བའི་ལུས་ཐོབ་ཀྱང་། །དལ་བརྒྱད་དང་འབྱོར་བཅུ་ཚང་བ་དགོས།
དེའི་རྗེས་སུ་མང་པོར་ཡོད་ཀྱང་ཐུགས་དྲན་མི་གསོས་ལ། མགུར་གྱི་མཐར། ཕྱི་
མ་དང་ཨོ་རྒྱན་མཁའ་འགྲོའི་གླིང་། །ངོ་ཤེས་ལྷར་མཇལ་བའི་སྨོན་ལམ་འདེབས།
།ཨ་སྐད་ཅིག་ལ་འགྲུབ་པའི་བཀྲ་ཤིས་ཤོག ༔ཨ་ཨ། །ཅེས་སོགས་མང་པོ་ཡོད་
གསུངས། དྲིན་ཅན་བླ་མས་མགུར་འདི་གསུངས་རིང་སྤྱན་ཆབ་ཉིལ་ཉིལ་མཛད་
དོ། །རོང་པོའི་དཔོན་སྡེ་ལྷ་བོད་ཧུ་ལྷ་ཁོ་ནི་གླང་དར་མའི་སྤྲུལ་པ་ཡིན་པར་གྲགས།
གླང་དར་གྱི་སྐྱེ་བ་ཡིན་པའི་རྟགས་སུ་མགོ་ལ་ར་ཅོ་ཆུང་དུར་སྐྱེས་ཡོད། སྟོན་ལས་ཀྱི་
སྒྲིག་ལན་ཡོད་པའི་ཕྱིར་ན་སྡེ་ལྷ་བེ་ཧུས་རི་གྲུར་སྤྲུལ་སྐུ་བགྲོངས་པར་བརྩམས་ནས་
མཚོན་ཆ་སོགས་ཇི་ལྟར་བེད་སྤྱད་ཀྱང་མ་གྲོངས་པས། སྐུ་ལུས་ཀོ་བའི་ནང་དུ
གཏུམ་སྟེ་མགུལ་ལ་མཆིག་ཡ་ལོ་བཏགས་ནས་འབྲི་ཆུའི་ནང་དུ་འཕངས་པས།
རྗེས་མར་ཀོ་ཐམ་ཧྲེད་སྐབས། ཀོ་བའི་ནང་དུ་གསེར་གྱི་རྡོ་རྗེ་འོད་འབར་བ་ཞིག་
ལས་སྐུ་གདུང་མི་སྣང་བས། ཐམས་ཅད་ཞལ་མཐུན་པར་རི་གྲུར་སྤྲུལ་སྐུ་གསེར་
གྱི་རྡོ་རྗེ་ལ་འགྱུར་བར་རྟོགས་ཤིང་། རི་གྲུར་གྱི་དོན་གོང་བཞིན་ལ། གསེར་གྱི་རྡོ་
རྗེ་ཐོགས་པའི་རྒྱུ་མཚན་དེ་ཡིན་ནོ། །དེའི་རྗེས་སུ་ཉིན་ཞིག་གི་སྔ་དྲོར་ཁྲ་ལེབ་རིན་
པོ་ཆེའི་ཆིབས་པ་གཉིས་ཀ་རྟ་ལ་ནག་འཕྱུར་ཞིང་གཞན་གྱིས་ཆིབས་སོང་བ་འདྲ་བ་
ཞིག་མཐོང་བས། ཁྲ་ལེབ་ཧ་རྗིའི་སེམས་ལ་ཆིབས་རྟ་གཉིས་རྐུན་མས་བརྐུས་པར་
དོགས་ནས་དེའི་ནུབ་ཆིབས་རྟའི་ར་བའི་ནང་དུ་ཉལ་རྩིས་སྐབས། ཁྲ་ལེབ་རིན་པོ་
ཆེ་ཕེབས་ནས་གང་བྱེད་ཀྱི་ཡོད་དམ་གསུངས། གོང་གི་ལོ་རྒྱུས་ཞུས་པས། ཞལ་

ནས་མདང་ནུབ་ངས་ཁོ་འཇོ་གྲུབ་ཐོབ་ལྷ་སའི་ལམ་ཕྱེད་བར་སྐྱེལ་མ་ཞུས་པས་ཆིབས་པ་གཉིས་ལ་རྡུལ་ནག་ཡོང་བའི་རྒྱུ་མཚན་དེ་ཡིན་གསུངས། གཞན་ཡང་མི་མང་པོས་གྲུབ་ཐོབ་མཆོག་གི་ཞལ་དངོས་ལྷ་ས་དང་གཙང་ནས་མཇལ་བའི་ལོ་རྒྱུས་ཡོད། སྔོ་ལྷ་བེ་ཧུས་དོན་དེ་རྟོགས་རྗེས་ཤིན་ཏུ་འགྱོད་ནས། ར་ཉག་དགོན་གྱི་བླ་མ་རྡུ་མཐའ་སྐྱབས་མགོན་དང་ཁྲ་ལེབ་སྐྱབས་མགོན་གཉིས་ལ་ཁོ་རང་ངན་སོང་དུ་མི་འགྲོ་བའི་སྐྱབས་འཇུག་ནན་ཞུས་བྱས་པས། སྐྱབས་མགོན་གཉིས་ནས་ཁས་ལེན་མཛད་དགོས་བྱུང་། སྔོ་ལྷ་གྲོངས་སྐབས་སྐྱབས་མགོན་གཉིས་ཀྱང་གྲོངས་དགོས་པ་བྱུང་བ་དང་། དེའི་རྗེས་སྐབས་སྐབས་སུ་རྡུ་མཐའ་སྐྱབས་མགོན་ཁྲ་དགོན་ལ་འཁྲུངས་ཤིང་། ཁྲ་ལེབ་སྐྱབས་མགོན་ར་ཉག་དགོན་ལ་འཁྲུངས་པ་སོགས་རེས་མོས་མཛད་པར་གྲགས། མཐའ་བྲལ་དབུ་མའི་དོན་རྟོགས་ཤིང་། །གཟུགས་ཅན་གཟུགས་མེད་འདུལ་བ་ལ། །མཛད་པའི་རྣམ་འཕྲུལ་ཆུ་ཟླ་བཞིན། །གྲུབ་ཐོབ་ཁྱེད་ལ་སུ་མི་གུས། དེ་ཡང་ཁྲ་ལེབ་སྐྱ་ཕྲེང་དང་པོ་ཉི་མ་བཀྲ་ཤིས་ཀྱི་མགུར་ལས། གཙོང་རོང་ཁམས་ཀྱི་མི་ནག་ཕོ་མོ་ཡིས། །སངས་རྒྱས་དངོས་སུ་བྱོན་ཀྱང་སྐྱོན་ཞིག་བཏགས། །བསམ་མི་ཤེས་པས་གྲུབ་མཐའི་ཕྱོགས་རིས་འཛིན། །ཆགས་སྡང་སྤྱོད་པས་ཕ་རོལ་ག་ལ་ནོན། །ཚུར་ལ་རང་ཉིད་ལྟུང་བ་ནག་འབྱམས་ཐོག །ཅེས་དང་། ཕྱོགས་རིས་མེད་པའི་དག་སྣང་མ་བྱས་པས། །ཕྱོགས་སྡེའི་འདོད་གཏམ་དམྱལ་བ་རང་གིས་སྒྲུབ། །ངེས་པར་རང་གི་སེམས་རྒྱུད་མ་བཏུལ་ན། །།ཁ་རྒྱངས་ཆོས་གཏམ་ཆགས་སྡང་ཕྱུང་པོ་ཡིན། །སངས་རྒྱས་བསྟན་པའི་སྒྲུབ་སྡེ་ཆེན་པོ་དང་། །མཚན་དང་ལྡན་པའི་བླ་མ་དམ་པ་ལ། །མདོན་ལྐོག་མེད་པའི་ཞབས་ཕྱི་སྒྲུབ་པ་ནི། །འདི་ཕྱི་གཉིས་ཡོད་རང་གི་བསོད་ནམས་རྒྱས། ཅེས་དང། ད་ནས་བཟུང་སྟེ་དུས་རྣམས་ཐམས་ཅད་ལ། །ཕྱོགས་རིས་ཆགས་སྡང་ཀུན་བྱེད་གློང་ནས་སྤོངས། །དག་སྣང་ཕྱོགས་མེད་ཀུན་བྱེད་གློང་ནས་སྦྱོངས། །དགེ་

དང་མི་དགེ་ཀུན་བྱེད་གླིང་ནས་འབྱུང་། །ད་ལྟའི་དུས་ཀྱི་གྲུབ་མཐའ་བཟང་ངན་འདི། །བཟང་པོ་གང་ཡིན་ངན་པ་གང་ཡིན་པ། །ཀུན་བྱེད་རྒྱལ་པོའི་གླིང་ནས་བཟང་ངན་འབྱུང་། །དཀར་པོའི་དགེ་བ་བྱུང་ན་ཉམས་རེ་མཚར། །ནག་པོའི་སྡིག་པ་བྱུང་ན་ཡི་རེ་མུག །སྐྱེ་བ་མང་པོ་འཛམ་གླིང་ཡུལ་དུ་བླངས། །ཆོས་ལུགས་བཞི་ལ་མ་བརྒྱུད་གང་ཡང་མེད། །ཆོས་སྒོ་བཞི་ལ་མ་ཞུགས་གང་ཡང་མེད། །བཟང་པོ་འདི་ཡིན་ངན་པ་འདི་ཡིན་ཞེས། །བཟང་ངན་དབྱེ་བ་ང་ལ་མ་བྱུང་བས། །ཆོས་རྣམས་ཐམས་ཅད་སངས་རྒྱས་ཡུལ་དུ་གཅིག །བྱུང་བ་སངས་རྒྱས་རྣམས་ཀྱི་ཐུགས་ལས་བྱུང་། །ཐུགས་ལས་བྱུང་ཞིང་ཞལ་ནས་གསུངས་པའི་ཆོས། །གཅིག་ལ་བཟང་བའི་ཆོས་ཤིག་གསུངས་པ་དང་། །ངན་པའི་ཆོས་ཤིག་གཅིག་ལ་གནང་བ་མིན། །སངས་རྒྱས་ཡུལ་ནས་བཟང་ངན་མ་བྱུང་ཡང་༑ །མ་རིག་ཡུལ་ནས་བཟང་པོ་ངན་པ་བྱུང་། །ང་ཡིས་སྐྱེ་བ་མང་པོ་བརྒྱུད་པ་ལས། །ཕྱག་ཆེན་ལམ་འབྲས་དབུ་མ་ལྷ་ལྷན་དང་། །བཀའ་གདམས་རྫོགས་པ་ཆེན་པོ་ལ་སོགས་པའི། །ཆོས་ལུགས་གྲུབ་མཐའ་སོ་སོའི་འགྲོ་དོན་ནི། །ཐམས་ཅད་ང་ཡིས་མ་བསླབས་གང་ཡང་མེད། །དེ་ཕྱིར་རང་ལ་གྲུབ་མཐའ་ཕྱོགས་རིས་མེད། །ཕྱོགས་རིས་ཆགས་སྡང་སྤངས་པས་རང་སར་གྲོལ། །མ་འོངས་ཕྱི་རབས་རྗེས་འཇུག་བུ་སློབ་རྣམས། །ཕྱོགས་རིས་སྤྱོངས་ལ་དག་སྣང་ཕྱོགས་མེད་སྦྱོངས༑ །སྐྱབས་གནས་བསླུ་མེད་ཡིན་ནོ་ཡིད་ལ་ཞོག། །ཅེས་གསུངས་པ་ལྟར་དམ་པ་འདི་རྣམས་ཀྱི་སྐྱེ་བའི་སྤྲུལ་འཕྲུལ་ལ་བསམ་གྱིས་མི་ཁྱབ་བོ།།

༼༢༨༽ བཀའ་བརྒྱུད་ཁྲ་འགུ་དགོན་གྱི་གྲྭ་བླ་མ་གཉྫ། རྣམ་དག་ཚུལ་ཁྲིམས་གཙང་མའི་ས་གཞི་ལ། །ཐུགས་བསྐྱེད་བྱང་ཆུབ་སེམས་ཀྱི་བདུད་རྩིས་བརླན། །བསྐྱེད་རྫོགས་སྔགས་ཀྱི་འབྲས་བུ་མཛེས་ཤིང་དུད། །སུམ་ལྡན་བླ་མ་མཆོག་ལ་ལན་བརྒྱར་བཏུད། བླ་མ་གཉྫ༼༡༩༣༡༽ལོའི་སྤྱི་ཟླ༼༤༽ཚེས༼༡༣༽ཉིན་སྐུ་འཁྲུངས། དགུང་ལོ༼༡༣༽ལ་སྐྲ་སྟོད་ཁྲ་འགུ་དགོན་ལ་རབ་ཏུ་བྱུང་། འགོ་རི་

སྒྲུབ་དཔོན་ལ་བསྟེན་ནས་དགོན་གྱི་སྒྲོལ་བཞིན་འདོན་ཆོག་བློ་འཛིན་སོགས་ལ་སློབ་སྦྱོང་གནང་། དགུང་ལོ(༡༨)དཔལ་ལྡན་མཁྱེན་བརྩེའི་མདུན་ནས་དགེ་ཚུལ་སློང་གི་སྡོམ་པ། བྱང་ཆུབ་སེམས་སྡོམ། གསང་སྔགས་སྨིན་བྱེད་ཀྱི་དབང་རྣམས་ལེགས་པར་ཐོབ། དེའི་རྗེས་སུ་ནཱ་རོའི་ཆོས་དྲུག་སྒྲུབ་ཁང་དུ་སྒྲུབ་དཔོན་ཁ་བཏགས་ཨོ་རྒྱན་མཛད་ནས་ཚར་གསུམ་བཞུགས། (༡༩༥༨)ལོའི་དུས་ཀྱི་འགྱུར་བ་ལ་བརྟེན་ནས་ཁྲ་འགུའི་བླ་གྲྭ་རྣམས་དང་མཉམ་དུ་རྒྱ་གར་དུ་ཕེབས། རྒྱ་གར་ཌྷ་ས་རུ་དྲིན་ཅན་བླ་མ་སོགས་དང་མཉམ་དུ་ལོ་དགུའི་རིང་ལ་རིས་མེད་ནང་པའི་ཆོས་ཀྱི་རིག་གཞུང་ཁག་ལ་སློབ་སྦྱོང་གནང་། སྐྱབས་རྗེ་ཀ་ལུ་རིན་པོ་ཆེའི་མདུན་ནས་རིན་ཆེན་གཏེར་མཛོད་ཀྱི་དབང་ཡོངས་རྫོགས་གསན། (༡༩༧༦)ལོར་༧རྒྱལ་དབང་ཡིད་བཞིན་ནོར་བུའི་བཀའ་བཞིན་དྲིན་ཅན་བླ་མ་སོགས་དང་མཉམ་དུ་ཨ་རིར་ཕེབས། དེ་ནས་རིམ་བཞིན་ཀ་ལི་ཕོ་ཉའི་ཀརྨ་ཐེག་གསུམ་ཆོས་གླིང་ཆོས་ཚོགས་ཀྱི་བླ་མ་མཛད། (༡༩༨༠)ལོར་བཀའ་བརྒྱུད་བསམ་ཡས་གླིང་གི་སྒྲུབ་ཁང་གི་སྒྲུབ་དཔོན་མཛད་པ་དང་ཀ་ལི་ཕོ་ཉའི་ཆོས་ཚོགས་ཀྱི་འགན་ཡང་གཟིགས། ༧རྒྱལ་དབང་ཀརྨ་པ་རིག་པའི་རྡོ་རྗེ་མཆོག་ཨ་རིའི་ཡུལ་དུ་སྟོང་ཚུལ་བསྟན་སྐབས། བླ་མ་གནྡ་ནས་ཞབས་ཕྱི་ལེགས་པར་ཞུས་པས། ༧རྒྱལ་དབང་མཆོག་གི་ཞལ་ནས། སོ་སོའི་སྔོན་ལས་ཀྱི་མཐུས། མི་འདིས་ང་རང་ལ་ཕན་ཐོགས་ཆེན་པོ་བྱུང་ཞེས་གསུངས་ནས་ཐུགས་དགྱེས་དགྱེས་མཛད། (༨༦)དང་(༨༧)ལོར་སྐྱབས་རྗེ་ཁྲ་འགུ་རིན་པོ་ཆེ་དང་མཉམ་དུ་བོད་ཁྲ་འགུ་དགོན་ལ་ཕེབས། སླར་ཡང་(༨༨)ལོར་དྲིན་ཅན་བླ་མ་དང་མཉམ་དུ་བོད་ལ་ཕེབས། དེའི་སྔོན་ཙམ་ལ་ཁོང་གི་དབྱིན་ཇིའི་དངོས་སློབ་ཁ་ཤས་ལ། ད་ལོ་བོད་ལ་འགྲོ་རྗེས་ཚུར་འོངས་ཐུབ་ཀྱི་མ་རེད། བོད་ལ་ཤི་གི་རེད་ཅེས་གསུངས་པ་དང་། གཞན་ཡང་སྐུ་ཞབས་བསྟན་འཛིན་ལགས་ཀྱི་ཞབས་ཕྱི་ཡེ་ཤེས་རྣམ་དག་ནས། སྐུ་ཉིད་བོད་ནས་མར་ཕེབས་མཚམས་མཁན་རིན་པོ་ཆེ་

དང་མཉམ་དུ་ང་ཚོའི་ཚང་སའི་སྟོན་མོ་ལ་ཕེབས་རོགས་གནང་ཞུས་པས། ཧ་གོད་ཀྱི་བཞད་མོ་དང་བཅས། སྣང་བ་མཚར་པོ། དེ་དུས་ང་རང་ཤི་ཚར་རེད་ཅེས་གསུངས། ཁོང་གི་ལྟག་མགུལ་ལ་གཉན་འབུར་ཞིག་དོན་ནས། ང་རང་གཉན་འབུར་འདིའི་འོག་ནས་ཐར་ཀྱི་མ་རེད་ཅེས་གསུངས་པས། དྲིན་ཅན་བླ་མས། ཁྱེད་རང་གཉན་འབུར་ཆུང་ཆུང་ཞིག་ལ་དེ་འདྲའི་ཞེ་སྐྲག་བྱེད་དགོས་དོན་གང་ཡོད་ཅེས་ཞལ་རྩེད་ཀྱི་ཚུལ་དུ་ཞུས། གཉན་འབུར་འདི་གཞན་དང་མི་འདྲ་བ་ཞིག་འདུག །རེད་གཉིས་མགྱོགས་པོར་ཁྲ་དགོན་ལ་སླེབས་པ་བྱེད་དགོས། ཁྲ་དགོན་འགྱོར་མཚམས་ང་རང་ལ་གང་འདྲ་བྱུང་ཡང་ཁྱེད་ལ་དཀའ་ངལ་ཡོད་མ་རེད་ཅེས་བསྟུད་མར་གསུངས། ཁྲ་དགོན་སླེབས་རྗེས་གཉན་འབུར་ཇེ་ཆེ་དང་སྟོང་གཞི་ཇེ་ལོད་སོང་ནས་སྐྱེ་རྒྱུའི་སྨན་ཁང་ཆེན་མོར་གདན་དྲངས། དྲིན་ཅན་བླ་མ་ཡང་སྨན་ཁང་དུ་གཟིགས་པར་ཕེབས་པས། ཁོང་གི་མགུལ་དུ་རྨ་དགྲིས་གཡོགས་ཡོད་པས། ཞལ་ནས་སྐུ་རྩེད་ཙུང་ཟད་གསུངས་པའི་ཚུལ་དང་བཅས་གཟེར་ཟུག་སོགས་གང་ཡང་མེད་པར་ཞིང་དུ་གཤེགས། དེ་ནས་གདུང་ཁྲ་དགོན་དུ་གདན་དྲངས་ནས་སྐུ་ལ་ཆོས་གོས་དང་ཞྭ་ཁྲ་གསོལ་ནས་ཅོག་པུར་བཞག་པས། སྐུ་དྲང་པོར་བཞུགས་ཀྱང་མགུལ་པ་ལ་སྔོན་ནས་གཉེན་འབུར་གྱི་སྐྱོན་གྱིས་དྲང་པོར་བཞུགས་མི་ཐུབ་སྐབས། འདས་རྗེས་སུ་ཡང་དབུ་མར་ལྷུང་བས། ཁོང་དང་མཉམ་དུ་སྒྲུབ་ཁང་དུ་བཞུགས་མྱོང་བའི་མཆེད་གྲོགས་རྒྱ་རའི་དགེ་རྒན་ཀརྨ་བདུད་འདུལ་ནས་ཐུགས་དམ་གསལ་འདེབས་གསུངས་པས། དེ་ནས་དབུ་སྒྱུར་མི་དགོས་པར་ཐད་ཀར་བཞུགས་ནས་ཐུགས་དམ་ཉིན་ལྔའི་རིང་བཞུགས། རྗེས་མར་གདུང་བཞུ་བའི་འགན་གཙོ་བོ་ཁོང་གི་སྐུ་ཚ་དགེ་རྒན་རིན་ཆེན་ནོར་བུ་མཆོག་གིས་འཁུར་མཛད་ནས་སྐུ་གདུང་མཆོད་རྟེན་ཡང་བཞེངས། རྒྱ་རའི་དགེ་རྒན་ཀརྨ་བདུད་འདུལ་ཡང་ནཱ་རོའི་ཆོས་དྲུག་སྒྲུབ་ཁང་གྲོལ། ཁོང་གི་ཁུ་བོ་དབུ་མཛད་རྒྱ་ར་དཔལ་དགའི་མདུན་ནས་དབུ་མཛད་སོགས་ཆོ་ག་ཕྱག་ལེན་རྣམས་

མ་ལུས་པར་གསན་པས། ད་ལྟ་ཁྲ་དགོན་དུ་ཆོ་ག་ཕྱག་ལེན་གྱི་རྒྱུན་མ་ཉམས་པ་
བཞུགས་པ་འདི་ཉིད་གཙོ་བོ་ཁོང་གི་སྐུ་དྲིན་ཡིན། མ་ཚད་སྐུ་ཚེ་གང་པོར་ཁྲ་དགོན་
གྱི་དབུ་མཛད་དང་ཆོས་ཁྲིམས་ཚར་གཉིས་སོགས་ཀྱི་ཐུགས་འགན་བཞེས་པ་དང་།
དུས་ཀྱི་འགྱུར་བ་བྱུང་བའི་རྗེས་སུ། ད་ར་ཀརྨ་རིན་ཆེན། སྒྲུབ་དཔོན་ཚེ་དབང་རྡོ་
རྗེ། བན་ཁྲ་ཀརྨ་མཐུ་སྟོབས་དང་ཆོས་འཕེལ། རྨོ་རའི་དགེ་རྒན་ཀརྨ་ཚུལ་ཁྲིམས།
དགེ་རྒན་ཀར་ཚེ། འདན་ཤུལ་དགེ་རྒན་ཀརྨ་བདུད་འདུལ། སྨན་པ་དགེ་རྒན་རིན་
ཆེན་ནོར་བུ་སོགས་རྣམ་སྣང་དུ་རུབ་རུབ་མཛད་ནས་འདུས་ཏེ། མི་རིང་བར་ཐུགས་
རྩོལ་ཆེན་པོས་ཁྲ་དགོན་གྱི་ལྷ་ཁང་སོགས་བཞེངས། ཉེ་ཆར་ལོ་ཤས་རིང་ལ་རྒྱ་རའི་
དགེ་རྒན་ཀརྨ་བདུད་འདུལ་སྟོང་གཞི་ཆེན་པོ་ཐེབས། སྨན་པ་རྣམས་གཅིག་མཐུན་
གྱིས། སྐུ་ལུས་ལ་དཔགས་ན་མགྱོགས་པོར་གྲོང་དེས་འདྲ་ཞེས་ལབ། འོན་ཀྱང་
ཁོང་གི་ཞལ་ནས་ཁྲ་ལེབ་རིན་པོ་ཆེ་མ་མཇལ་བར་དུ་སྒྲུག་གི་ཡིན་ཅེས་བསྟུད་མར་
གསུངས། དེ་ནས་༼༢༠༠༩༽ཕྱི་ཟླ་༼༤༽པའི་ནང་ནས་ཁྲ་དགོན་གྱི་འདུ་ཁང་འབྱུང་
བཞི་གེགས་མེད་བདུད་ལས་རྣམ་རྒྱལ་གསར་བཞེངས་གྲུབ་པའི་མཛད་སྒོའི་སྐབས།
སྐྱབས་རྗེ་ཁྲ་ལེབ་རིན་པོ་ཆེ་ཕེབས་ནས་ཁོང་ལ་འཕོ་བ་གསུངས་མཛད། འཕོ་བ་
གྲུབ་ཚར་བའི་དགོང་མོར་སྒྲུབ་དཔོན་རིན་ཆེན་ཚེ་རིང་ལ། ང་རང་སྤྲོ་ཐུང་བའི་རྐྱེན་
གྱིས་ཉིད་ལ་ཚིག་རྩུབ་མང་པོར་སྨྲ་བ་ལ་དགོངས་པ་མ་ཚོམ། ཁྱེད་རང་ཡང་སྒྲུབ་
ཁང་དུ་ཡར་ཕེབས་ནས་སྙིད་པོ་གཟིམས་མཛོད། ང་རང་ཡང་རེ་སྒྲུག་བཞིན་སྐྱབས་
རྗེ་རིན་པོ་ཆེའི་མདུན་ནས་འཕོ་བ་ཐོབ་པས་དོ་ནུབ་སྙིད་པོ་ཉལ་གི་ཡིན་སོགས་ཐུགས་
བརྩེ་བའི་བཀའ་མོལ་ལྷུག་པོར་གསུངས་ནས་གཟིམས། དེ་ནུབ་ཞིང་དུ་གཤེགས་ནས་
ཆོས་གོས་དང་ཞྭ་ཁྲ་གསོལ། ཐུགས་དམ་ལ་ཉིན་ཤས་བཞུགས་རྗེས་ཡང་དབེན་
བདེ་མཆོག་ཕོ་བྲང་དུ་གདུང་བཞུས་པའོ། །བན་ཁྲ་དགེ་རྒན་ཀརྨ་ཆོས་འཕེལ་ཡང་
ནཱ་རོའི་སྒྲུབ་ཁང་གྲུབ། སྐུ་ཚེ་གང་པོར་ཐུགས་མཐུན་ཁྲིམས་གཙང་དང་། དགོན་

པའི་སྒྲོག་ཤིང་ལྷ་བུར་གྱུར། འདའ་ཁར་ད་ལྟ་ཁྲ་འགུ་དགོན་གྱི་མཁན་པོ་ཕྲིན་ལས་དཔལ་བཟང་གིས་ཞབས་ཕྱི་ཞུས་ནས་ལྷ་ས་དང་མཚུར་ཕུ་ནས་བཟུང་སྟེ། ལྷོ་གནས་རྒྱས་པར་བསྐོར། བལ་ཡུལ་དང་རྒྱ་གར་གྱི་གནས་རྣམས་ལེགས་པར་གྲུབ་རྗེས་སླུང་གཞི་ཡོག་ནས། བལ་ཡུལ་གནས་མཆོག་སྟག་མོ་ལུས་སྦྱིན་དུ་སྐུ་གདུང་བཞག་སའི་ས་དཔྱད་རྣམས་ཁོང་རང་གིས་ལེགས་པར་གཟིགས་ནས་དེ་རུ་སྐུ་གདུང་བཞུ་དགོས་པའི་ཞལ་ཆེམས་དང་བཅས་ཞིང་དུ་གཤེགས། ཁོང་གི་ལུམ་བྲིང་ཨ་ནེ་ཞིང་དུ་གཤེགས་སྐབས་ཀྱང་ཐུགས་དམ་བཞུགས། གཞན་ཡང་དགེ་རྒན་ཀར་ཚེ་དང་འདན་ཤུལ་བདུད་འདུལ། ཀརྨ་ཚུལ་ཁྲིམས་རྣམས་ཞིང་དུ་གཤེགས་སྐབས་ཀྱང་ཐུགས་དམ་བཞུགས། ཟུར་རུ་གོང་མའི་མགོན་བླ་བལ་ཡུལ་སྟག་མོ་ལུས་སྦྱིན་དུ་སྐུ་གཤེགས་སྐབས་ཐུགས་དམ་བཞུགས་པ་སོགས་དམ་པ་འདི་རྣམས་ནི་ཤིན་ཏུ་ངོ་མཚར་བའི་ཡུལ་དུ་གྱུར་བཞིན་པ་འདི་འོ། །དེ་ལྟར་གོང་དུ་བྲིས་པའི་ཁམས་མདོ་སྨད་ཀྱི་སྦས་པའི་རྣལ་འབྱོར་ཙུང་ཤས་ཀྱི་ཕྱི་ནང་གསང་གསུམ་གྱི་རྣམ་ཐར་རྒྱ་མཚོ་ལྟ་བུ་ལས་ཐུན་མོང་འཇིག་རྟེན་གྱི་ངོ་སྐལ་དུ་ཇི་ལྟར་བསྟན་གནང་ཚུལ་མདོར་བསྡུས་པ་འདི་ནི། སྐྱབས་བརྒྱུད་བསྟན་པའི་སྒྲོག་ཤིང་མཁས་གྲུབ་གཉིས་ལྡན་གྱི་མཁན་པོ་ཚུལ་ཁྲིམས་རྒྱ་མཚོ་མཆོག་གི་ཕྲིན་ལས་ཤར་ནུབ་ཀྱི་རྒྱལ་ཁབ་ཀུན་ལ་ཁྱབ་ཅིང་། གང་འདུལ་གྱི་ཆོས་འཁོར་མཐའ་ཡས་པ་བསྐོར་ནས་ནུབ་ཕྱོགས་ཨ་རིའི་ཡུལ། རབ་འབྱམས་རྒྱལ་བ་ཀུན་གྱི་ཕྲིན་ལས་ཀྱི་ཟློས་གར་དཔལ་༧རྒྱལ་བའི་དབང་པོ་ཀརྨ་པའི་གདན་ས་གསུམ་པ། ཀརྨ་ཐེག་གསུམ་ཆོས་ཀྱི་འཁོར་ལོའི་དགོན་པར་ཐེབས་སྐབས། དགོན་དེའི་མཁན་པོ་དྲིན་ཅན་བླ་མ་དང་མཉམ་དུ་ཁམས་སྣ་ཡི་གྲུབ་ཐོབ་རྣམས་ཀྱི་རྣམ་ཐར་གྱི་སྐོར་ལ་བགྲོ་གླེང་གནང་བས། བླ་མ་མཆོག་གིས་ཐུགས་མཉེས་པའི་སྒོ་ནས་སྦས་པའི་རྣལ་འབྱོར་ཁ་ཤས་ཀྱི་ངོ་མཚར་བའི་མཛད་རྣམ་གསུངས་པས། མཁན་པོ་ཚུལ་ཁྲིམས་རྒྱལ་མཚན་ནས་བདག་ལ་

རྣམ་ཐར་དེ་ཚོ་འབྲི་དགོས་པར་བཀའ་ཕེབས། སྤྱིར་སྟོན་མ་ནས་རང་གིས་ཀྱང་ཕྱོགས་བསྡུ་བྱ་རྒྱུའི་འཆར་གཞི་ཡོད་ཕྱིར་ཁ་ཤས་བྲིས་ཟིན་ལ། ལྷག་པར་དུ་མཁན་པོ་མཆོག་གི་བཀའ་ལུང་གྲུབ་པའི་སྒོ་ནས་དང་དུ་བླངས་ནས་བླ་མས་གསུངས་པ་རྣམས་སྐབས་གཅིག་ཏུ་བྲིས་ནས་མཁན་པོ་མཆོག་ལ་ཕུལ་ཟིན། འོན་ཀྱང་དེ་ཙམ་གྱིས་ཚོག་ཤེས་མ་བྱས་པར། བླ་མས་རི་ཁྲོད་དུ་བཀའ་ཆོས་གསུངས་སྐབས་ཀྱི་རྣམ་ཐར་གསུངས་པ་རྣམས་དང་། གཞན་ཡང་རང་སློབ་ཁང་དུ་འདུག་པའི་སྐབས་སུ་སློབ་བླ་རྣམས་ཀྱིས་བཀའ་འདྲི་དང་བཀའ་མོལ་གྱི་ཞོར་དུ་བླ་མས་གསུངས་པ་རྣམས་གཅིག་ཀྱང་ཡན་གར་དུ་མ་བཞག་པར་ཕྱོགས་གཅིག་ཏུ་བསྡུས་ཤིང་། དེ་རྣམས་ཀྱང་ཡང་ནས་ཡང་དུ་བཀའ་འདྲི་དང་། ཚ་ཚད་གྲུབ་པའི་རྗེས་སུ་ཡང་བསྐྱར་གཟིགས་འབུལ་ཞུས་ཏེ། བླ་མས་འགྲིག་འདུག་གསུངས་པའི་བཀའ་ཡི་གནང་བ་ཐོབ་མཚམས་པར་བསྒྲུན་བྱས་པ་ལས། གོ་ལོ་དང་ཐོས་ལོ་ཙམ་ལ་ཡིད་ཆེས་བྱས་པའམ། ཡང་ན་བྱེ་བས་བསགས་པའི་ནས་འབྲུ་བཞིན་འབྲི་རྒྱུ་ཅི་རྙེད་བྱས་ནས་རྣམ་ཐར་ཁ་ཤས་ཤིག་པར་ཐུབ་པ་ལ་ངས་བྱས་ཀྱི་ཁེངས་པ་ནི་ནམ་ཡང་སྤྱང་ཞིང་བློ་གཟུ་བོར་གནས་པས་བྲིས་པ་ཡིན་ལ། རྣམ་ཐར་རེ་རེའི་དབུ་དང་མཇུག་ཏུ་མཆོད་བརྗོད་དང་དགེ་བསྔོའི་ཕྱིར་དུ་ཤློ་ཀ་ཁ་ཤས་རེས་བརྒྱན་པ་ཡང་དམ་པའི་སྐྱེས་བུ་འདི་རྣམས་ཀྱི་རྣམ་ཐར་ཐོས་པ་དཀའ་བས་དེ་རྣམས་ཀྱི་ཆེ་བ་བརྗོད་པའི་ཕྱིར་དང་། དེ་ཡང་མང་ཆེ་བ་ནི་རང་དགོན་སྣ་སྐོད་ཁྲ་འགུ་བཀྲ་ཤིས་ཆོས་གླིང་དགོན་གྱི་སློབ་བླ་དང་ཆོ་མཚམས་རྣམས་ཀྱི་རྣམ་ཐར་དང་། གཞན་ཡང་ས་དགེ་བཀའ་རྙིང་རིས་མེད་ཀྱི་ཆོས་བརྒྱུད་འཛིན་པའི་དམ་པ་ཁ་ཤས་ཀྱི་རྣམ་ཐར་ཡང་ཡོད་ཅིང་། བླ་མ་མཆོག་གི་ཞལ་ནས་ཀྱང་། ང་རང་ཁྲ་དགོན་གྱི་གྲྭ་ཡིན་པའི་རྒྱུ་མཚན་གྱིས་རང་དགོན་གྱི་སྐྱེས་བུ་རྣམས་ཀྱི་རྣམ་ཐར་མང་

ཙམ་ཤེས་པས་སླས་པ་ཡིན་ལ། ས་དགེ་བཀའ་རྙིང་གྲུབ་མཐའ་རིས་མེད་ཀྱི་རྣལ་འབྱོར་པ་རྣམས་ཀྱི་རྣམ་ཐར་མང་ཙམ་ཤེས་ན་དགའ་ཞིང་གུས་པས་འདིར་འགོད་འདོད་ཡོད་ཀྱང་དེ་ཙམ་ལས་མི་ཤེས་པས་ཅི་བྱ་གསུངས། དེ་ཡང་དགོས་པ་ནི་གྲུབ་མཐའ་རིས་མེད་ཀྱི་ཆོས་བརྒྱུད་འཛིན་པའི་དམ་པའི་སྐྱེས་བུ་འདི་རྣམས་ཀྱི་རྣམ་ཐར་ཉུང་ཤས་ཤིག་འགོད་ཐུབ་ནའང་། རྒྱལ་བ་དགྱེས་པའི་མཆོད་སྤྲིན། འགྲོ་དྲུག་ཕ་མའི་དྲིན་ལན། མོས་གུས་ཅན་ལ་བདུད་རྩི། ངེས་འབྱུང་ཅན་ལ་སྐྱུལ་ལྕགས། དམ་ཆོས་སྒྲུབ་པའི་རྒྱུ་རྐྱེན། དམ་པའི་ཆོས་ཀྱི་ཆེ་བ། བླ་མ་མཉེས་པའི་རྒྱ་མཚོག །ཀུན་ལ་དག་སྣང་དགོས་ཚུལ་སོགས་དང་། ཁྱད་པར་དུ་དམ་པའི་ཆོས་ལ་ཡིད་ཆེས་དང་མོས་གུས་སྐྱེ་བའི་རྒྱུ་རྟུ་འགྱུར་བ་ངེས་ལ། རང་ནི་ཐོས་བསམ་གྱི་དཔྱད་པ་རྒྱ་ཆེན་པོ་དབེན་པས། རྫོང་བྱེད་ཚིག་ལ་སྦེབ་སྦྱོར་དང་སྙན་ངག་གིས་བརྒྱན་པའི་རྩོམ་ཚིག་སོགས་ལ་ཆ་རྒྱུས་ཆུང་བས་མཁས་པའི་དབང་པོ་རྣམས་ཁྲེལ་བའི་རྒྱུ་ལས་མེད་མོད། འོན་ཀྱང་རང་འདྲའི་སྐལ་མཉམ་རྣམས་ལ་གོ་སླ་བའི་ཚིག་གཙོ་བོར་བྱས་ནས་བྲིས་པས། དེས་ན་ཐུན་མོང་འཇིག་རྟེན་པ་རྣམས་ཀྱིས་ཀྱང་རྟོགས་སླ་ཞིང་རྒྱུད་ལ་དད་གུས་ཀྱི་ཐར་པའི་ས་བོན་ཐེབ་པའི་ཆེད་དང་། གཞན་ཡང་མ་འོངས་པ་ལ་ཐོས་བསམ་དང་ལྡན་པའི་སྐྱེ་སེར་དག་གིས། ང་ཚོ་ལོ་རྒྱུས་ཀྱི་ཆུ་ཀླུང་རིང་མོ་ཁྲོད་ན་གནས་པའི་གངས་ཅན་བོད་ཞེས་སྙན་གྲགས་འཛིན་མར་ཁྱབ་པ་འདི་འང་གཙོ་བོ་དམ་པའི་ཆོས་ཀྱི་བཀའ་དྲིན་ཡིན་ཞིང་། དམ་པའི་ཆོས་དེ་ཉིད་ཀྱང་སྟོན་པ་ཐུགས་རྗེ་ཅན་གྱིས་གསུངས། རིས་མེད་ཀྱི་བསྟན་འཛིན་རྣམས་ཀྱིས་སྤེལ་བས། དེའི་ཕྱིར་ན་ས་དགེ་བཀའ་རྙིང་གྲུབ་མཐའ་རིས་མེད་ཀྱི་མཁས་གྲུབ་ཀྱི་སྐྱེས་བུ་རྣམས་དང་། ཁྱད་པར་དུ་དགོས་པའི་དབང་གིས་གང་ལ་གང་འདུལ་གྱིས་གཟུགས་སྐུར་སྟོན་པར་མཛད་པའི་སྤྲས་པའི་རྣལ་འབྱོར་ཕོ་མོ་འདི་རྣམས་ཀྱི་རྣམ་ཐར་ཉུང་ཤས་ཤིག་གཟུ་བོའི་བློ་ཡིས་འགོད་ཐུབ་

ནའང་རྒྱལ་བའི་བསྟན་ལ་བྱ་བ་བྱས་པ་ཡིན་ཞེས་རང་གིས་མགྲིན་པ་གཟེངས་སུ་བསྟོད་དེ་བརྗོད་པ་ཡིན་སྟེ། གང་ཞེ་ན། རྣམ་ཐར་འདི་ཚོ་ལ་བསྟེན་ནས་སྤྱིར་རྒྱལ་བས་ལེགས་པར་གསུངས་པའི་དམ་པའི་ཆོས་དང་། ལྷག་པར་དུ་གསང་སྔགས་ཀྱི་སྨིན་ལམ་ཟབ་མོ་ལ་ཡིད་ཆེས་དང་མོས་གུས་སྐྱེ་ཞིང་། རྣམ་ཐར་རང་གིས་ཀློག་པའམ། གཞན་གྱིས་ཀློག་པ་ཐོས་ན་རྒྱུད་ལ་དད་པ་དུང་དུང་ངང་གིས་སྐྱེ་ཞིང་། དེ་ཙམ་གྱིས་ཀྱང་ཐར་པའི་ས་བོན་ལེགས་པར་རྒྱུད་ལ་ཐེབས་པ་དང་། དད་པ་ནི་རྒྱལ་བས་གསུངས་པའི་ཆོས་ཀྱི་སྙིང་པོ་ཡིན་པའང་མདོ་རྒྱུད་དག་ལས་རྒྱ་ཆེར་གསུངས་ལ། ལྷག་པར་དུའང་གཉུག་མ་ལྷན་ཅིག་སྐྱེས་པའི་ཕྱག་རྒྱ་ཆེན་པོ་རྟོགས་པར་བྱེད་པ་ལ། མོས་གུས་ནི་ཡེ་ཤེས་ཀྱི་སྒོ་འབྱེད་པར་བྱེད་པའི་ལྡེ་མིག་ལྟ་བུར་ཡིན་པར་གསུངས་པས། དེས་ན་མོས་གུས་ཕྱག་རྒྱ་ཆེན་པོ་ཞེས་སྒྲུབ་བརྒྱུད་འདི་པའི་དམ་པ་རྣམས་ཀྱི་ཆོས་སྐད་གཙང་མ་དང་གཙིགས་ཆེན་དུ་འཛིན་ལ། དེ་ཉིད་ཚུལ་བཞིན་རྒྱུད་ལ་སྐྱེ་བར་བྱེད་པ་ལ་ཐུན་མོང་དང་ཐུན་མོང་མ་ཡིན་པའི་དམ་པ་འདི་རྣམས་ཀྱི་རྣམ་ཐར་ཐོས་པ་ལ་རག་ལས་པས། རིས་སུ་མ་ཆད་པའི་རྒྱལ་བའི་བསྟན་པ་ལ་ལྷག་བསམ་ལྡན་པའི་གངས་ལྗོངས་ཀྱི་རིག་གསར་རྣམ་པས། སོ་སོའི་དགོན་པ་དང་བླ་མ། རྣལ་འབྱོར་ཕོ་མོ་རྣམས་ཀྱི་རྣམ་ཐར་གཞན་ལས་ཐོས་པའམ། ཡང་ན་གཞན་གྱིས་རང་ལ་བསྙད་པ་སོགས་ལ་དཔྱད་པ་ཞིབ་མོ་དང་། ལྷག་བསམ་མོས་གུས། གཟུ་བོའི་བློ་ཡིས་འགོད་ཐུབ་ན། རང་ཅག་ཁ་བ་གངས་ཅན་ལྗོངས་ཀྱི་ལོ་རྒྱུས་ཀྱི་དཔལ་ཡོན་འཛིན་མའི་ཁྲོན་ན་ཡོངས་སུ་ཁྱབ་པས། འཛམ་གླིང་གོ་ལའི་ཁྲོན་ན་གནས་པའི་མི་རིགས་ཡོངས་ལ་ཡང་ཕན་ངེས་ལ། དེང་སང་གྲུབ་པའི་གནས་མཆོག་དང་། ས་དགེ་བཀའ་རྙིང་གི་དགོན་པ་དང་བླ་མ་སྐྱེས་ཆེན་དམ་པ་མང་པོའི་ལོ་རྒྱུས་སྔར་ཡོད་རྣམས་བོར་བརླག་སོང་བའམ་གཏན་ནས་མེད་པ་དང་། དེ་རྣམས་ཀྱི་རྣམ་ཐར་ལྟ་ཅི། སྐུ་ཕྲེང་དང་མཚན་ཡང་ཤེས་དཀའ་བའི་དུས་སྐབས་

འདི་ལ། མུ་མཐུད་ནས་དཀའ་ངལ་འཛེམས་མེད་ཀྱིས་སྔར་ཡོད་རྣམས་རྩད་འཚོལ་དང་། ཡོད་པ་རྣམས་གོང་འཕེལ་དུ་གཏོང་རྒྱུ་ནི་རང་ཅག་རྣམས་ཀྱི་འོས་འགན་ཡིན་ཞིང་། ད་ལྟ་རང་ཅག་རྣམས་ཀྱིས་གཟུགས་སྐུའི་མཚན་དཔེ་མཇལ་བཞིན་པའི་མཁན་སྤྲུལ་རྣམས་དང་རྣལ་འབྱོར་ཕོ་མོ་རྣམས་ལ་མཉམ་འགྲོགས་ཀྱི་མིག་བརྙས་དང་ལོག་ལྟ་སྤྲངས་ལ་སྐུ་ཆེའི་རྣམ་ཐར་དང་ལོ་རྒྱུས་ལྷུག་པོར་འགོད་གནང་ཞེས་ལྷག་བསམ་དག་པས་སོར་གཉིས་ཐལ་མོ་སྦྱར་ནས་ཞོར་དུ་བྲིས་ཐལ་ལོ། སླར་སླས་པ། དོན༷་ཀུན་གྲུབ་པའི་སྟོན་པ་སངས་རྒྱས་མཆོག །དོན༷་གཉིས་མཐར་ཕྱིན་ཆོས་སྐུའི་རང་ཞལ་མཇལ། །དོན༷་མེད་ཞི་བའི་དབྱིངས་སུ་མ་བཞུགས་པར། །དོན༷་ལྡན་ཆོས་སྒོ་ཟབ་རྒྱས་མཐའ་ཡས་གསུངས། །འཁོར༷་མེད་བཀའ་དྲིན་ཅན་གྱི་སྟོན་པ་དེས། །འཁོར༷་གྱི་ཐོག་མ་ལྔ་སྡེ་བཟང་པོ་སོགས། །འཁོར༷་བའི་གཅོང་རོང་འཇིགས་པའི་མུན་ནག་ནས། །འཁོར༷་བའི་སེམས་ཅན་གང་འདུལ་ཐར་ལམ་འདྲེན། །ཆོས༷་རྒྱལ་མེས་དབོན་རྣམ་གསུམ་ནས་བཟུང་སྟེ། །ཆོས༷་མེད་ཀླུ་ཀློ་བོད་ཀྱི་ཡུལ་དུ་ཡང་། །ཆོས༷་ཀྱི་ཞིང་ས་དམ་པ་འདི་བསྐྲུན་པས། །ཆོས༷་ལྡན་བོད་ཅེས་མཚན་སྙན་ཐ་གྲུར་ཁྱབ། །ཁྱད༷་པར་མཁན་སློབ་ཆོས་གསུམ་བཀའ་དྲིན་གྱིས། །ཁྱད༷་ཆོས་གཞན་ལས་ཆེ་བའི་གསང་སྔགས་བསྟན། །ཁྱད༷་མེད་བོད་ཀྱི་ཡུལ་ཁམས་ཀུན་ཁྱབ་པས། །ཁྱད༷་མཚར་སྤྲས་པའི་རྣལ་འབྱོར་ཕོ་མོ་ཕེབས། །རྣམ༷་རྟོག་ཆོས་སྐུར་དག་པའི་རྟོགས་ལྡན་རྣམས། །རྣམ༷་པ་གཟུགས་སྐུའི་བཀོད་པ་ཅིར་ཡང་སྟོན། །རྣམ༷་གྲངས་ཉུང་ངུར་བཀོད་པའི་ངོ་མཚར་གྱི། །རྣམ༷་ཐར་རིན་ཆེན་དང་པོ་འདི་ན་མཆིས༔ །སྣ༷་སྣ༷་ཚིག་གི་སྦྱིབ་སྦྱོར་བདག་ལ་མེད། །འགྲིག༷་འགྲིག༷་སུམ་རྟགས་དག་གསུམ་འདིར་མ་མཆིས། །རྒྱུས༷་རྒྱུས༷་ལུང་རིགས་སྦྱོས་པ་ཡང་མེད་པས། །མཁས༷་མཁས༷་ལུང་རིགས་མཁན་རྣམས་འདིར་མ་གཟིགས། །འགྲོ༷་དྲུག་གནས་ལས་ཐར་འདོད་ངེས་འབྱུང་

ཅན། །འགྲོ་ཀུན་ཕ་མར་ཤེས་པའི་བྱམས་སེམས་ཅན། །འགྲོ་རྣམས་ལྷ་རུ་ཤེས་པའི་དག་སྣང་མཁན། །འགྲོ་མགོན་རྣམས་ཀྱི་རྣམ་ཐར་ཀློག་པར་ཞུ། །འདི་བགྱིས་དགེ་བས་འདི་ཕྱི་བར་གསུམ་དུ། །བདག་དང་ཕ་མ་གྱུར་རྣམས་བདག་འཛིན་གྱིས། །ཉེས་ལྟུང་གང་བགྱིས་ཉེས་པར་མཐོང་ནས་ནི། །སྙིང་ནས་བཤགས་པས་སྙིང་རྗེའི་ལྷ་རྣམས་དགོངས། །རིས་མེད་བསྟན་པ་ཕྱོགས་དུས་ཀུན་ཏུ་དར། །རིས་མེད་སྐྱེས་ཆེན་སྐུ་ཚེ་སྲིད་མཐར་བརྟན། །རིས་མེད་མ་གྱུར་འགྲོ་བ་ཐམས་ཅད་ཀུན། །རིས་མེད་རྣམ་མཁྱེན་གོ་འཕང་ཐོབ་པར་ཤོག །ཅེས་པ་འདི་འང་དྲིན་ཅན་བླ་མ་མཁན་པོ་ཀར་མཐར་རིན་པོ་ཆེའི་སྐུ་ཚ་དང་སློབ་འབངས་ཀྱི་མིང་ཙམ་དང་། དགའ་ཡུལ་ཁྲ་འགུ་བཀྲ་ཤིས་ཆོས་གླིང་དགོན་གྱི་གྲྭ་མཐར་སྐྱེས་པ། གུས་པ་ཀརྨ་འགྲོ་འདུལ་འབོད་པས། སྔར་ནས་རྣམ་ཐར་ཚང་མ་བྲིས་ཟིན་པས་དེ་རྣམས་ལ་དཔྱད་པ་དང་འབྲི་བསྐྱུན་སོགས་དྲིན་ཅན་བླའི་མའི་དགོངས་བཞེད་བཞིན་ཞུས་ནས་སྤྱི་ལོ༼༢༠༠༥༽དང་། བོད་རྒྱལ་ལོ་༼༢༡༣༢༽རབ་གནས་ཤིང་བྱའི་ཧོར་ཟླ་དགུ་པའི་ཚེས་བཟང་ཉིན། ནུབ་ཕྱོགས་ཨ་རིའི་ཡུལ། དཔལ་༧རྒྱལ་བའི་དབང་པོ་ཀརྨ་པའི་སྒྲུབ་སྡེ་ཡིད་འོང་བསམ་གཏན་གླིང་དུ་སྒྲུབ་ཐེངས་གཉིས་པར་འདུག་སྐབས། རྒྱལ་ཡུམ་རྡོ་རྗེ་ཕག་མོའི་ནང་སྒྲུབ་སྐབས་སུ་རྫོགས་པར་གྲུབ་ནས་པར་སྐྲུན་ཞུས་པ་དགེ།

May all beings be happy!